Atheism and Agnosticism

Recent Titles in Religion in Politics and Society Today

Islam in America: Exploring the Issues
Craig Considine

Religion and Environmentalism: Exploring the Issues
Lora Stone

Antisemitism: Exploring the Issues
Steven Leonard Jacobs

Atheism and Agnosticism

Exploring the Issues

Peter A. Huff

Religion in Politics and Society Today

ABC-CLIO®

An Imprint of ABC-CLIO, LLC

Santa Barbara, California • Denver, Colorado

Copyright © 2021 by ABC-CLIO, LLC

All rights reserved. No part of this publication may be reproduced, stored in a retrieval system, or transmitted, in any form or by any means, electronic, mechanical, photocopying, recording, or otherwise, except for the inclusion of brief quotations in a review, without prior permission in writing from the publisher.

Library of Congress Cataloging-in-Publication Data

Names: Huff, Peter A., author.
Title: Atheism and agnosticism : exploring the issues / Peter A. Huff.
Description: Santa Barbara, California : ABC-CLIO, an imprint of ABC-CLIO, LLC, [2021] | Series: Religion in politics and society today | Includes bibliographical references and index.
Identifiers: LCCN 2021023085 (print) | LCCN 2021023086 (ebook) | ISBN 9781440870828 (hardcover) | ISBN 9781440870835 (ebook)
Subjects: LCSH: Atheism—Encyclopedias. | Agnosticism—Encyclopedias. | Atheism—United States—Encyclopedias. | Agnosticism—United States—Encyclopedias.
Classification: LCC BL2747.3 .H84 2021 (print) | LCC BL2747.3 (ebook) | DDC 211/.803—dc23
LC record available at https://lccn.loc.gov/2021023085
LC ebook record available at https://lccn.loc.gov/2021023086

ISBN: 978-1-4408-7082-8 (print)
       978-1-4408-7083-5 (ebook)

25 24 23 22 21   1 2 3 4 5

This book is also available as an eBook.

ABC-CLIO
An Imprint of ABC-CLIO, LLC

ABC-CLIO, LLC
147 Castilian Drive
Santa Barbara, California 93117
www.abc-clio.com

This book is printed on acid-free paper ∞

Manufactured in the United States of America

In Memory of Thomas J. J. Altizer (1927–2018)

Contents

Alphabetical List of Entries

Series Foreword

Religion is a pervasive and powerful force in modern society, and its influence on political structures and social institutions is inescapable, whether in the United States or around the world. Wars have been fought in the name of faith; national boundaries have been shaped as a result; and social policies, legislation, and daily life have all been shaped by religious beliefs. Written with the reference needs of high school students and undergraduates in mind, the books in this series examine the role of religion in contemporary politics and society. While the focus of the series is on the United States, it also explores social and political issues of global significance.

Each book in the series is devoted to a particular issue, such as anti-semitism, atheism and agnosticism, and women in Islam. An overview essay surveys the development of the religious dimensions of the subject and discusses how religion informs contemporary discourse related to that issue. A chronology then highlights the chief events related to the topic. This is followed by a section of alphabetically arranged reference entries providing objective information about people, legislation, ideas, movements, events, places, and other specific subjects. Each entry cites works for further reading and in many cases provides cross-references. At the end of each volume is an annotated bibliography of the most important print and electronic resources suitable for student research.

Authoritative and objective, the books in this series give readers a concise introduction to the dynamic interplay of religion and politics in modern society and provide a starting point for further research on social issues.

Preface

Some people will welcome this book with enthusiasm and relief. Some will be shocked to see that it exists at all. It is hard to be neutral on the topic. Atheism and agnosticism stimulate both fear and fascination. What no one can deny is this: together they represent an enormously significant feature of our life today. Unbelief and nonreligion are growing dramatically in all parts of society. For millions of people around the world, this is the age of atheism and agnosticism.

The form of this book is related to its subject. Atheism, agnosticism, and encyclopedias share a kinship that goes way back. The French *Encyclopédie* (1751–1772), the collective literary project that set the type for all future encyclopedias, was the Western world's—and possibly the whole world's—first major platform for atheist and agnostic, or near-atheist and near-agnostic, voices. The editor, Denis Diderot, intended to gather the human knowledge available to his time and place into a vast circle of insight—hence the term *encyclopedia* (from the Greek *en* [in] + *kyklos* [circle] + *paideia* [learning]). The writers covered a wide range of scientific, philosophical, social, political, and cultural issues, all from the perspective of natural human curiosity. What a character in Aldous Huxley's *Brave New World* (1932) would later describe as the "thing called God" received little attention. Medieval mystics had defined God as a circle whose center was everywhere and whose circumference was nowhere. Diderot's *Encyclopédie*, with some seventy thousand entries, made it clear that God was being edged out of the circle of human concern.

Diderot's age was an era of revolution—revolutions, that is: the American (1775–1783), the French (1789–1799), and the Haitian (1791–1804). Ours is a revolutionary time too. This encyclopedia is necessary because of what Diderot's *Encyclopédie* and hundreds of other books in its wake helped to produce: generations of people who explain, enjoy, or endure life without need of or desire for God. They call themselves atheists and agnostics. Many identify as humanist or freethinking, skeptical or secular. Some use terms such as *godless* or *god-free*. Others, rejecting labels, say they are simply human beings confronting life as it is. What they share is a worldview unmixed with the supernatural. There is discernible shape to the world of atheism and agnosticism but no uniformity. Atheists and agnostics represent all ages, all nationalities, all ethnicities, all genders, all classes, and a broad spectrum of political loyalties. There are atheists and agnostics in education, politics, business, the arts, entertainment, and, yes, foxholes and—contra Isadore Wing in Erica Jong's novel *Fear of Flying* (1973)—on turbulent airplanes too. There are even atheists and agnostics in temples, synagogues, churches, mosques, covens, seminaries, ashrams, and monasteries. Many who inhabit this worldview put great faith in math and science, but the varieties of atheist and agnostic experience are virtually without number.

This book investigates the ways in which atheists and agnostics have enriched, challenged, and revolutionized public life in the modern period, especially in the United States. It concentrates on individuals, groups, and themes relevant to the present moment, but it also reaches back to figures and developments in the twentieth and nineteenth centuries, decades crucial to the evolution of atheist and agnostic outlooks. Occasionally, the book narrates the long background to a problem or aspiration, reminding us that, while in many ways preeminently modern (and postmodern), atheism and agnosticism have deep roots in the universal human story—a story too often tangled with the history of hate (Diderot himself was incarcerated in solitary confinement for publishing a book on atheism).

Given the nature of an encyclopedia, this book's entries are to be read in the order of the reader's interest, not by order of the alphabet or page number. Each entry is designed to be a whole by itself.

Every book has its roots in a social context, a political debate, or a moment of awakening. This book came to completion during the coronavirus pandemic of 2020 and the global Black Lives Matter movement that brought millions of people into the streets demanding an end to systemic racism—ironically, one of the modern forms of racism traceable to Diderot's "enlightened" generation.

In Albert Camus's novel *The Plague* (1947), on the reading list of many during the time of COVID-19, what sets the atheist narrator Dr. Bernard Rieux apart is his resolve to bear witness to truth in a time of crisis. Not every atheist or agnostic is a hero. Many balk at the category of prophet. Bearing witness or fighting for the right to bear witness, though, is a theme that cuts across the whole panorama of atheist and agnostic experience—from *A* to *Z*.

Acknowledgments

Several people have provided kind assistance and encouragement during the production of this book. I am grateful to George Butler for initiating the project and to my editor, Erin Ryan, for her expert care and guidance. My wife, Mary Huff, deserves great appreciation for her unfailing support and her generous review of my prose. I also thank friends and colleagues, especially Steven Burgess, Lissa McCullough, Marc Davidson, Cesraéa Rumpf, and Todd Fuist, who have offered many helpful criticisms and suggestions. Valued readers of all or significant parts of the text include Courtney Lacy, Harold Kasimow, Jeffrey Marlett, Anne Marie Smith, and Karen Van Fossan. According to my calculation, one dissertation, one memoir, and at least two novels have been delayed by this encyclopedia. The dialogue we shared, exhibiting the "affinity of ideas" that Simone de Beauvoir cherished so profoundly, has made the writing of this book a great adventure. The book is dedicated to the memory of one whose own adventure has been an inspiration for years.

Overview

Atheism and agnosticism are essential to the modern experience. They help to make the modern world what it is, in word and deed. Without these two ideas or sets of ideas, these two ways of seeing the world or being in the world, everything we call modern (and postmodern) would be dramatically different, perhaps unrecognizable. The entire modern project, springing from what historians have long called the Enlightenment of the seventeenth and eighteenth centuries, revolves around freedom: freedom to question authority, freedom to reject oppressive institutions, and freedom to invent new ways of constructing selfhood, organizing community, pursuing happiness, and achieving fulfillment. Atheism and agnosticism express these defining freedoms of the modern age: inquiry, revolution, invention. They permeate every dimension of modernity—from politics, economics, and science to literature, education, entertainment, art, and religion.

Recognizing the importance of atheism and agnosticism is one thing. Understanding what they are is another. Both are difficult to define. Many discussions of atheism and agnosticism suffer from simplistic assumptions about the meaning of the terms and the phenomena to which they point. Routinely, atheism and agnosticism are reduced to questions of belief. According to conventional wisdom, atheism is belief in the nonexistence of God or disbelief in the existence of God. Agnosticism, sometimes caricatured as timid or tepid atheism, is seen as the inability or unwillingness to believe with any degree of certainty in God's existence or nonexistence.

These common approaches to atheism and agnosticism tell only a fraction of the story. As intellectual shorthand, they get a conversation started. For people who identify as atheist or agnostic, they may get the conversation started in the wrong way or aimed in the wrong direction. They may not only tell just a fraction of the story but may actually tell the fraction of the story in a way that is misleading, forestalling any hope of holistic understanding.

Concentrating on belief or unbelief (not to mention the concept of God with a capital *G*)—categories borrowed largely from Christian theology—contributes to narrow and distorted portraits of atheism and agnosticism. A brief review of atheist and agnostic literature reveals a number of other factors shaping these distinctive outlooks and orientations: critique, defiance, disenchantment, discovery, liberation, and exhilaration, just to name a few. These themes offer not only a sense of atheist and agnostic beliefs or ideas but also a glimpse of the many moods and concerns that make atheist and agnostic experiences so multifaceted. Defining a worldview in terms borrowed from another worldview is never a reliable way to grasp its angle of vision or hear its voice. Acknowledging that beliefs about God may not necessarily constitute the main characteristics of atheism and agnosticism is an important first step toward allowing these important realities to speak for themselves.

Grammar itself is a challenge when it comes to understanding atheism and agnosticism. Too often, atheism and agnosticism and their adherents have been pictured exclusively in terms of negation or lack: not believing something, not having something, not being something. A long train of synonyms with negative prefixes or suffixes reinforces this trend: unbeliever, nonbeliever, irreligious, antireligious, nonreligious, antitheist, nontheist, infidel, godless, ungodly, and misotheist ("hater" of God). Even twenty-first-century nicknames such as None (as in "none of the above [religions]") and Done (as in "done with religion") fit the pattern. This trend goes back to the Greek basis for each word: *atheos* (*a* + *theos* = "without god") and *agnosis* (*a* + *gnosis* = "without knowledge"). Today, any number of atheists and agnostics may capitalize on the negative flavor of the root terms, boldly defying what they take to be the oppressive nature of religion and the God idea. Some people who find religion meaningless and God a useless hypothesis, however, avoid *atheist* and *agnostic* precisely because of the negative stigmas associated with the labels. Many gravitate toward substitutes such as *freethinker, humanist,* and *secularist,* or the twenty-first-century neologism *Bright,* promoted by supporters of the New Atheist movement. Others attempt to remind the general public and fellow atheists and agnostics that grammatically negative terms need not be construed as signifying undesirable states of being at all. A *non*addictive drug is a good thing, as is an *un*injured body or a flaw*less* performance of music. Some participants in this terminological debate suggest that God-*free* or god-*free* (the issue of letter case always entering into the discussion too) may be the best way to state in a positive way what appears to be a negative.

The twenty-first century has witnessed the appearance of a new class of confident advocates for secularity and nonreligion, eager to present atheism and agnosticism in a positive and compelling light. For them, atheism and agnosticism are far more than a nay-saying to a question of belief or a refutation of somebody else's worldview. Social scientist Phil Zuckerman exemplifies this approach in *Living the Secular Life* (2014). He maintains that atheism is not a reversal of something or a rejection of a competing viewpoint. It is a constructive, affirmative way of being in the world, based on courage and awe and yielding authenticity and contentment. Lesley Hazleton, in *Agnostic: A Spirited Manifesto* (2017), argues that cultivated not-knowing can be, and long has been, the effective basis for a life marked by intellectual adventure and generous empathy for other human beings. Questioning and questing, she says, lead to richer ends than what rigid avowal or denial can provide.

Such forthright recommendations of atheism and agnosticism have been extremely rare in history. They are stark reminders of how modern—how new, that is—open, organized, socially active, and legally protected atheism and agnosticism truly are. The track record of atheophobia, fear or hatred of atheists, is as long as the history of atheism itself. In some countries, blasphemy and apostasy laws still exist and still exact severe punishment on the individual who will not conform to fixed standards of belief and behavior. Even in societies with protections for freedom of speech and conscience, outspoken atheism can wreck a career or relationship. The history of doubt and dissent—things that generally fall under the category of agnosticism—has also been accompanied by suspicion, accusation, and penalties for individuals who fail or refuse to endorse reigning orthodoxies.

The academic study of the history of atheism and agnosticism is in its early stages. Until the late twentieth century, it was little more than a footnote to the history of philosophy and religious thought. Too often it was blurred with accounts of religious heresies and other deviations from ecclesiastically defined creeds. Greater acceptance of intellectual diversity in present-day society has fueled growing interest in atheism and agnosticism's past. Unfortunately, undisciplined quests for atheist and agnostic forebears, sometimes portrayed as trendsetters or heroes, have been only exercises in wishful thinking. Twentieth-century theologian Karl Barth once described the then-fashionable quest for the historical Jesus as the process by which liberal Christian scholars, looking down the well of history, discovered not an eccentric first-century radical but simply the reflection of their own faces—and their own modern values and desires. The contemporary search for atheist and agnostic ancestors risks a similar process of projection and anachronism.

At least three significant challenges face the historian of atheism and agnosticism. One is the convention of the periodization of history. Carving history into preconceived chapters, such as ancient, medieval, Renaissance, Enlightenment, modern, and the like, is still a standard practice in the academy and the media. These titles are frequently woven into the stories of atheism and agnosticism. Freighted with a load of assumptions that may distort more than they describe, the labels should be employed with caution and self-awareness. Referring to the intellectual innovation of highly literate male European thinkers in the seventeenth and eighteenth centuries as the "Enlightenment" highlights that era's revolutionary new ways of studying nature and imagining society. At the same time, "Enlightenment" and its equivalents in French and German, *Siècle des lumières* and *Aufklärung*, grant cover for notions of race, gender, and progress that subsidized the African slave trade, the genocide of Indigenous peoples, colonialism, and government exclusively by white, property-owning men. The myth of the Enlightenment as the Age of Reason obscures the era's self-contradictions and ignores its injustices.

Another challenge to the historical study of atheism and agnosticism is, again, terminology itself. *Atheism* first appeared in English, and *athéisme* in French, in the mid-1500s. Each was initially a term of derision, not self-description. *Agnosticism*, by contrast originally a matter of self-identification, was coined only in 1869. These terms, while remarkably flexible, have come to be seen as relatively reliable indicators of recognizable positions or mindsets in various phases of modern history. It is a matter of debate, though, whether the terms effectively correspond to states of mind harbored by some people in earlier periods of history. If no language existed to describe the state of affairs, and especially if the danger to person and freedom was so grave that admission of atheism or agnosticism would have meant possible prison or death, how can anyone point to individuals in the premodern past, individuals lacking words or safety to speak up, and confidently identify those figures as atheists or agnostics? One standard principle in the study of language is the appearance of words only when societies need them—to aid in the discussion of realities that are socially or psychologically noticeable or undeniably relevant for the first time. Could this mean that there might be something peculiarly modern about atheism and agnosticism themselves? Is modernity the age of atheism and agnosticism? Or is the modern period one chapter in the story of these worldviews?

A third challenge to the construction of atheist and agnostic lineages is the built-in Eurocentrism of most inquiries into their backgrounds. The vast majority of histories of atheism and agnosticism have been written by Western writers, for Western readers, about a certain set of Western people. The standard narrative arc, tracing a line of skepticism and unbelief from ancient Greek suspicion about the gods to twenty-first-century North Atlantic New Atheism, tends to confirm this conclusion. Haunting every study of atheism and agnosticism, past and present, is the question of the relationship between atheism and agnosticism and the specific forms, assumptions, and styles of Western intellectual life. Are atheism and agnosticism, in other words, primarily Western phenomena? If they are, then atheism and agnosticism, like Protestant Christianity, modern science, and rock music, would appear to be not only some of the most important products of the Western world's cultural economy but also some of its chief exports. If they are not essentially Western, then what are the signs of atheism and agnosticism in cultures that have not been substantially influenced by such Abrahamic traditions as Judaism, Christianity, and Islam—in cultures, that is, without a history of obsession with the concept signified by the singular term *God*? Are there compelling reasons to describe certain forms of philosophical outlook in, say, African or Australian or American Indigenous cultures, or in South or East Asian cultures, as varieties of the things we call atheism and agnosticism?

Despite the challenges, a number of historians have attempted to narrate a chronicle of atheism and agnosticism stretching from ancient to modern times and around the globe. Most efforts of this kind begin their narratives in the first millennium BCE. Few examine the full time of *Homo sapiens* on Earth (about three hundred thousand years). Almost none consider the lives and strivings of other *Homo* species, which would extend the story of the human mind back to around 2,500,000 BCE. The best archaeological evidence suggests that magic and religion have shaped human experience for millennia. God and gods, however, have been relatively recent additions to human cultural life.

Depending exclusively on written evidence, many historians identify possible first signs of atheism and agnosticism in India's nontheist Sankhya philosophy or the traditions of Jainism and Buddhism, dating from around 500 BCE. Some point to folk traditions in ancient China that evolved into Daoism and Confucianism, some to systems of thought that planted the seeds for the human-centered African *ubuntu* ethic. Many historians, writing from a Western perspective, claim to find atheist and agnostic ancestors in a handful of ancient Mediterranean nonconformists: three Greeks from the fifth century BCE—Protagoras of Abdera, Theodorus of Cyrene, and Diagoras of Melos, author of the skeptical *On the Gods*—and two Romans from the first century BCE—Cicero, author of *On the Nature of the Gods*, and Lucretius, author of *On the Nature of Things*. The supreme difficulty entailed in these efforts is the problem of demonstrating the connection between ancient people who thought gods to be irrelevant and modern people who see God and gods as imaginary. The quest for the world's first atheist or first agnostic, while tantalizing, is fraught with trouble. Many critics say it is wrongheaded from the start. Atheism and agnosticism have no origins, they contend. They are names for the natural state of the human mind, as old as the human species.

The student of atheism and agnosticism is on firmer ground investigating the phenomena today. One of the most striking features of these ways of life and thought is their variety. A diversity of types of atheism and agnosticism confronts the open-minded researcher. Often the types can be grouped into pairs of contrasting forms: rational versus emotional, organic versus organized, active versus passive, naive versus sophisticated. Some atheists and agnostics are raised in nonreligion. Some have transformations of mind and heart along the lines of a religious conversion. Some are in the closet, some out. Some have no argument with religion. Others wrestle with gods for a lifetime. Some struggle to figure out what all the fuss is about. Some insist that atheism and agnosticism have intellectual content—specific ideas. Others say the positions represent independence from all creeds, even anticreeds. Some treat science like a substitute deity. Others are suspicious of scientism. Some are progressives seeking radical social change. Others are aloof and elitist, content with the status quo. Some are happy. Others are nostalgic, mourning a lost faith. Some could not believe if they wanted to. Others, spiritually homeless, dwell between belief and unbelief, half conscious, as philosopher Martin Heidegger put it, of the "trace of the fugitive gods."

Counting these diverse individuals is becoming less daunting. More social scientists are specializing in the study of nonreligion. More atheists and agnostics are speaking up. An obstacle to demographic accuracy, however, remains terminology, distinguishing the difference between *atheist* and *agnostic, humanist, secularist,* and *freethinker*—terms often used interchangeably by the same person.

Self-declared atheists are the easiest to quantify. Some estimates place the worldwide atheist population at five hundred million to seven hundred million. Factoring in covert atheists would raise the number exponentially. Nations reporting the highest percentages of people who identify as atheists, all in double digits, include China, Japan, the Czech Republic, Australia, Iceland, Belgium, Denmark, and France.

In the United States, the many forms of nonreligion are rapidly growing. According to the Pew Research Center (https://pewresearch.org), from 2009 to 2019, the percentage of adults who identify as atheists doubled, from 2 percent to 4 percent. Agnostics increased from 3 percent to 5 percent. People with no religious affiliation, the so-called Nones, grew from 12 percent to 17 percent. By 2019, over one-quarter of the U.S. adult population claimed no religion—an unprecedented moment in the history of a country still described by some as Christian. Every study indicates that the highest rates of unbelief and nonaffiliation, and the fastest rates of change, are among young adults. Even the most sober analysts are forced to imagine a soon-to-be majority American population for whom the national motto "In God We Trust" is not only a relic of the past but a bewildering and insulting one at that.

All of this confirms that atheism and agnosticism have enormous social, political, and cultural significance, especially, as French philosopher Michel Onfray has said, "when private belief becomes a public matter." The growing visibility and normality of unbelief affect everything in contemporary life—from the way people raise children and count their years to the way they relate to their planet and respond to someone who sneezes. At stake is the definition of the good life for the individual and the community. Perhaps atheism and agnosticism have been options for all humans throughout the storied past of the species. They definitely have intimate ties to modernity and the yearning for freedom at the heart of the conflicted and litigious Enlightenment legacy. The study of atheism and agnosticism is the study of people striving to think and live in freedom without supernatural help or hindrance.

Further Reading

Baggini, Julian. *Atheism: A Very Short Introduction.* Oxford: Oxford University Press, 2003.

Berman, Marshall. *All That Is Solid Melts into Air: The Experience of Modernity*. New York: Penguin, 1988.

Buckley, Michael J. *At the Origins of Modern Atheism*. New Haven, CT: Yale University Press, 1987.

Bullivant, Stephen, and Michael Ruse, eds. *The Oxford Handbook of Atheism*. Oxford: Oxford University Press, 2013.

Eagleton, Terry. *Culture and the Death of God*. New Haven, CT: Yale University Press, 2015.

Gosden, Chris. *Prehistory: A Very Short Introduction*. Oxford: Oxford University Press, 2003.

Gray, John. *Seven Types of Atheism*. New York: Farrar, Straus and Giroux, 2018.

Hazleton, Lesley. *Agnostic: A Spirited Manifesto*. New York: Riverhead Books, 2017.

Hecht, Jennifer Michael. *Doubt: A History*. San Francisco: HarperSanFrancisco, 2003.

Heidegger, Martin. *Poetry, Language, Thought*. Trans. Albert Hofstadter. New York: Harper and Row, 1971.

Hyman, Gavin. *A Short History of Atheism*. London: I. B. Tauris, 2010.

Le Poidevin, Robin. *Agnosticism: A Very Short Introduction*. Oxford: Oxford University Press, 2010.

Martin, Michael, ed. *The Cambridge Companion to Atheism*. Cambridge: Cambridge University Press, 2007.

Marty, Martin E. *Varieties of Unbelief*. New York: Anchor Books, 1966.

McGowan, Dale. *Atheism for Dummies*. Mississauga, ON, Canada: John Wiley and Sons, 2013.

Onfray, Michel. *Atheist Manifesto: The Case against Christianity, Judaism, and Islam*. Trans. Jeremy Leggatt. New York: Arcade, 2011.

Taylor, Charles. *A Secular Age*. Cambridge, MA: Belknap Press of Harvard University Press, 2007.

Watson, Peter. *The Age of Atheists: How We Have Sought to Live Since the Death of God*. New York: Simon and Schuster, 2014.

Yolyon, John W., Roy Porter, Pat Rogers, and Barbara Maria Stafford, eds. *The Blackwell Companion to the Enlightenment*. Oxford: Blackwell, 1995.

Zuckerman, Phil. *Living the Secular Life: New Answers to Old Questions*. New York: Penguin, 2014.

Chronology

1811—Percy Bysshe Shelley, known as the "Eton Atheist," is expelled from Oxford University for writing *The Necessity of Atheism*.

1829—Radical printer Richard Carlile, publisher of Thomas Paine, and freethinking Rev. Robert Taylor, known as the "Devil's Chaplain," conduct the Infidel Home Missionary Tour of England.

1832—Pantheist and former Universalist minister Abner Kneeland founds the free-thought journal *Boston Investigator*.

1835—David Friedrich Strauss publishes *Das Leben Jesu, kritisch bearbeitet* (*The Life of Jesus, Critically Examined*).

1838—The last person tried for blasphemy in the United States, Abner Kneeland, serves sixty days in a Boston jail.

1841—Ludwig Feuerbach publishes *Das Wesen des Christentums* (*The Essence of Christianity*).

1843—Karl Marx calls religion the "opium of the people" in *Critique of Hegel's Philosophy of Right*.

1845—The first National Convention of Infidels is held in the United States.

1846—George Eliot publishes an English translation of David Friedrich Strauss's *Das Leben Jesu, kritisch bearbeitet* (*The Life of Jesus, Critically Examined*).

1848—Karl Marx and Friedrich Engels publish *The Communist Manifesto*.

1850—Alfred, Lord Tennyson publishes the poem *In Memoriam*, speaking of nature as "red in tooth and claw" and the value of "honest doubt."

1854—George Eliot publishes an English translation of Ludwig Feuerbach's *Das Wesen des Christentums* (*The Essence of Christianity*).

1859—Charles Darwin publishes *The Origin of Species*.

1866—Charles Bradlaugh founds the National Secular Society in the United Kingdom.

1867—Matthew Arnold publishes the poem "Dover Beach," on the "melancholy, long, withdrawing roar" of the once high "Sea of Faith."

1869—Thomas Henry Huxley coins the term *agnostic*.

1871—Britain abolishes the religious test for universities.

1877—Charles Bradlaugh publishes *A Plea for Atheism*.

Felix Adler founds the Society for Ethical Culture in the United States.

1878—Annie Besant publishes *My Path to Atheism*.

1880—Fyodor Dostoevsky publishes *The Brothers Karamazov*.

1882—Friedrich Nietzsche publishes *The Gay Science*, announcing "God is dead."

1883–1885—Friedrich Nietzsche publishes *Thus Spoke Zarathustra*.

1885—The Rationalist Association (originally Rationalist Press Association) is founded in the United Kingdom.

1886—Charles Bradlaugh, Britain's first openly atheist elected member of Parliament, takes his seat in the House of Commons.

1888—British Parliament passes the Oaths Act, permitting members of Parliament to affirm the Oath of Allegiance without swearing on a Bible to God.

Theodore Roosevelt calls Thomas Paine, author of *The Age of Reason*, a "filthy little atheist."

1889—Thomas Henry Huxley publishes his essay "Agnosticism."

1892—American ex-Quaker atheist and Dianist free-love advocate Elmina D. Slenker launches the children's magazine *The Little Freethinker*.

1895—Elizabeth Cady Stanton publishes *The Woman's Bible*.

1896—Elizabeth Cady Stanton publishes *The Degraded Status of Woman in the Bible*.

Richard Strauss's symphonic tone poem *Also Sprach Zarathustra*, inspired by Nietzsche's *Thus Spoke Zarathustra*, premieres in Frankfurt.

1907—H. L. Mencken publishes *The Philosophy of Friedrich Nietzsche*, the first book on Nietzsche in English.

1912—Thomas Hardy publishes the poem "God's Funeral."

1913—Sigmund Freud publishes *Totem and Taboo*.

1916—Emma Goldman publishes *The Philosophy of Atheism and the Failure of Christianity*.

1925—The League of Militant Atheists is founded in the USSR.

Clarence Darrow serves as defense attorney at the antievolution Scopes trial in Dayton, Tennessee.

1927—Sigmund Freud publishes *The Future of an Illusion*.

1933—The first Humanist Manifesto is published.

1939—Sigmund Freud publishes *Moses and Monotheism*.

1940—Bertrand Russell, declared "unfit to teach philosophy," is dismissed from College of the City of New York.

1941—The American Humanist Association is founded.

1943—Jean-Paul Sartre publishes *Being and Nothingness*.

1945—Sartre delivers his "Existentialism Is a Humanism" lecture at Club Maintenant, Paris.

1948—The BBC broadcasts a debate between Bertrand Russell and Jesuit philosopher Frederick Copleston on the existence of God.

1950—Bertrand Russell receives the Nobel Prize in Literature.

Antony Flew presents a paper titled "Theology and Falsification" at the Socratic Club, Oxford University.

1952—The first World Humanist Congress is held.

The International Humanist and Ethical Union (now Humanists International) is founded.

The Amsterdam Declaration is released.

1953—The American Humanist Association inaugurates the Humanist of the Year Award.

1954—"Under God" is added to the U.S. Pledge of Allegiance.

1955—*Inherit the Wind*, a play based loosely on the Scopes trial, premieres.

1956—"In God We Trust" is declared the official motto of the United States.

1960—A film version of *Inherit the Wind* is released.

1961—The First Secretary of the Communist Party of the USSR, Nikita Khrushchev, claims that the first human in space, Soviet cosmonaut Yuri Gagarin, said he saw no God while orbiting Earth.

1962—Prayer in public schools is declared unconstitutional by the U.S. Supreme Court.

The Fellowship of Religious Humanists (later, the Unitarian Universalist Humanist Association) is founded in the Unitarian Universalist Association.

1963—Bible reading in public schools is declared unconstitutional by the U.S. Supreme Court.

Anglican Bishop John A. T. Robinson publishes *Honest to God*.

Madalyn Murray O'Hair founds American Atheists.

1964—The U.S. Supreme Court classifies secular humanism as a religion.

Jean-Paul Sartre refuses the Nobel Prize in Literature.

1965—The Vatican establishes the *Secretaria Pro Non Credentibus* (Secretariat for Nonbelievers).

Harvey Cox publishes *The Secular City*.

Leslie Weatherhead publishes *The Christian Agnostic*.

1966—Thomas J. J. Altizer publishes *The Gospel of Christian Atheism*.

Time magazine publishes an Easter issue with a red-and-black "Is God Dead?" cover.

Playboy magazine publishes radical theologian William Hamilton's essay "God Is Dead."

1967—Albania becomes world's first avowed atheist nation-state.

1969—Paul Kurtz founds Prometheus Books.

Sherwin Wine founds the Society for Humanistic Judaism.

1971—John Lennon and Yoko Ono's song "Imagine" is released.

1973—The Humanist Manifesto II is published.

1976—Antony Flew publishes *The Presumption of Atheism*.

1977—Harvard University establishes a humanist chaplaincy.

1978—Anne Nicol Gaylor and Annie Laurie Gaylor establish the Freedom from Religion Foundation.

1980—Paul Kurtz and over fifty signatories release *A Secular Humanist Declaration*.

1984—The BBC airs Don Cupitt's *The Sea of Faith* series.

1987—President George H. W. Bush reportedly says he does not think atheists "should be regarded as citizens" of the United States of America.

1988—Salman Rushdie publishes the novel *The Satanic Verses.*

1989—The "Rushdie Affair" begins, as Iran's Ayatollah Ruhollah Khomeini issues a *fatwa* calling for the death of novelist Salman Rushdie.

African Americans for Humanism is founded by Norm R. Allen Jr.

1991—The death metal band Atheist releases its *Unquestionable Presence* album.

1995—The Dutch philosopher Herman Philipse publishes *Atheïstisch Manifest.*

1999—Lana and Lilly Wachowski's science fiction film *The Matrix* is released.

2002—The Amsterdam Declaration 2002 is promulgated at the World Humanist Congress.

The Godless Americans March is held in Washington, DC.

The Secular Coalition for America is formed.

2003—*Humanism and Its Aspirations* (Humanist Manifesto III) is published.

2004—Sam Harris publishes *The End of Faith.*

2005—Barry Kosmin establishes the Institute for the Study of Secularism in Society and Culture at Trinity College, Hartford, Connecticut.

Gregory Epstein is appointed humanist chaplain at Harvard University.

Science writer Rebecca Watson founds the *Skepchick* blog and website.

2006—Richard Dawkins publishes *The God Delusion.*

The Richard Dawkins Foundation for Reason and Science is founded.

U.S. journalist Gary Wolf coins the term *New Atheism.*

The Pastafarian parody-religion founder Bobby Henderson publishes *The Gospel of the Flying Spaghetti Monster.*

2007—Ayaan Hirsi Ali publishes *Infidel.*

California representative Pete Stark becomes the first openly atheist member of U.S. Congress.

The film *The Great Debaters,* based on the career of Wiley College professor Melvin B. Tolson, an African American humanist and defender of evolution, is released.

2008—The Nonreligion and Secularity Research Network is founded by University of Kent scholar Lois Lee.

The term *None* is first used to designate religiously unaffiliated individuals.

Bill Maher's film *Religulous* is released.

The first Skepticon is held in the United States.

Comedian/writer Ariane Sherine organizes the Atheist Bus Campaign in Britain.

2009—Hemant Mehta begins The *Friendly Atheist* blog for Patheos.

Jon Amiel's film *Creation* is released.

2010—The first Global Atheist Convention is held in Melbourne, Australia.

2011—Susan Jacoby inaugurates the *Washington Post*'s "Spirited Atheist" column.

Alain de Botton presents his "Atheism 2.0" TED talk.

Mandisa L. Thomas founds the nonprofit Black Nonbelievers Inc.

The Nonreligion and Secularity Research Network launches the journal *Nonreligion and Secularity*.

Australian singer/songwriter Shelley Segal releases *An Atheist Album*.

The metal band Gaytheist is founded.

Phil Zuckerman establishes the first department of secular studies (Pitzer College) in U.S. higher education.

The World Atheist Convention is held in Dublin, Ireland.

2012—The International Humanist and Ethical Union (now Humanists International) launches its annual Freedom of Thought Report.

The second Global Atheist Convention is held in Melbourne, Australia.

The first Women's Secular Conference is held.

Secular Woman Inc. is founded.

Jennifer McCreight founds Atheism Plus (Atheism+).

The first Reason Rally is held in Washington, DC.

2013—October 5 is named annual Atheist Appreciation Day.

The Black Secular Rally is held in New York.

The first atheist monument is erected on U.S. government property.

Sylvia Broeckx's documentary *Hug an Atheist* is released.

2014—AtheistTV is launched by American Atheists.

2016—Sweden opens the nation's first atheist cemetery.

The Frank W. Wolf International Religious Freedom Act extends protection to atheists and nonreligious individuals.

The second Reason Rally is held in Washington, DC.

2018—*Humanist* magazine publishes a cover story on "Five Fierce Humanists: Unapologetically Black Women Beyond Belief."

The U.S. Congress bars a secular humanist from serving as a Navy chaplain.

Sam Harris releases the documentary film *Islam and the Future of Tolerance*.

2019—The Women of Color beyond Belief Conference is held.

2020—Mubarak Bala, president of the Humanist Association of Nigeria, is arrested and detained by Nigerian authorities.

Agnosticism

Agnosticism, as a way of thinking and a way of being in the world, has been a part of human experience for centuries. Around 500 BCE, Confucius, in China, and the historical Buddha, Siddhartha Gautama, in India, were famously hesitant to pronounce definitive answers to abstract questions about metaphysics, gods, ghosts, and the afterlife. According to the *Analects*, Confucius (Kongzi) did not speak of "prodigies, force, disorders, or spirits." In ancient Greece just a few decades later, the pre-Socratic philosopher Protagoras, in his now lost work *On the Gods*, admitted he possessed no way of knowing whether deities existed.

As a word, *agnosticism* has been a part of human discourse just since the nineteenth century. Thomas Henry Huxley, British biologist and champion of Charles Darwin's theory of evolution, invented the term in 1869. Sweeping adoption of the term in the Victorian age established it as an essential component of communication and self-identification in the modern world. Today, agnosticism is seen as a distinctive response to the question of religious belief and compared with one or more of the varieties of atheism or nonreligion. A-to-Z surveys on religious affiliation, which usually end with Zen or Zoroastrianism, often begin with Agnosticism.

While atheism is popularly defined as belief in the nonexistence of God or disbelief in the existence of God, agnosticism is typically caricatured as timid or tame atheism, a soft or passive or even lazy form of unbelief. Theologian John Courtney Murray called it "atheism by default." The term is sometimes associated with an inability or unwillingness to believe with any degree of certainty in God's existence or nonexistence. The Greek basis for the modern word—*agnosis* (*a* + *gnosis* = "without knowledge")—suggests this quality of uncertainty or ambiguity. For philosopher John Dewey, agnosticism, in contrast to the cloudless sky of atheism, was the "shadow cast by the eclipse of the supernatural."

Huxley, impatient with ideological labels, coined the term as an antidote to such confining categories. As he indicated in his 1889 essay "Agnosticism," he did not intend to name a position on the spectrum of responses to the question of God. Agnosticism, he said, represented a general approach to all questions facing human beings—not itself an answer, and certainly not a creed or flight into indecision, but rather a disciplined way of thinking through problems, a posture of openness before the unknown and the possibly unknowable. For Huxley, the true agnostic was one who put faith in the power of reason as far as it would go and respected the questions reason could not fully clarify or explain.

Huxley's original meaning of the term is found in the methodological agnosticism of present-day natural and social sciences—the attitudinal quality that allows empirical scientific method to operate according to its own principles and in tune with its own integrity. At its best, this practice incorporates a stance of intellectual honesty before an open question or line of inquiry. Such a suspension of belief, along with awareness of implicit bias, allows the researcher to analyze a question as impartially as possible, contemplate the merits of a hypothesis patiently, and follow evidence wherever it might lead, no matter what the outcome. In this sense, agnosticism is little more than the proper exercise of academic freedom and scholarly responsibility, withholding judgment until all the evidence has been collected, scrutinized, and interpreted.

More often than not, agnosticism takes the form of a particular sort of response to the subject of God, distinct from both atheism and theism. Drawing from the root meaning of the word, many who claim to be agnostic, when faced with the question of God's existence, say they simply do not know. The terms of the God-question, they say, lack proper clarity, or the evidence by which one would settle the question is incomplete, unconvincing, or incredible. Some agnostics claim that such questions are beyond the capacity of human beings to answer precisely or persuasively. Others, peeling back multiple layers of not knowing, admit that they not only do not know but that they also do not know how anyone could ever know. If God is infinite mind or spirit, they ask, what kind of data would grant knowledge of such a mystery's existence or nonexistence? Many different kinds of agnostics apply the same criteria to questions of miracles, revelations, and life after death.

Individuals who have adopted the term to describe their own intellectual or psychological position have included many artists, writers, educators, scientists, philosophers, business leaders, entertainers, activists, and other public figures. Huxley's idol, Darwin, was one of the earliest and most eminent. According to a 2019 Pew Research Center survey, 5 percent of the U.S. adult population self-identify as agnostic.

Since the early twentieth century, theologians, clergy, and other religious individuals have also found the term helpful in expressing their complex positions. Agnosticism does not exist only outside religious traditions. Forms of agnosticism can be found within religious communities. After World War II, German émigré and liberal Protestant thinker Paul Tillich represented a theological sea change during that age of anxiety. In his *Dynamics of Faith* (1957) and three-volume *Systematic Theology* (1951–1963), he defined doubt as a necessary and valuable component of genuine faith or ultimate concern—this, after German theologian Rudolf Bultmann had revolutionized New Testament studies with his program of demythologization, translating the biblical message into secular terms. Likewise, Leslie Weatherhead's *The Christian Agnostic* (1965) answered a great need among believers struggling to make sense of the clash between the prescientific truth claims of their heritages and the realities of their everyday lives in modernity. The creedless Unitarian Universalist movement has for decades honored doubt and uncertainty as natural companions to the responsible search for truth. For centuries, doubt and skepticism have played venerable roles in the great dharma traditions stemming from South Asia. Author of *The Faith to Doubt: Glimpses of Buddhist Uncertainty* (1990), Stephen Batchelor calls the built-in agnosticism of Buddhism an effective form of intellectual and psychological therapy.

With the appearance of New Atheism and the rise of the Nones, a contemporary rediscovery of the breadth and depth of Huxley's agnosticism is underway in late modern, or postmodern, society. In *The Unknown God* (2004), British philosopher Anthony Kenny describes agnosticism as an attitude of intellectual humility equidistant from the hard-to-defend certainties of both faith and antitheism. Lesley Hazleton's *Agnostic: A Spirited Manifesto* (2017) argues that cultivated not-knowing can be the effective basis for a life marked by intellectual adventure and generous empathy. Still, agnosticism is routinely pictured as atheism's irresolute cousin. In contrast to both the faith of unconditional assent and unbelief styled as absolute denial or rejection, agnosticism points to a third way of negotiating the questions that make human experience human.

See also: Christianity, Atheism and Agnosticism in; Darwin, Charles; Huxleys, The; Nones

Further Reading

Batchelor, Stephen. *Buddhism without Beliefs: A Contemporary Guide to Awakening*. New York: Riverhead Books, 1997.

Batchelor, Stephen. *The Faith to Doubt: Glimpses of Buddhist Uncertainty*. Berkeley, CA: Counterpoint, 2015.

Church, F. Forrester, ed. *The Essential Tillich: An Anthology of the Writings of Paul Tillich*. New York: Collier Books, 1987.

Confucius. *The Analects*. Trans. Raymond Dawson. Oxford: Oxford University Press, 2008.

Dewey, John. *A Common Faith*. New Haven, CT: Yale University Press, 1934.

Goodin, David. *An Agnostic in the Fellowship of Christ: The Ethical Mysticism of Albert Schweitzer*. Lanham, MD: Lexington Books/Fortress Academic, 2019.

Hazleton, Lesley. *Agnostic: A Spirited Manifesto*. New York: Riverhead Books, 2017.

Hecht, Jennifer Michael. *Doubt: A History*. San Francisco: HarperSanFrancisco, 2003.

Kenny, Anthony. *The Unknown God: Agnostic Essays*. London: Continuum, 2004.

Le Poidevin, Robin. *Agnosticism: A Very Short Introduction*. Oxford: Oxford University Press, 2010.

Murray, John Courtney. *The Problem of God*. New Haven, CT: Yale University Press, 1964.

Weatherhead, Leslie. *The Christian Agnostic*. Nashville, TN: Abingdon Press, 1990.

Amsterdam Declarations

Two important documents, advancing the cause of worldwide humanism, bear the title *Amsterdam Declaration*. The first was released in 1952, the second in 2002. Both documents communicate the essentials of the humanist vision of life and its relevance for the contemporary world. The complete text of each declaration is posted on the website of Humanists

International, a nongovernmental organization recognized by the United Nations (https://humanists.international/what-is-humanism/the-amsterdam -declaration).

The initial Amsterdam Declaration was a product of the first World Humanist Congress, which convened in 1952 in the Dutch capital city. The event was the launch of the International Humanist and Ethical Union (IHEU), a consortium of humanist, atheist, free thought, and secularist groups from around the world. Founders included two future signers of the second Humanist Manifesto (1973): Julian Huxley, author of *Religion without Revelation* (1927), and Harold Blackham, author of *Six Existentialist Thinkers* (1952). In 2019, the IHEU changed its name to Humanists International.

The 1952 Amsterdam Declaration was framed in the context of a double crisis: the aftermath of World War II and the initial years of the Cold War. In five short paragraphs, the document portrayed humanism as a third way toward global peace and community, in contrast to both revealed religions and modern totalitarian systems. Humanism, it maintained, is a holistic philosophy of life, an undogmatic faith, that unites "all those who cannot any longer believe the various creeds and are willing to base their conviction on respect for man [*sic*] as a spiritual and moral being." Humanism's core values, the declaration said, are democratic decision-making, the wedding of science to human welfare, recognition of the dignity and freedom of each human person, promotion of social responsibility through nonsectarian education, and creation of a community offering all people meaningful opportunities for self-expression and self-realization.

The second declaration was prepared for Humanists International's fiftieth anniversary convention, also held in the Netherlands. The 2002 document was an updating and expansion of the original. The exclusive language of the first declaration was eliminated, and expressions drawn from mid-twentieth-century religious humanism that described humanism as a faith were also removed or modified. The natural world was given greater prominence, the "transforming power of art" was allotted its own section, and a full paragraph was devoted to a critique of the alleged historic attempt of the world's major religions to impose their worldviews of divine revelation on all of humanity. Issues not explicitly mentioned include sexism, gender diversity, racism, colonialism, and climate change. Designed, like its prototype, to be a brief document trading in universal themes, the 2002 declaration, in seven economical paragraphs, highlighted the moral concern at the heart of humanism and represented an effort to balance reverence for reason and science with appreciation for the role of imagination and creativity in human experience. Along with the three official Humanist Manifestos (1933, 1973, and 2003), the Amsterdam Declarations serve as core documents in humanism's evolving canon of classics.

See also: Humanism; Humanist Manifestos; Huxleys, The; Organizations, Atheist and Agnostic

Further Reading

Gasenbeek, Bert, and Babu Gogineni, eds. *International Humanist and Ethical Union 1952–2002: Past, Present and Future.* Utrecht, Netherlands: De Tijdstroom Uitgeverij, 2002.

Atheism

Atheism is a major factor in modern and postmodern society. It is both a way of seeing the world and a way of being in the world. For centuries, atheism has been described by people who have not been atheists. Often they have been opponents, censuring atheism on religious, social, political, psychological, and ethical grounds. Too often they have been people speculating about what other people think or feel, without concrete knowledge of the lived experience of atheism. Atheists themselves talk about atheism in many different ways. Just as there are varieties of religious experience, there are varieties of atheist experience. The meaning of atheism is neither obvious nor simple.

The term *atheism* and its equivalents first appeared in European languages during the sixteenth century. The words were based on the Greek *atheos* (*a + theos* = "without god"). In ancient Mediterranean cultures, people stigmatized with this label, including Socrates, around 400 BCE, promoted not a worldview antagonistic to divine beings but a critical approach to ideas, seeing value in the free examination of society's unquestioned assumptions. In the first century CE, Roman elites called Jews and Christians atheists. The allegiance to only one deity—an unknown deity from western Asia, invisible and male but seemingly celibate—rivaled the folk religions of the empire, threatened the cult of the emperor, and stumped the Roman imagination. Once the Christian church gained worldly power, it turned the tables and called practitioners of the older religions atheists, saying pagan gods were not gods at all. Muslim authorities, after the rise of Islam in the seventh century, issued similar declarations. By the early modern period, Western writers and their Arab, Turkish, and Persian counterparts used words derived from *atheos* as all-purpose terms of abuse, not precise references to a specific point of view. Cambridge theologian Henry More's *An Antidote against Atheisme* (1653) was as much about witchcraft and religious fanaticism as what people today call atheism. Due to widespread blasphemy and obscenity laws, few people before 1800 openly described themselves as atheist.

Conventional wisdom speaks of atheism as belief in the nonexistence of God or disbelief in the existence of God. Many atheists agree. They associate atheism with issues of belief and identify many reasons for nonbelief. Debates hinge on what is not believed. Some atheists approach the question in abstract terms, claiming atheism means repudiation of all gods, from Apollo to Wotan. Others acknowledge that modern Western atheism springs from an intellectual culture shaped by Christianity. They relate today's atheism directly to the God of Christian theism (who is almost always referred to with a capital *G*). In many respects, the atheism of many atheists is a mirror image of Christianity.

The vast literature on atheism by atheists reveals many more nuanced understandings of atheism. Some writers recognize that the God denied by atheists does not always correspond to the God affirmed by believers. Aware of the complexities within theism, they share Jewish philosopher Martin Buber's conviction that *God* is the "most loaded of all words." Others, especially since Friedrich Nietzsche's proclamation of the death of God in the nineteenth century, have endeavored to move the discussion of atheism beyond belief—especially beyond the categories of rationalism. Contemporary atheism is frequently portrayed as a life orientation or the default position of the human mind, not simply a set of ideas. Atheist novelists, playwrights, artists, composers, and poets express atheism as a cluster of moods, intuitions, and sentiments. Criticism of religion and religious institutions, especially accompanied by disappointment or outrage in light of religion's intellectual incoherence or moral failure, can be interpreted as a mode of atheism. Even anger at God can be a kind of atheism.

Scholars have attempted to create typologies of the variations of atheism. The types are commonly grouped into pairs of contrasting forms such as rational versus emotional, organic versus organized, active versus passive, and naive versus sophisticated. Some atheists are raised in nonreligion.

Some have transformations of mind and heart along the lines of a religious conversion. Some atheists are public, some private. Some have no argument with religion. Others wrestle with gods for a lifetime. Some insist atheism has intellectual content. Others say it represents independence from all creeds. Some treat science like a substitute deity. Others are wary of scientism. Some seek social change. Others are indifferent, content with the status quo. Some are happy. Others are nostalgic, reluctant atheists mourning a lost faith. Some could not believe even if they wanted to.

Forms of everyday atheism include the methodological atheism that reigns in the natural sciences (evident every time researchers assume that no supernatural force will influence their experiments) and the pragmatic atheism found in religious communities (when, as the saying goes, people pray as if everything depends on God and act as if everything depends on them).

One issue that illustrates the diversity within atheism is morality. Critics wonder how atheists can be responsible without religion. Nietzsche's *Beyond Good and Evil* (1886) fueled such suspicions, as did the widely quoted comment by a character in Fyodor Dostoyevsky's *The Brothers Karamazov* (1880): "If there is no God, everything is permitted." Some atheists do, in fact, embrace hedonism, rejecting all values except the pursuit of pleasure. Others believe in moral relativism, understanding morality as an invention of society, constantly evolving. Still others identify as nihilists, convinced that the universe is devoid of ultimate meaning. In contrast, a significant number of atheists believe that reason, science, and experience can lead to the adoption of universal ethical principles that, despite changes in society or shifting insights into human nature, religious and nonreligious people can share. *Good without God* (2009) by Harvard and MIT's humanist chaplain Greg Epstein, *The Most Good You Can Do* (2015) by philosopher Peter Singer, and *What It Means to Be Moral* (2019) by sociologist Phil Zuckerman, echoing the three Humanist Manifestos (1933, 1973, 2003), represent the current state of this conversation within atheist and humanist circles. A body of self-help literature, by atheists for atheists, focuses on issues such as life-cycle ceremonies and parenting in nonreligious homes. Many atheists are active in campaigns for racial justice, women's rights, reproductive rights, LGBTQ+ rights, freedom of conscience, and environmental justice.

Estimates place the worldwide atheist population at five hundred million to seven hundred million. Factoring in covert atheists, unidentified often due to atheophobia in society, would raise the number significantly.

Nations reporting the highest percentages of people who identify as atheists, all in double digits, include China, Japan, the Czech Republic, Australia, Iceland, Belgium, Denmark, and France. In the United States, atheism is rapidly growing. According to the Pew Research Center (https://pewresearch.org), from 2009 to 2019, the percentage of adults who identify as atheists doubled, from 2 percent to 4 percent. The expansion of atheism's social media presence and the proliferation of atheist organizations in recent years testify to the mainstreaming of multiple forms of atheism in many societies.

See also: Atheism, New; Atheism 2.0; Atheophobia; Humanist Manifestos; Nietzsche, Friedrich; Organizations, Atheist and Agnostic; Singer, Peter; Zuckerman, Phil

Further Reading

Baggini, Julian. *Atheism: A Very Short Introduction*. Oxford: Oxford University Press, 2003.

Buckley, Michael J. *At the Origins of Modern Atheism*. New Haven, CT: Yale University Press, 1987.

Bullivant, Stephen, and Michael Ruse, eds. *The Oxford Handbook of Atheism*. Oxford: Oxford University Press, 2013.

Eagleton, Terry. *Culture and the Death of God*. New Haven, CT: Yale University Press, 2015.

Epstein, Greg. *Good without God: What a Billion Nonreligious People Do Believe*. New York: HarperCollins, 2009.

Gray, John. *Seven Types of Atheism*. New York: Farrar, Straus and Giroux, 2018.

Hyman, Gavin. *A Short History of Atheism*. London: I. B. Tauris, 2010.

Küng, Hans. *Does God Exist? An Answer for Today*. Trans. Edward Quinn. New York: Doubleday, 1980.

Kurtz, Paul. *Forbidden Fruit: The Ethics of Secularism*. Amherst, NY: Prometheus Books, 2008.

Martin, Michael, ed. *The Cambridge Companion to Atheism*. Cambridge: Cambridge University Press, 2007.

Marty, Martin E. *Varieties of Unbelief*. New York: Anchor Books, 1966.

McGowan, Dale, Molleen Matsumura, Amanda Metskas, and Jan Devor. *Raising Freethinkers: A Practical Guide for Parenting beyond Belief*. New York: AMACOM, 2009.

Onfray, Michel. *Atheist Manifesto: The Case against Christianity, Judaism, and Islam*. Trans. Jeremy Leggatt. New York: Arcade, 2011.

Singer, Peter. *The Most Good You Can Do: How Effective Altruism Is Changing Ideas about Living Ethically*. New Haven, CT: Yale University Press, 2015.

Watson, Peter. *The Age of Atheists: How We Have Sought to Live since the Death of God*. New York: Simon and Schuster, 2014.

Zuckerman, Phil. *Living the Secular Life: New Answers to Old Questions*. New York: Penguin, 2014.

Zuckerman, Phil. *What It Means to Be Moral: Why Religion Is Not Necessary for Living an Ethical Life*. Berkeley, CA: Counterpoint, 2019.

Atheism, New

The term *New Atheism* refers to the resurgence of interest in atheism and a forceful articulation of atheist ideas on a mass scale during the first years of the twenty-first century. New Atheism was sparked in part by the success of the New Religious Right in U.S. society, the rise of Islamic extremism around the world, and the terrorist attacks of September 11, 2001. It brought renewed fervor to age-old critiques of religion and attempted to mount fresh defenses of secularity based on reason, science, and the conviction that global peace and survival depend on a forthright assessment of religion's threats to humanity and the planet. The features of the movement that have made New Atheism particularly new have been its sense of urgency, its crusading style, its prodigious confidence, its scientific credentials, its media savvy, and its reliance on celebrity spokespersons. American journalist Gary Wolf coined the term *New Atheism* in 2006. A decade later, some observers were wondering if the movement had run its course.

Four individuals, described as the "four horsemen" of the movement (alluding to an apocalyptic image from the book of Revelation in the New Testament), have been identified as the principal leaders and definers of New Atheism—all of them best-selling authors and skilled debaters: biologist Richard Dawkins, philosopher Daniel C. Dennett, neuroscientist Sam Harris, and journalist and literary critic Christopher Hitchens. Other prominent writers and speakers associated with the movement have included physicist Victor Stenger, author of *God: The Failed Hypothesis* (2007) and *The New Atheism* (2009), and human rights champion Ayaan Hirsi Ali, author of *The Caged Virgin* (2004) and *Infidel* (2007). Novelist Philip Pullman, whose *His Dark Materials* fantasy trilogy (1995–2000) sparked censorship controversies, is sometimes seen as a fellow traveler of the movement. Prevalent themes addressed by all New Atheist representatives include what they believe to be religion's appalling moral record, its collusion with intellectual dishonesty, its reliance on outdated ideas, its incompatibility with scientific inquiry, and its inferiority to atheism when it comes to issues of human happiness, human rights, and human understanding of the natural world.

Richard Dawkins (b. 1941) was arguably the first to put New Atheism on the cultural map. Born in Nairobi, Kenya, he received a conventional British education that led eventually to a PhD in biology and an award-winning Oxford academic career. In the first volume of his autobiography, *An Appetite for Wonder* (2013), he traced his atheism to a decisive teenage encounter with the thought of Charles Darwin, who from that time on became Dawkins's "greatest scientific hero." Dawkins's *The Selfish Gene* (1976) earned him international renown in the field of gene-centered evolutionary theory. *The Blind Watchmaker* (1986) attacked the claims and methods of intelligent design, and his blockbuster *The God Delusion* (2006) has served for many as the manifesto for New Atheism. *Outgrowing God: A Beginner's Guide* (2019) covers similar ground for a new generation of readers. Throughout the twenty-first century, Dawkins has been a model of the scholar-activist, seeking, often through popular means—notably his support for Ariane Sherine's Atheist Bus Campaign of 2008–2009, with its "There's Probably No God" ads—to raise awareness about what he sees as the cultural promise of nonreligion. The Richard Dawkins Foundation for Reason and Science (www.richarddawkins.net), established in 2006, pursues his goals of fostering at all levels of society greater scientific literacy and appreciation for a secular view of the world.

Like Dawkins, Daniel C. Dennett (b. 1942) had gained a solid reputation in the academy long before the events of 9/11. Trained in philosophy, he brought a well-honed expertise in the philosophy of science to the New Atheist project. A native of Boston, he studied at Harvard and received an Oxford PhD in philosophy. Since 1971, he has taught at Tufts University, specializing in cognitive studies and philosophy of the mind. *Darwin's Dangerous Idea* (1995), the sixth of his many books, established his place in the history of science. In his tenth book, *Breaking the Spell* (2006), his most significant contribution to New Atheism, he offered a scientific appraisal of religion itself, describing the origins and development of religion as phenomena within the evolutionary process having nothing to do with supernatural or otherworldly forces. Belief in God or gods, according to Dennett, is a natural—if not logical—outcome of millennia of human experiences and choices. His coauthored *Caught in the Pulpit: Leaving*

Belief Behind (2015), a study of religious leaders who are closet unbelievers, brought new depth to New Atheist research.

Sam Harris (b. 1967) is perhaps the better-known American-born member of the "four horsemen." Raised in a nonreligious household in California, he studied philosophy at Stanford University and received his PhD in neuroscience from the University of California, Los Angeles. His *New York Times* best seller *The End of Faith* (2004), an aggressive critique of the fundamentalism that fueled the 9/11 suicide attacks and a long line of atrocities before them, was in many ways a precursor for New Atheism. In *Letter to a Christian Nation* (2006), he sought to convince conservative U.S. Christians, as well as their moderate and liberal coreligionists, of the self-deception required to be both a Christian faithful to ancient scripture and a member of modern society benefiting from science. He defined atheism as not another faith or worldview but simply the recognition of what is obvious. In TED talks and his regular *Making Sense* podcasts, Harris especially defends the notion of morality without God and the claim that science can tackle ethical questions. More interested in Asian traditions than other New Atheist figures, he has advocated for disciplined meditation practice, based on Tibetan models, and what he describes as "spirituality without religion."

The fourth of the "four horsemen" was Christopher Hitchens (1949–2011), the least academic of the famous quartet but arguably its greatest literary talent and sharpest wit. A product of the British boarding-school system and Balliol College, Oxford, Hitchens was a prolific journalist and social critic, publishing over twenty books and scores of essays, perfecting a signature blend of the discerning public intellectual and the consummate contrarian. In his iconoclastic bombshell *god is not Great* (2007), intentionally displaying the lowercase *g*, Hitchens scrutinized creeds and codes from a broad spectrum of faiths—especially the Abrahamic traditions of Judaism, Christianity, and Islam—and found them all intellectually defective or morally depraved. Individuals surveyed represented for him a sampling of the world's most notorious charlatans, and the populations mentioned he saw as history's most duped and devilish. His anthology *The Portable Atheist* (2007) offered connoisseurs of and newcomers to the history of atheist literature five hundred pages of classic unbelieving authors, from the ancient Greek Lucretius to television's science personality Carl Sagan. *Mortality* (2011), the essays Hitchens published when he was dying from esophageal cancer, showed the world how one convinced atheist faced life's ultimate challenge. His death, some suggest, took the steam—or at least the fun—out of New Atheism.

The New Atheism phenomenon has been one half of a lively war of words. The "four horsemen" and their allies unleashed a torrent of words in books, articles, blogs, podcasts, and videos. Their adversaries, for the most part conservative Christians, have not been shy in responding—with titles such as *Answering the New Atheists, Atheism's New Clothes, The Dawkins Delusion, Atheist Delusions*, and *Why God Won't Go Away*. Well-publicized debates between New Atheists and high-profile Christian, mainly evangelical, apologists, such as William Lane Craig, Dinesh D'Souza, Rick Warren, and Alister McGrath, have attracted enthusiastic audiences in university auditoriums and a host of digital formats.

Critics, even those sympathetic with the New Atheist agenda, have pointed out that the face of the movement has been overwhelmingly white and male. Feminist scholar Sikivu Hutchinson decries the "major divide between white atheist discourse and the lived experiences of humanists of color." Some observers have been troubled by the movement's dismissal of "political correctness," religious toleration, and interfaith dialogue and what appears to be its inclination toward Islamophobia. Many commentators have noted that the movement's militant style mirrors the missionary and fundamentalist qualities of its sternest opponents. Specialists in religious studies, both religious and nonreligious, criticize New Atheism for reducing religion to a set of ideas, equating religious moral teaching with ancient scriptural codes, ignoring the wealth of religious studies scholarship in the contemporary academy, and overlooking religion's contributions to art, education, medicine, and social reform. Some call New Atheist readings of the history of Christianity and the history of science amateurish. Humanities scholars detect in the movement's respect for science an uncritical idolatry of science, or scientism. At their weakest, the New Atheists resemble old-fashioned freethinkers declaiming the crimes and contradictions of the Bible in the village square. No New Atheist has approximated the secular empathy for faith expressed in Bruce Sheiman's *An Atheist Defends Religion* (2009) and Alain de Botton's *Religion for Atheists* (2012).

The impact of New Atheism on culture is difficult to calculate. Anecdotal evidence suggests significant influence in North America and the United Kingdom. Since the dawn of the twenty-first century, atheism, especially organized atheism, has taken on a new public presence in nearly all facets of society—including entertainment and commerce, with merchandise ranging from secular-themed T-shirts and coffee mugs to atheist Christmas-tree ornaments. As catalyst or cause, New Atheism represents a new idiom for a proud and ambitious atheist voice.

See also: Dawkins, Richard; Dennett, Daniel C.; Harris, Sam; Hirsi Ali, Ayaan; Hitchens, Christopher; Hutchinson, Sikivu; Organizations, Atheist and Agnostic

Further Reading

Dawkins, Richard. *The God Delusion*. Boston: Houghton Mifflin, 2008.

Dawkins, Richard. *Outgrowing God: A Beginner's Guide*. New York: Random House, 2019.

Dennett, Daniel C. *Breaking the Spell: Religion as a Natural Phenomenon*. New York: Viking, 2006.

Dennett, Daniel C., and Linda LaScola. *Caught in the Pulpit: Leaving Belief Behind*. Durham, NC: Pitchstone, 2015.

Harris, Sam. *The End of Faith: Religion, Terror, and the Future of Religion*. New York: W. W. Norton, 2004.

Harris, Sam. *Letter to a Christian Nation*. New York: Vintage, 2008.

Haught, John F. *God and the New Atheism: A Critical Response to Dawkins, Harris, and Hitchens*. Louisville, KY: Westminster John Knox Press, 2008.

Hitchens, Christopher. *god is not Great: How Religion Poisons Everything*. New York: Twelve, 2007.

Hitchens, Christopher, ed. *The Portable Atheist: Essential Readings for the Nonbeliever*. Philadelphia: Da Capo, 2007.

Hitchens, Christopher, Richard Dawkins, Daniel C. Dennett, and Sam Harris. *The Four Horsemen: The Conversation that Sparked an Atheist Revolution*. New York: Random House, 2019.

Hutchinson, Sikivu. *Moral Combat: Black Atheists, Gender Politics, and the Values Wars*. Los Angeles: Infidel Books, 2011.

Khalil, Mohammad Hassan. *Jihad, Radical Islam, and the New Atheism*. Cambridge: Cambridge University Press, 2017.

Ryan, Paul. *After the New Atheism Debate*. Toronto: University of Toronto, 2014.

Atheism 2.0

Atheism 2.0 is a twenty-first-century version of atheism conceived, named, and promoted by best-selling British writer and philosopher Alain de Botton (b. 1969). In contrast to New Atheism and other more traditional forms of atheism, Atheism 2.0 is atheism calibrated for the postmodern era. It does not concentrate primarily on the question of the existence of God, the truth claims of religious creeds, the reliability of ancient sacred texts, the alleged conflict between religion and science, or the moral record of religious institutions in society. Atheism 2.0 assumes the nonexistence of God but sees the religious heritages of the world as valuable sources of culture and useful wisdom for people of all ideologies, worldviews, and time periods.

An independent scholar and entrepreneur engaged in publishing and education, de Botton holds a BA in history from Cambridge and a master's degree in philosophy from Oxford. He is the author of fourteen books, fiction and nonfiction, and is well known for the clarity of his prose and the elegance of his style. His titles include *Essays in Love* (2006), *How Proust Can Change Your Life* (2006), *Status Anxiety* (2005), *How to Think More about Sex* (2012), and *Art as Therapy* (2013). He is founder of the School of Life (www.theschooloflife.com), an adult education project exploring new approaches to topics such as self-knowledge, work, and leisure, and a space-based wellness venture called Living Architecture (www .living-architecture.co.uk), part tourist agency, part multisite retreat center, fostering reflection on meaningful living through immersive experiences in experimental homes designed by specially commissioned architects. Raised in a secular Jewish family with Swiss roots, de Botton is a lifelong atheist who finds universal and nonreligious value in the religious traditions of the world.

Atheism 2.0 is based on de Botton's 2011 TED talk "Atheism 2.0," viewed nearly three million times on YouTube, and his book *Religion for Atheists: A Non-Believer's Guide to the Uses of Religion* (2012). Its core principle is the distinction between wisdom and doctrine. "The most boring and unproductive question one can ask of any religion," he says, "is whether or not it is *true*." De Botton identifies creativity and generosity in the religious traditions that have filled the world with striking architecture and institutions such as hospitals, libraries, orphanages, and schools. Imagining a world with no religion, he argues, would require picturing human experience stripped of most of its art, literature, and music—even its calendars. For centuries, he asserts, religious thinkers have mined the depths of human consciousness and, despite limitations and errors, have granted enduring insights to people of all creeds and no creed, people facing the same great mysteries of life bound by no borders of culture or belief.

According to de Botton, nonreligion need not be antireligion. He aims to reconcile antipathy to supernaturalism with admiration for religion's genius and openness to an as yet unconstructed religion of humanity, such as that proposed by nineteenth-century French theorist Auguste Comte, one of the founders of modern sociology. De Botton's type of atheism maintains that religions, irrespective of their dogmatic claims and missionary impulses, function as do languages, artistic performances, or therapies—ultimately neither true nor false, but culturally enriching and potentially humanizing, playing necessary roles in society, even for the most dedicated citizens of the secular city.

Empathetic audiences have encountered in de Botton's Atheism 2.0 a candor, equanimity of mind, and an impressive level of religious literacy rarely found among modern atheism's militant defenders. Critics dismiss his conclusions as self-evident, based on selective investigation, or restatements of attempts at demythologization found in many varieties of agnosticism, religious liberalism, and religious humanism.

See also: Agnosticism; Atheism, New; Humanism; Media, Atheism and Agnosticism and the

Further Reading

De Botton, Alain. *Religion for Atheists: A Non-Believer's Guide to the Uses of Religion.* New York: Vintage, 2012.

Atheism and Agnosticism, African American

The multifaceted African American experience has produced rich and enduring forms of atheism and agnosticism. Distinctive ways of living and thinking without God and without certain faith have accompanied the quest for justice and the search for identity that have made the stories of Black Americans so exceptional in world history. Throughout the centuries of those stories, individuals from many different walks of life have contributed to the expression of modern unbelief, the formation of secular communities of support and advocacy, and critical reflection on the way ethnic self-understandings intersect with the varieties of nonreligion in the modern world.

African American atheism and agnosticism have always existed in a culture notable for its religious engagement. Since 1619, people of African descent have profoundly shaped religious life and thought in what is now the United States. The first Africans in America, engulfed in modern

Christian Europe's transatlantic enterprise of human trafficking, brought with them Indigenous traditions and variants of Islam deeply rooted in the African past. By the second half of the seventeenth century, forced dismantling of belief and practice had become a strategic component of Euro-America's international trade in human beings. The eventual retrieval of old creeds and rites and the creation of new ones, first under slavery and then under segregation and systemic racism, were indicators of the ways in which generations of African Americans resisted injustice with mind and body.

Today, the nation's religious music, preaching, worship, theology, denominational pluralism, and diverse styles of ecclesiastical organization—from storefront churches to megachurches—would be unrecognizable without the influence of centuries of African American religious imagination and innovation. Religiously informed judgments of America itself—communicated by prophets such as nineteenth-century rebel leaders Denmark Vesey and Nat Turner and twenty-first-century revolutionary theologians James Cone, Cornel West, and Thandeka— underscore the importance of African American perspectives for U.S. religious history.

At present, African Americans constitute the most religious ethnic group in the country. Black Americans rank high on questions regarding belief in God, daily prayer, Bible reading, religious membership, and church attendance. According to the Pew Research Center, nearly 80 percent of African American adults identify as Christian, with the vast majority participating in historic Black churches associated with Baptist, Methodist, Holiness, Pentecostal, and nondenominational traditions.

In contrast to such high levels of religious belief and behavior, African American culture has also fostered strains of skepticism, humanism, and nonbelief. Some may have existed unrecognized in the early phases of the slavery era. Interviews with formerly enslaved individuals indicate that religion was never universally or uniformly embraced before the end of the Civil War. Like freethinkers in other inhospitable environments, early Black nonbelievers rarely enjoyed anything close to the safety, opportunity, and leisure required in order to make their presence known and ideas understood.

In the nineteenth century, abolitionist, reformer, and slavery survivor Frederick Douglass gave voice to the mounting criticism of the Christianity that justified and colluded with racial injustice for centuries. "It is against religion," he declared in *Narrative of the Life of Frederick Douglass* (1845), "that I have felt it my duty to testify." Douglass contrasted the Christianity of America with the Christianity of Christ. He saw Christian slaveholders as far more menacing than nonreligious. With German-Jewish feminist and abolitionist writer Ottilie Assing, his friend and collaborator, he discovered common themes in the literature of Christian modernism and Christian atheism then streaming out of Europe. Two busts of contemporary radical German thinkers adorned the mantelpiece of his Washington, DC, home: one of David Friedrich Strauss, author of *The Life of Jesus, Critically Examined* (1835), which explained much of the Jesus story as myth, and one of Ludwig Feuerbach, author of *The Essence of Christianity* (1841), famous for its description of God as a psychological projection of human wishes.

In the twentieth century, African American atheism and agnosticism came of age. Writers, artists, academics, and activists, many associated with the Harlem Renaissance of the 1920s and '30s, spoke openly of their sense of betrayal by traditional Christianity and the anguish they experienced dealing with the spiritual consequences of what poet Langston Hughes called a "dream deferred." Novelists such as Zora Neale Hurston, author of *Their Eyes Were Watching God* (1937), portrayed the supernaturally charged environment of the Black church and the psychological wasteland of a society plagued by white supremacy. Many, including former youth-preacher James Baldwin a generation later, wrote autobiographically of the "slow crumbling" of childhood faith and the lonely quest for satisfying alternatives. His friend Lorraine Hansberry put the brutality of both atheophobia and racism on stage in her highly acclaimed *A Raisin in the Sun* (1959). Before and during the civil rights movement of the 1950s and '60s, Black unbelievers searched for postreligious sources of meaning in science, depth psychology, existentialism, Marxism, and the work of anticolonial thinkers throughout the African diaspora, then laying the groundwork for Afrocentric thought. For many years, Pan-African scholar W. E. B. Du Bois served as unofficial dean of America's evolving Black humanism.

Women have been especially important in the development of African American atheism and agnosticism. Alice Walker, author of *The Color Purple* (1982) and many other volumes of fiction, poetry, and nonfiction, stimulated great interest in the Black humanist past with the book that commemorated her hunt for Zora Neale Hurston's forgotten gravesite: *In Search of Our Mothers' Gardens* (1983). Named Humanist of the Year for 1997 by the American Humanist Association, Walker also coined the term *womanist* to convey the distinctive cluster of insights, inclinations, and apprehensions associated with the experiences of feminists of color.

Today, women are prominent in the publication of secular perspectives and the organization of venues for the support and advocacy of Black nonreligious causes. One special concern is the relative neglect of gender and racial injustice issues in some branches of the global atheist and agnostic network. Another is the set of challenges faced by Black women participating in what therapist Candace Gorham has called the "Ebony Exodus" from religion—a coming-out experience that can place relationships, employment, social status, personal reputation, and physical well-being in jeopardy. Black Nonbelievers Inc. (www.blacknonbelievers .com), founded by Mandisa Thomas, and Black Skeptics of Los Angeles (www.freethoughtblogs/blackskeptics.com), founded by Sikivu Hutchinson, author of *Humanists in the Hood* (2020), constitute two areas of significant growth within African American communities of unbelief. The cover story of the June 2018 issue of *Humanist* magazine, "Five Fierce Humanists: Unapologetically Black Women Beyond Belief," featured Gorham, Thomas, Hutchinson, and two other leading voices among African American freethinkers: animal rights activist Liz Ross, founder of Vegan Advocacy Initiative, and LGBTQ+ advocate Bridgett Crutchfield, founder of Minority Atheists of Michigan. At 18 percent of the contemporary Black population in the United States, African American atheists, agnostics, and Nones of all genders represent a visible and vocal dimension of twenty-first-century nonreligion.

See also: Atheophobia; Christianity, Atheism and Agnosticism in; Du Bois, W. E. B.; Feminism, Atheism and Agnosticism and; Feuerbach, Ludwig; Hurston, Zora Neale; Hutchinson, Sikivu; Nones; Organizations, Atheist and Agnostic; Pinn, Anthony B.

Further Reading

Alexander, Nathan G. *Race in a Godless World: Atheism, Race, and Civilization, 1850–1914*. Manchester: Manchester University Press, 2019.

Allen, Norm R., Jr., ed. *African American Humanism: An Anthology*. New York: Prometheus Books, 1991.

Allen, Norm R., Jr., ed. *The Black Humanist Experience: An Alternative to Religion*. New York: Prometheus Books, 2003.

Blain, Keisha N., Christopher Cameron, and Ashley D. Farmer, eds. *New Perspectives on the Black Intellectual Tradition*. Evanston, IL: Northwestern University Press, 2018.

Cameron, Christopher. *Black Freethinkers: A History of African American Secularism*. Evanston, IL: Northwestern University Press, 2019.

Douglass, Frederick. *The Narrative and Selected Writings*. Ed. Michael Meyer. New York: Modern Library, 1984.

Evans, D. K. *Emancipation of a Black Atheist*. Durham, NC: Pitchstone, 2017.

Garst, Karen L., ed. *Women beyond Belief: Discovering Life without Religion*. Durham, NC: Pitchstone, 2016.

Gorham, Candace R. M. *The Ebony Exodus Project: Why Some Black Women Are Walking Out on Religion—and Others Should Too*. Durham, NC: Pitchstone, 2013.

Hutchinson, Sikivu. *Godless Americana: Race and Religious Rebels*. Los Angeles: Infidel Books, 2013.

Hutchinson, Sikivu. *Humanists in the Hood: Unapologetically Black, Feminist, and Heretical*. Durham, NC: Pitchstone, 2020.

Hutchinson, Sikivu. *Moral Combat: Black Atheists, Gender Politics, and the Values Wars*. Los Angeles: Infidel Books, 2011.

Pinn, Anthony B. *African American Humanist Principles: Living and Thinking Like the Children of Nimrod*. New York: Palgrave MacMillan, 2004.

Pinn, Anthony B., ed. *By These Hands: A Documentary History of African American Humanism*. New York: New York University, 2001.

Pinn, Anthony B. *The End of God-Talk: An African American Humanist Theology*. New York: Oxford University Press, 2012.

Pinn, Anthony B. *Writing God's Obituary: How a Good Methodist Became a Better Atheist*. Amherst, NY: Prometheus Books, 2014.

Raboteau, Albert J. *Canaan Land: A Religious History of African Americans*. New York: Oxford University Press, 2001.

Winn, Jason. *The Black Atheist in America*. Parker, CO: Outskirts Press, 2012.

Zuckerman, Phil, ed. *Du Bois on Religion*. Walnut Creek, CA: AltaMira Press, 2000.

Atheopaganism

Atheopaganism connects some of the world's oldest spiritual currents with some of humanity's newest intellectual developments. The term is one name for the phenomenon of Earth-based philosophies and spiritual traditions that do not depend on the supernatural or belief in deities. *Atheopaganism* refers to a cluster of nontheist and humanist forms of paganism in contemporary culture, including atheist or god-free versions of witchcraft. Practitioners of atheopaganism distinguish themselves and their worldviews from pagan and Wiccan traditions that are centered on the reverencing of gods and goddesses, especially pantheons once worshipped by ancient Mediterranean, Germanic, Scandinavian, and Celtic peoples.

Modern paganism, also called neo-paganism, has deep roots in human history. Pagans today see themselves as keepers of sacred traditions that predate the great dharma traditions of South and East Asia and the Abrahamic religions that originated in western Asia. Pagan traditions avoided extinction in the West by going underground or blending creatively with ostensibly exclusive dominant patterns of monotheist orthodoxy. Their esoteric, occult, astrological, and alchemical traditions enriched the mystical dimensions of the Abrahamic religions for centuries. In some cases, the same person sought both the Philosopher's Stone and the beatific vision. Many practitioners of ancient magical arts paid dearly for their craft. Witch trials in premodern and early modern Europe and its colonies led to the execution of some forty thousand people, mainly women. Present-day pagan writers, teachers, and spokespersons, looking to this past for inspiration, tend to avoid the term *neo-pagan*. They emphasize continuity with the past rather than novelty or innovation.

Pagan revivals have occurred periodically in Western culture since the Renaissance. Some historians insist that vernacular forms of paganism have always existed in Western culture—beneath, beside, or within Christian traditions. Contemporary paganism stems largely from the intensifying interest in alternatives to mainstream religious culture that defined so much of the intellectual history of the nineteenth and twentieth centuries. Some pagans trace the modern revitalization of their ancient tradition to the work of three British writers: anthropologist Margaret Murray, author of *The Witch-Cult in Western Europe* (1921); folklorist and coven organizer Gerald Gardner, author of *Witchcraft Today* (1951); and self-proclaimed "Great Beast 666" Aleister Crowley, author of *Magick in Theory and Practice* (1930). Never a single movement, paganism now exists in multiple forms, some organized, systematic, and public, some individualized, eclectic, and private. Many variants are interlaced with ideas, practices, narratives, insights, and institutions associated with cognate movements, such as gnosticism, Rosicrucianism, spiritualism, Theosophy, and New Age spirituality. A point of ongoing controversy among modern pagans, their allies, and their critics is the degree to which beliefs and rituals from Native American traditions and the classical Asian traditions of Hinduism, Buddhism, Daoism, and Sufism may be appropriated with integrity.

In the second half of the twentieth century, second-wave feminism, coupled with burgeoning ecological and green political movements, generated great interest in the rediscovery of paganism and witchcraft on a worldwide scale. By the early 1970s, *McCall's* magazine was showcasing an "Occult Explosion" (1970) and *Time* an "Occult Revival" (1972). Goddess worship especially characterized the pagan resurgence. One version of the Gaia theory, seeing Earth itself as a living being manifesting the primal Mother Goddess long honored by various premodern peoples, became a prominent feature of some strains of modern pagan sentiment. The publication of three important books in 1979—*Drawing Down the Moon*, by National Public Radio journalist and pagan practitioner Margot Adler; *The Spiral Dance*, by pagan leader Starhawk; and *Changing of the Gods*, by psychologist of religion Naomi Goldenberg—marked a watershed moment in North American religious and cultural history. An earlier landmark publication, Merlin Stone's *When God Was a Woman* (1976), encouraged spiritual seekers and social activists to recognize the deep historical and psychological affinities between women's experiences and what historians now call the misogynist turn in the history of the world's religions, that is, the shift from matriarchies to patriarchies some 12,000 years ago. In her breakthrough study, anticipating similar works by Riane Eisler, Marija Gimbutas, and Gerda Lerner, Stone revealed how the "suppression of women's rights began with the suppression of women's rites."

For decades, modern paganism has been an influential force shaping new movements in psychology, peace and social justice, health and wellness, literature, fashion, entertainment, foodways, sexual performance, and the arts. Increasing interest in paganism and witchcraft among millennials and Gen Z individuals has inspired some observers to speak of the early twenty-first century as the age of Generation Hex. In the academy, pagan studies and the history of magic are gaining ground as respected and substantive areas of scholarly research. Cherry Hill Seminary in South Carolina (www.cherryhillseminary.org) is the world's first institution offering graduate degrees in pagan ministry. *The Pomegranate* (https:// journals.equinoxpub.com/POM/index) is the first international, peer-reviewed journal of pagan studies.

The best-known type of contemporary paganism is Wicca (from the Old English for "to bend or alter"). Some estimates place the current pagan population in the United States around 340,000 and the current Wiccan population around 350,000. According to the Pew Research Center, the combined U.S. population could be as high as 1.5 million. Estimates for the international pagan population hover around 3 million. The demographics of modern paganism, however, will continue to be only approximate as long as persecution of pagans remains a threat to full revelation of pagan identity and practice in any culture. In the United States, negative stereotypes of paganism and witchcraft can be found at virtually every point on the contemporary sociopolitical spectrum. At the same time, annual Witchfests and Pagan Pride events in major cities, global pagan festival gatherings, and a thriving, pagan-themed tourism industry offer evidence of the mainstreaming of pagan identity and practice.

Within the pagan community, atheists constitute a distinct minority. Criticism of historic Christianity and its immaterial, masculine-portrayed God typically accompanies interest in pagan wisdom, especially as pagan identity often involves an ongoing assessment of traditional Christian notions of original sin, shame, misogyny, homophobia, and mind-body dualism, along with the religion's suspicion of the erotic and its ambivalent attitude toward mirth. Disbelief or nonbelief in sacred or supernatural entities within the pagan community, however, is rare.

Atheist pagans, such as the contributors to John Halstead's anthology *Godless Paganism: Voices of Non-theistic Pagans* (2016), often see themselves as doubly affiliated—associated with both ancient Earth-based traditions and modern forms of Western skepticism. Atheopagans and humanist pagans stress the overlap between naturalist pagan rituals and evolving modern science and the distinction between their secular outlook and explicitly religious pagan pathways. They seek to avoid both the uncritical mythological supernaturalism they find in religious paganism and the narrow rationalism and antipagan discrimination they encounter in conventional humanism. Organizers in the field of nontheist, science-based paganism include Mark Green, author of *Atheopaganism* (2019) and founder of the Atheopaganism website (www.atheopaganism.com), and writer-teacher B. T. Newberg, founder of Humanistic Paganism (www .humanisticpaganism.com).

Atheist and agnostic witchcraft is a growing phenomenon too. Some practitioners locate themselves within atheopaganism. Others avoid the paganism category. Gabriela Herstik, the Jewish-Latinx author of *Inner Witch* (2018) and the "weed and witchcraft" columnist for *High Times*, represents a trend among contemporary witches, linking the ancient-modern craft to no specific religious system or set of beliefs. Kristen J. Sollée, gender studies scholar and author of *Witch Hunt: A Traveler's Guide to the Power and Persecution of the Witch* (2020), identifies as a witch and agnostic. Alex at www.diywitchery.com self-describes as an agnostic secular witch. So do participants in the Facebook "Agnostic

Witch" community. Prominent atheist witches include YouTube personality Sedna Woo; *Medium* blogger Vi La Bianca, author of "7 Questions for a Queer Atheist Witch"; and Anna Mist, host of the blog site *I, Medusa* ("for atheist witches, by atheist witches"). Atheist witches speak of nontheist witchcraft ceremonies as life-giving exercises in mindfulness meditation, communion with natural Earth and lunar cycles, and rites of self-care much needed in postmodern society. The podcast *The Atheist and the Witch* (www.theatheistandthewitch.com) provides one of many examples of the creativity sparked by the meeting of skepticism and magic. Despite rising levels of acceptance, individuals who are both witches and atheists or agnostics face immense prejudice from multiple sources in contemporary culture.

See also: Atheophobia; Feminism, Atheism and Agnosticism and; Humanism; LGBTQ+ Persons, Atheist and Agnostic

Further Reading

Adler, Margot. *Drawing Down the Moon: Witches, Druids, Goddess-Worshippers, and Other Pagans in America Today*. New York: Penguin, 2006.

Berger, Helen A. *A Community of Witches: Contemporary Neo-Paganism and Witchcraft in the United States*. Columbia: University of South Carolina Press, 1999.

Davies, Owen, ed. *The Oxford Illustrated History of Witchcraft and Magic*. London: Oxford University Press, 2017.

Davy, Barbara Jane. *Introduction to Pagan Studies*. Lanham, MD: AltaMira Press, 2007.

Eisler, Riane. *The Chalice and the Blade: Our History, Our Future*. New York: HarperCollins, 1995.

Goldenberg, Naomi. *Changing of the Gods: Feminism and the End of Traditional Religions*. Boston: Beacon Press, 1979.

Gosden, Chris. *Magic: A History*. New York: Farrar, Straus and Giroux, 2020.

Green, Mark A. *Atheopaganism: An Earth-Honoring Path Rooted in Science*. Santa Rosa, CA: Green Dragon, 2019.

Halstead, John, ed. *Godless Paganism: Voices of Non-Theistic Pagans*. Lulu, 2016.

Herstik, Gabriela. *Inner Witch: A Modern Guide to the Ancient Craft*. New York: TarcherPerigee, 2018.

Hutton, Ronald. *The Triumph of the Moon: A History of Modern Pagan Witchcraft*. Oxford: Oxford University Press, 2001.

Louv, Jason, ed. *Generation Hex*. New York: Disinformation, 2005.

Mist, Anna. *The Atheist Witch's Guide to Energy*. Independently Published, 2019.

Mist, Anna. *Godless Magick: A Brief Guide on Atheistic Witchcraft*. Amazon Digital Services, 2017.

Sollée, Kristen J. *Witch Hunt: A Traveler's Guide to the Power and Persecution of the Witch*. Newburyport, MA: Weiser Books, 2020.

Sollée, Kristen J. *Witches, Sluts, Feminists: Conjuring the Sex Positive*. Berkeley, CA: ThreeL Media, 2017.

Starhawk. *The Spiral Dance: A Rebirth of the Ancient Religion of the Great Goddess*. New York: HarperCollins, 1999.

Stone, Merlin. *When God Was a Woman: The Landmark Exploration of the Ancient Worship of the Great Goddess and the Eventual Suppression of Women's Rites*. New York: Houghton Mifflin Harcourt, 1976.

Atheophobia

Atheophobia is the fear, suspicion, or hatred of atheists. The term comes from the Greek *atheos* ("without god") and *phobos* ("fear"). It refers to all forms of prejudice and discrimination against atheists and people perceived to be atheists, especially other secular and nonreligious persons. Atheophobia, expressed in repressive acts, hate speech, and active persecution and violence, has appeared in many forms throughout the centuries. It continues to be a present reality in many cultures around the world.

Before *atheist* was a term of description, it was a term of derision and demonization. Only since the nineteenth century has the word assumed the meaning it carries today: a person who does not, will not, or cannot believe in God (almost always put in the singular with a capital *G*)—or someone who does not live with a God- or god-concept at all. The term *atheist* originated in ancient Greece and was initially used more generally than it is in contemporary society. It accused individuals, in a wholesale way, of impiety, immorality, and other forms of antisocial sentiment. The pre-Socratic philosopher Protagoras (fifth century BCE), who questioned the ability of humans to achieve knowledge of the gods, was denounced as a threat to society. According to some accounts, the Athenian authorities burned his books and banished him from the city. Socrates (469–399 BCE) was accused of impiety and atheism (being godless), charges that did not reckon with the aims of his self-imposed role as society's gadfly. Socrates saw it as his mission to criticize secondhand knowledge and to investigate relentlessly all ideas, especially those communicating society's most fundamental assumptions. Centuries later, his death sentence serves as an abiding symbol of the tragedy of all attempts to police the mind. Ironically, in his last book, *Laws*, the elderly Plato, once a disciple of Socrates, included atheism in his list of offenses against society that deserved punishment.

Atheophobia is rooted in the premodern conviction that ideas have spiritual power. It was a presupposition consistent with the once near-universal worldview of animism, the belief that all things, seen and unseen, possess spiritual force. According to this view, ideas, along with the words that express them, can be beneficial or menacing, depending on the degree to which they conform to established religious, political, or social orthodoxies. Ideas and words can heal or harm. Bad or incorrect thoughts and words, it was believed, possess the potential to subvert society and the souls of its citizens.

In the premodern West, pagan magic and Christian worship agreed on this basic point. Virtually everyone believed that thoughts and language, sometimes accompanied by ceremonial gesture, were efficacious: they could make things happen. The witch's spell could change the course of nature—in garden, market, or bed. The priest's prayer could change bread into human flesh. It was no accident that the cunning words *hocus pocus* came from a bending of the ritual formula in the Roman Mass: *Hoc est corpus meum* ("This my body").

The Hebrew Torah's taboo against pronouncing, and thereby abusing, the divine name, the provision in the Ten Commandments prohibiting the taking of Yahweh's name "in vain," captures this distinctive understanding of ideas and words. For ancient Israel, avoidance of the ineffable name was not a matter of manners but of metaphysics. The full backdrop for this view was set in the Western mind by the first creation myth of the book of Genesis, where Elohim brings the "heavens and the earth" into being simply by speaking—or thinking out loud. Words, and the thoughts behind them, the peoples of many cultures taught for centuries, can create a world out of nothing or cast a cosmos into chaos.

Atheophobia is one extreme example of this approach to reality. The belief that thinking or saying the wrong thing about God—especially denying God completely—could be hazardous for everyone has led repeatedly throughout history to the felt need for laws to protect the public from dangerous ideas and for methods to punish those considered to be society's wrong-thinkers as well as its wrongdoers. The history of atheophobia is intertwined with the history of heresy hunting, witch trials, inquisitions, censorship, and codes against blasphemy and obscenity. Ironically, the history of intellectual surveillance and intolerance has linked religion's detractors with its most daring innovators, revealing the vulnerable ground shared by both antireligious doubters and hyperreligious dissenters. Unbelievers and society's unorthodox believers, skeptics and self-declared seers alike, have both suffered from external power structures seeking to govern internal belief in the name of one system of purported truth.

What made atheophobia a public possibility for centuries was the combination of three factors: monotheism, a centralized religious teaching authority, and a single-option religious society—the dominion of one religion backed by political power, patronage, and prestige. Not every culture has been hospitable to these factors. Indigenous cultures in Africa, Australia, and the Americas have traditionally recognized the legitimacy of different spiritual paths for different individuals and no firm demarcation between human beings and other life-forms, including deities and spirits. Before the modern period, South Asia was generally resistant to atheophobia because of its principle of the one and the many—in the words of the Rig Veda, "the one truth sages call by many names." In ancient India, Hinduism's nontheist Sankhya philosophical system was judged to be orthodox due to its respect for the Vedic scriptures. *Nāstikas* (usually translated "atheists"), such as Jains and Buddhists who did not revere the ancient scriptures, were seen as unorthodox but never subjected to persecution. Similarly, traditional East Asian cultures have never fostered atheophobia due to the alien nature of monotheism itself and the cultures' traditionally humanist approach to religion and relative agnosticism on questions about supernatural beings. Policies of religious toleration in premodern Asia date back to India's third-century BCE Magadhan emperor Ashoka, whose famous stone inscriptions encouraged respect for all dharmas.

Atheophobia has appeared most often in cultures shaped by Christianity and Islam, each of which not only aligned with political powers but generated empires, colonial systems, and modern nation-states in its own image. Both traditions have demonstrated the exclusivist inclinations within the monotheist worldview and distinct tendencies to beget various forms of theocracy (*theos* ["god"] + *kratos* ["rule"]), governance by religious authorities in the name of divine law and in collusion with secular magistrates. Beginning with the age of Constantine (c. 272–337), in the Christian world, and the caliphs after Muhammad (571–632), in the Islamic world,

Christian and Muslim legal codes designed to protect society from allegedly treacherous ideas targeted four things: heresy (defined as incorrect or distorted belief within the religious community), idolatry (understood as the worship of false gods), blasphemy (an all-inclusive concept entailing irreverence and contempt toward God), and apostasy (the rejection of one's birth religion). Apostasy has sometimes been seen as a crime against society, sometimes a crime against family—and therefore often handled with the brutal violence of private vengeance.

For centuries, pure atheism in the modern sense was unthinkable and therefore rarely a specific charge leveled against anyone judged to be a deviant thinker. Atheism functioned as a gratuitous condemnation supplementing and emphasizing the gravity of other more particular indictments. The greatest heretics in Christianity were those who, like fourth-century North African priest Arius, denied the full divinity of Christ; in Islam, those who challenged Muhammad's final-prophet status or who, like Sufi poet Al-Hallaj (executed 922), reportedly claimed to be God. Atheism remained an abstract intellectual crime and a phantom source of fear.

Punishments meted out for heresy, idolatry, blasphemy, and apostasy in Christian and Muslim societies have included fines, confiscation of property, incarceration, torture, banishment, and death. From late antiquity to early modernity, religious and civil authorities cooperated in the processes of accusation, arrest, interrogation, trial, and sentencing. The number of atheists executed as heretics, idolaters, blasphemers, or apostates is unknown.

The earliest pleas for religious toleration and intellectual freedom in the modern sense ignored atheism. They were written by Christians to Christian readers and were based on Christian principles. Most were composed by Christians suffering at the hands of other Christians. During the period of the sixteenth-century Reformation, Anabaptists, Quakers, Unitarians, and others penned arguments against religious persecution and in favor of what they called "soul liberty." The 1553 burning of anti-Trinitarian physician-theologian Michael Servetus in John Calvin's Protestant Geneva had a profound effect on these efforts. It created a crisis in the Western Christian conscience. French theologian Sebastian Castellio's response to the public execution, *Concerning Heretics* (1554), refuted all justifications for the death penalty in cases of supposed heresy and initiated a cascade of books questioning the morality of any attempt to control belief through physical and legal pressure. His conclusion—"To kill a human is not to defend a doctrine, it is to kill a human"—represented a major turning point in the history of Western thought and behavior.

In the wake of the Servetus's death, appeals for religious freedom poured off the world's new printing presses. Many framed their arguments in terms of toleration, seeking accommodations for religious minorities in the context of a society privileging one particular religious system or organization. Others argued for structural change in the shape of separation of church and state. Most of those stopped short of imagining separation of religion from public life. France's Edict of Nantes (1598), granting Protestants freedom from harassment, and England's Act of Toleration (1689), protecting nonconformists' right of worship, were important milestones. Virtually all documents and decrees of the period treated Christian theism as the norm. In British colonial America, Maryland's Act of Religious Toleration (1649) outlawed sectarian name-calling but continued to class blasphemy and denial of the Trinity as capital offenses. In Rhode Island, home of the first Jewish synagogue in what would become the United States, former Puritan turned Baptist and seeker Roger Williams invited readers to consider an expanded circle of freedom, promoting in *The Bloody Tenet of Persecution* (1644) the rights of Christians, Jews, and Muslims.

That same year in old England, poet and theologian John Milton, a modern follower of ancient Arius, released *Areopagitica*, an unprecedented plea for freedom of the press. During the Reformation, the Catholic church had invented modern censorship. Approval from church authorities was required for printing, and the Vatican's Index of Forbidden Books gave the world its first catalogue of banned books. New Protestant nations instituted similar measures, curbing publications that contained what leaders perceived to be unacceptable ideas. In language echoing Castellio, the author of *Paradise Lost* condemned the burning of both people and books. To kill a human being is to kill a reasonable creature, he said. Destroying a book "kills reason itself." Milton was confident no unorthodox book could ever intimidate truth. Paranoia about atheism, however, lurked in the background. The only note of reservation voiced in his bold proposal for unhindered speech was anxiety about books deemed "blasphemous and atheistical."

After a century of post-Reformation Christian warfare in Europe, writers and activists of the international Enlightenment movement brought the message of toleration to a new stage—from consideration of religious minorities to unrestricted freedom of thought and basic human rights. Pierre Bayle, John Locke, Voltaire, Thomas Paine, and many others produced writings that are now recognized as classics in the evolving literature on freedom of conscience—foundations of the literature of modernity itself. Many of the Enlightenment thinkers expressed strong anti-Catholic sentiments, seeing Rome as inimical to true liberty and church-state separation. Few of the male writers gave much attention to women's experiences of conscience. The best-known women writers of the movement—Mary Astell, Catharine Sawbridge Macaulay Graham, Judith Sargent Stevens Murray, Olympe de Gouges, and Mary Wollstonecraft—concentrated on intellectual freedom's relationship to a thick network of other inequity issues. No writer, of any sex or gender, had more than a rudimentary knowledge of the world's religions outside of Europe's warring sects. Virtually all failed to see the disconnect between their rhetoric of freedom and the Enlightenment's tendency toward racist ideas of white supremacy and its endorsement of the enslavement of Black and brown peoples from other continents.

Most Enlightenment writers continued to mount arguments for intellectual freedom within the framework of theism or what was coming to be known as deism, belief in an impersonal architect deity responsible for the universal laws of nature and morality. God, understood in generic terms, was regularly portrayed as the supreme underwriter of freedom, reason, and conscience. Because of the widespread practice of pragmatic self-censorship, it is impossible now to know how many of the writers held back from advancing a nontheist argument for intellectual liberty due to fears of exposing their own atheist or near-atheist views.

Thomas Jefferson, accused of atheism in his lifetime, argued for intellectual self-determination in two ways. As a reader of the Qur'an (one of the first in the United States), an editor of the New Testament (eliminating the supernatural parts), and a self-declared Unitarian (before the denomination was founded), he spoke of God as the ultimate guarantor of freedom. His Virginia Statute for Religious Freedom (1777) declared in a 547-word sentence that "Almighty God" had created the mind free—and so human governments should imitate the divine in their treatment of other people's thoughts. In his *Notes on Virginia* (1787), Jefferson went further. Contending that ideas on their own posed no threat to the security of society, and that the idea of no God deserved to be ranked as one idea among others, he took a step beyond the majority of his Enlightenment contemporaries. His reflection, this time articulated in less than 30 words and with *god* in lower case, represented nothing less than a new chapter in human thought: "But it does me no injury for my neighbor to say there are twenty gods, or no god. It neither picks my pocket nor breaks my leg."

Today, historians and social critics are engaged in an intense reevalu-ation of the Enlightenment legacy, exposing its self-contradictions and sorting through its far-reaching failures and influences. The pros and cons of modernity—and its offspring, globalization—are intricately tied up with the Enlightenment's complexities, inconsistencies, and errors. Living up to its highest standards, though, the Enlightenment has made the world safer for atheists. Atheophobia continues to exist, but where the Enlightenment heritage is present, its supports are weakened and its justi-fications open to greater scrutiny.

The political revolutions issuing from Enlightenment principles aimed toward greater interior freedom as well as the exterior freedoms of social organization, decision-making, and collective and individual action. Article VI of the U.S. Constitution (1787) outlawed religious requirements for public office. The Bill of Rights (1791), the Constitution's first ten amendments, guaranteed freedom of religious exercise, of speech, and of the press, as well as freedom from an established religion. The French Revolution's Declaration of the Rights of Man and Citizen (1789) pro-tected individual "opinions, including religious views" and the "free com-munication of ideas and opinions." The Constitution of the Russian Soviet Federated Socialist Republic (1918) enshrined "real freedom of con-science," separation of church and state, and the right of "religious and anti-religious propaganda." At what many interpreters consider the peak moment of high or late modernity, the Universal Declaration of Human Rights (1948), promulgated by the United Nations (UN), spoke of human beings as "endowed with reason and conscience" and possessing the rights to freedom of thought, freedom of expression, and the freedom to change religions and opinions without interference.

All these principles were reconfirmed in the International Covenant on Civil and Political Rights (1976) and the UN Declaration on the Elimination of All Forms of Intolerance and of Discrimination Based on Religion or Belief (1981). At least in theory, the Enlightenment legacy treated ideas in a way comparable to how one of its first economic products, capitalism, treated commercial trade—granting all ideas free interaction in a competi-tive intellectual marketplace, regulated not by the so-called invisible hand that Enlightenment theorists thought guided financial forces but by the power of reason available to all human beings.

In the United States, after ratification of the federal Constitution, some state constitutions continued to endorse one kind of religious privilege or another. Local law retained prejudice against some forms of religious faith and multiple forms of nonreligion. Massachusetts, in 1833, was the last state to disestablish religion—in that case, the Protestant churches dating back to the seventeenth-century Puritan era. Blasphemy laws remained on the books. The last person to be convicted of blasphemy in the United States was the former Universalist minister and freethinker Abner Kneeland, founder of the countercultural *Boston Investigator* journal. The court, which in 1838 sentenced him to sixty days in jail, showed little interest in distinguishing his professed pantheism, the belief that all reality is sacred, from still much-feared atheism. The petition to free Kneeland, signed by prominent figures such as Ralph Waldo Emerson, William Lloyd Garrison, and Bronson Alcott, was an indication of changing times and sentiments.

Atheophobia survived as one element of the Christian ethos that dominated U.S. culture for decades—the same ethos that enshrined compulsory chapel in colleges, prayer and Bible reading in public schools, "In God We Trust" as the nation's official motto, "under God" as a protected phrase of the Pledge of Allegiance, and White House prayer breakfasts. In 1940, U.S. courts declared British atheist Bertrand Russell unfit to teach philosophy at College of the City of New York. Atheism has been a convenient scapegoat or whipping post in American political rhetoric, especially verbal crusades against "godless communism." Accusations of atheism still smear individuals in all areas of social and private life—education, career, family, reputation, personal relationships, self-expression, and participation in social organizations and voluntary associations.

So far, no self-identified atheist has ever been elected president of the United States. According to a 2020 Gallup poll, a greater percentage of Americans would be more likely to vote for an LGBTQ+ or Muslim candidate than someone professing atheism. Despite legal action by the American Humanist Association and other groups for separation of church and state, six states preserve antiblasphemy codes on the law books, and seven state constitutions, in conflict with the federal ban on "religious tests," technically bar nontheists from public office.

In 2008, the British parliament rescinded all blasphemy laws in the United Kingdom. According to a 2011 Pew Research Center study, however, close to half the world's nations designate blasphemy or apostasy or both as illegal acts. The vast majority are Muslim or Muslim-majority countries in the Middle East, North Africa, or South Asia. Penalties for these alleged crimes include everything from public harassment and humiliation to state-approved execution or assassination. The rise of new fundamentalist forms of religion around the world, including Islamic State (ISIS or ISIL), in Iraq and Syria, and Boko Haram, based in Nigeria, has sparked fresh enthusiasm for old antiblasphemy ordinances. The spread of antiliberal and anti-Western sentiments has also contributed to climates that foster anti-atheist discrimination. Some European nations attempt to balance concerns for atheist rights with regulations against "defamation of religion" as a form of hate speech. Some ex-Muslim atheists, such as Ayaan Hirsi Ali, author of *Infidel* (2007), advocate for a twenty-first-century Enlightenment movement tailored to the needs and interests of Muslims.

The Freedom of Thought Report (https://fot.humanists.international), published since 2012 by Humanists International, shows that both atheism and anti-atheist persecution are on the rise worldwide. The annual reports identify atheists, agnostics, humanists, freethinkers, secularists, and other nonreligious people as collectively a "target minority" for persecution in multiple cultures. The 2020 arrest of Mubarak Bala in Nigeria, former Muslim and president of his country's Humanist Association, previously detained against his will in a psychiatric hospital, is one high-profile case signifying the ongoing threat facing nonbelievers globally. Atheophobia has evolved over time and is a part of the modern and postmodern experience. The rights and well-being of atheists and other nonreligious people continue to be endangered.

See also: Deism; Hirsi Ali, Ayaan; "In God We Trust"; Islam, Atheism and Agnosticism in; Media, Atheism and Agnosticism and the; "Under God"

Further Reading

Bainton, Roland H. *Hunted Heretic: The Life and Death of Michael Servetus, 1511–1553*. Rev. ed. Providence, RI: Blackstone Editions, 2005.

Bainton, Roland H. *The Travail of Religious Liberty: Nine Biographical Studies*. Eugene, OR: Wipf and Stock, 2008.

Christie-Murray, David. *A History of Heresy*. Oxford: Oxford University Press, 1991.

Erdozain, Dominic. *The Soul of Doubt: The Religious Roots of Unbelief from Luther to Marx*. Oxford: Oxford University Press, 2016.

Hecht, Jennifer Michael. *Doubt: A History*. San Francisco: HarperSanFrancisco, 2003.

Hughes, Merritt Y., ed. *John Milton: Complete Poems and Major Prose*. Indianapolis, IN: Bobbs-Merrill, 1957.

Kramnick, Isaac, ed. *The Portable Enlightenment Reader*. New York: Penguin, 1995.

Mansfield, Harvey C., Jr., ed. *Thomas Jefferson: Selected Writings*. Arlington Heights, IL: Harlan Davidson, 1979.

Stark, Rodney. *For the Glory of God: How Monotheism Led to Reformations, Science, Witch-Hunts, and the End of Slavery*. Princeton: Princeton University Press, 2003.

Stark, Rodney. *One True God: Historical Consequences of Monotheism*. Princeton: Princeton University Press, 2001.

Warburton, Nigel. *Free Speech: A Very Short Introduction*. Oxford: Oxford University Press, 2009.

B

Beauvoir, Simone de

Simone de Beauvoir (1908–1986) ranks as a preeminent figure in twentieth-century literature and an unparalleled shaper of modern feminist thought. With her companion and collaborator Jean-Paul Sartre, she made the philosophy of existentialism the emblem of a global movement seeking new and meaningful paths in social, political, personal, and artistic life. Her works of fiction and social commentary illuminate the infinite number of decisions that make authentic existence with responsibility and dignity both a possibility and a perpetual challenge. Her masterwork *The Second Sex* (1949), a landmark in feminist theory, sparked the second wave of the modern women's movement. An atheist from adolescence, Beauvoir fused the public and the private into a unified attempt to embody the philosophical ideal of the examined life in a world with no permanent values.

Beauvoir characterized her experience as a quest for genuine freedom, precisely the factor missing from her childhood. Her family exemplified the rigid standards of French bourgeois society before World War I. *Memoirs of a Dutiful Daughter* (1958), the first of four volumes of autobiography, chronicled her upbringing in a stifling atmosphere of patriarchal authority, prescribed social duty, and repressive Roman Catholic piety, moderated only by her father's genial skepticism. Gender roles were strictly enforced and knowledge of sexuality scrupulously controlled. Dubbed a promising student with a "man's brain," she discovered an attraction to the intellectual life, despite the conditions of her insular environment. One forbidden book led to another, and eventually she traded incense and candles for alcohol and tobacco, as she said, articulating her aspiration to be a writer.

Beauvoir pursued university degrees at a time when women still constituted a tiny minority in Western higher education. She studied at the

Institut Sainte-Marie, the Institut Catholique in Paris, the Sorbonne, and the Ecole Normale Libre, concentrating on mathematics, philosophy, and literature. She read deeply in continental philosophy, especially Gottfried Wilhelm Leibnitz and G. W. F. Hegel, and gained a reputation for original-ity and brilliance. Fellow students included future philosopher Simone Weil and anthropologist Claude Lévi-Strauss. With Sartre she formed a lifelong relationship as a writing couple. Their common grave in Mont-parnasse Cemetery in Paris is one of the world's much beloved literary pilgrimage sites.

Beauvoir's fifteen-year tenure of unrewarding lycée, or secondary school, teaching yielded to a promising career in writing, editing, and international lecturing during World War II and its aftermath. Existentialist legend places the birth of the new philosophical outlook at a moment in the 1930s, when Beauvoir, Sartre, and a mutual friend shared a memorable conversation and apricot cocktails in a Parisian bar. By the German inva-sion of France in 1940, the stage was set for bold new approaches to the promise and predicament of being human in the modern world. Beauvoir wrote a collection of stories, *When Things of the Spirit Come First* (not released until 1979); her first novel, *She Came to Stay* (1943); and the play *Useless Mouths* (1945), all addressing the unscripted and precarious nature of human life and love. In the process, she created existentialism's famous café literary scene as she searched for working environments with ade-quate heat in Nazi-occupied Paris.

Subsequent novels, especially the semiautobiographical Prix Goncourt winner *The Mandarins* (1954), explore the tensions felt in every individu-al's life between the free exercise of choice and commitment and the pres-sures exerted on freedom by chance occurrences, tragic circumstances, and the faceless forces of oppressive social structures. *The Ethics of Ambiguity* (1948), her clearest nonfiction exposition of the existentialist vision, counters the assumption that the nonexistence of God authorizes apathy and moral license. Her many contributions to *Les Temps Modernes*, the progressive journal she cofounded and coedited, reveal the extent to which she struggled to strike the proper balance between the postwar Left's allegiance to artistic and intellectual freedom and its obligation to support rising anticolonial movements around the globe.

The Second Sex, a mixture of encyclopedia, manifesto, and self-discovery, is Beauvoir's greatest act of research, reflection, and intellec-tual resistance. Over a half century after its publication, the book is still notable for its curiosity regarding the definition of *woman* and its thesis that a woman is not a matter of birth but something one becomes. Throughout the text, Beauvoir identifies religion as a serious threat to the health and full humanity of women. She portrays Christianity, in particular, as a major contributor to misogyny. The Catholic church, she maintains, has been, and still is, an agent of oppression, preaching the inferiority of women and perpetuating women's perilous situation in society—the same church that placed her books on the Vatican's Index of Forbidden Books. American feminist theologian and philosopher Mary Daly drew heavily upon Beauvoir's scholarship in her critique of Catholic sexism, *The Church and the Second Sex* (1968).

Beauvoir's atheism served as the foundation of her existentialist humanism and the point of departure for her life of active imagination and engagement. In many ways, she suggested, a life based on the recognition of the absence of God is both more demanding and more stimulating than a life founded on theist faith and devotion. As she put it in *The Ethics of Ambiguity*, atheism constitutes the ultimate position of human maturity, an austere but welcome form of enrichment, which brings with it great responsibility for the character of one's life and the life of society—a daunting view of human creativity so unlimited it blurs the distinction between the finite and the infinite.

See also: Feminism, Atheism and Agnosticism and; Sartre, Jean-Paul

Further Reading

Bair, Deirdre. *Simone de Beauvoir: A Biography*. New York: Summit Books, 1990.

Bakewell, Sarah. *At the Existentialist Café: Freedom, Being, and Apricot Cocktails*. New York: Other Press, 2016.

Bauer, Nancy. *Simone de Beauvoir, Philosophy, and Feminism*. New York: Columbia University Press, 2001.

Beauvoir, Simone de. *Adieux: A Farewell to Sartre*. Trans. Patrick O'Brian. New York: Pantheon, 1984.

Beauvoir, Simone de. *The Ethics of Ambiguity*. Trans. Bernard Frechtman. New York: Citadel Press, 1976.

Beauvoir, Simone de. *Feminist Writings*. Ed. Margaret A. Simons and Marybeth Timmerman. Urbana: University of Illinois Press, 2015.

Beauvoir, Simone de. *Memoirs of a Dutiful Daughter*. Trans. James Kirkup. New York: Harper Perennial, 2005.

Beauvoir, Simone de. *Philosophical Writings*. Ed. Margaret A. Simons. Urbana: University of Illinois Press, 2005.

Beauvoir, Simone de. *The Second Sex*. Trans. Constance Borde and Sheila Malovany-Chevallier. New York: Vintage Books, 2011.

Card, Claudia, ed. *The Cambridge Companion to Simone de Beauvoir*. Cambridge: Cambridge University Press, 2003.

Hengehold, Laura, and Nancy Bauer, eds. *A Companion to Simone de Beauvoir*. Hoboken, NJ: Wiley-Blackwell, 2017.

Moi, Toril. *Simone de Beauvoir: The Making of an Intellectual Woman*. 2nd ed. Oxford: Oxford University Press, 2008.

Rowley, Hazel. *Tête-a-Tête: The Tumultuous Lives and Loves of Simone de Beauvoir and Jean-Paul Sartre*. New York: Harper Perennial, 2006.

Besant, Annie

Annie Besant (1847–1933) was a writer, educator, social radical, public speaker, progressive political activist, and one of the most notable atheists of the nineteenth century. The range of her interests, abilities, and accomplishments still staggers the imagination of her biographers and disciples. The author of over three hundred books, pamphlets, and articles, she was an effective organizer, founding schools, including one university, and directing one of the modern world's most distinctive religious-philosophical movements. She agitated for socialism and women's rights and against her native Britain's colonial ambitions. Best known for her leadership of the international Theosophical movement that absorbed her later years, Besant played an especially important role in the development of modern atheism.

Besant's childhood and youth placed her squarely within Britain's Victorian experience, the era that made the nineteenth the century of Charles Dickens, Charles Darwin, John Henry Newman, Florence Nightingale, David Livingstone, and Karl Marx, the latter in his famous chair at the British Museum. The daughter of Irish parents in London, she came of age during the heyday of the Church of England's Oxford movement, when writers and thinkers such as Newman and Edward Pusey were attempting to transform the Anglican tradition into a vibrant alternative to both Catholicism and Protestantism. Intellectuals within the movement sought to fuse the best of the medieval and modern heritages, and architects adapted Gothic mystique to an age of coal and steam. Besant married a minister in the Anglican communion, but her growing interest in free thought, her literary aspirations, and her mounting concern over social injustice drew her away from Christianity, middle-class values, and what quickly became an unhappy marriage. Her first publication, written while still a vicar's wife, was a pamphlet questioning the divinity of Christ.

Legally separated from her husband, Besant studied briefly at the University of London and pursued work in journalism, labor organizing, and public speaking. She joined the National Secular Society, founded by writer-activist Charles Bradlaugh, and contributed regularly to the Society's free-thought newspaper *National Reformer*. With Bradlaugh, she published American physician Charles Knowlton's pamphlet on birth control, titled *The Fruits of Philosophy* (1877). Her own pamphlet *The Law of Population* (1878) made her the first woman in Britain to promote birth control publicly. The controversial publications brought charges of obscenity against Besant and Bradlaugh, with both barely avoiding sentences of hard labor due to a technical error in the legal proceedings. The courts were more successful in punishing Besant when they granted her estranged husband custody of their child.

Following the high-profile trial, Besant's unconventional friendship with Bradlaugh, also separated from his spouse, kept the partners continually in the public eye. She became active in the democratic socialist Fabian Society, the Irish home rule movement, the women's suffrage movement, and well-publicized strikes of women workers suffering in hazardous, low-paying jobs. She turned her many speeches, praised by George Bernard Shaw and even reluctant opponents, into published pamphlets such as *Why I Am a Socialist* (1886) and *Modern Socialism* (1886). Her companion and collaborator Bradlaugh became the first avowed atheist elected to serve as a member of the British House of Commons.

Besant was most active in public advocacy for atheism during the 1870s and '80s. In those years, she was arguably the most prominent female atheist in the world. In addition to her book *My Path to Atheism* (1878), she published numerous short works on atheism, including *The Gospel of Atheism* (1877), *A World without God* (1885), *Atheism and Its Bearing on Morals* (1887), and *Why I Do Not Believe in God* (1887). She offered a critique of her faith of origin in *Christianity: Its Evidences, Its Origin, Its Morality, Its History* (1881). In her *Autobiography* (1885), she explained how instinctive skepticism, the revolt against sexism, and insights into the evils of capitalism conspired to advance the evolution of her personal life philosophy. For her, atheism was not the denial or lack of belief—and certainly not the absence of a moral sense. She described the "noblest Atheism of our day" as the "joyous, self-reliant facing of the world with the resolute determination to improve it."

Her review of *The Secret Doctrine* (1888), by the Russian-born mystic and clairvoyant Helena Petrovna Blavatsky, turned Besant toward the new worldview of Theosophy. Informed by modern spiritualism, the Western legacy of hermetic and occult traditions, and selective appropriations of Hindu and Buddhist ideas and practices, Theosophy offered many seekers around the world a way to unite ancient wisdom with modern science. Besant became the second president of the Theosophical Society, cofounded in 1875 by Blavatsky and the American attorney-journalist Henry Steel Olcott. As the Society moved its headquarters to South Asia, she established residence in India. A supporter of Indian self-rule, she was once incarcerated for her work in the Indian independence movement. She also served as the first woman president of the Indian National Congress and founded Central Hindu College (later known as Banaras University). Her appearance as featured speaker for Theosophy at the 1893 interfaith World's Parliament of Religions in Chicago electrified the American audience, which was already entranced by a full roster of speakers from around the globe.

During the last decades of her life, Besant spoke and wrote on topics such as evolution, karma, reincarnation, yoga, and the Indian classic the Bhagavad Gita, never renouncing her earlier commitments to skepticism and social activism. Her *Case for India* (1917) remains one of the most significant indictments of British imperialism ever published by an ally of the independence movement. Her adopted son Jiddu Krishnamurti, author of *Freedom from the Known* (1969) and many other best sellers, became a beloved educator of the twentieth century, attracting people from all over the world to his school and retreat center in Ojai, California.

See also: Bradlaugh, Charles; Feminism, Atheism and Agnosticism and

Further Reading

Besant, Annie. *An Autobiography*. 2nd ed. London: Unwin, 1908.

Besant, Annie. *My Path to Atheism*. 3rd ed. London: Freethought Publishing Company, 1885.

Chandrasekhar, Sripati. *"A Dirty Filthy Book": The Writings of Charles Knowlton and Annie Besant on Reproductive Physiology and Birth Control and an Account of the Bradlaugh-Besant Trial*. Berkeley: University of California Press, 1981.

Manvell, Roger. *The Trial of Annie Besant and Charles Bradlaugh*. New York: Horizon Press, 1976.

Nethercot, A. H. *The First Five Lives of Annie Besant*. Chicago: University of Chicago Press, 1960.

Nethercot, A. H. *The Last Four Lives of Annie Besant*. Chicago: University of Chicago Press, 1963.

Screenivas, Mytheli. "Birth Control in the Shadow of Empire: The Trials of Annie Besant, 1877–1878." *Feminist Studies* 41 (2015): 509–37.

Taylor, Anne. *Annie Besant: A Biography*. Oxford: Oxford University Press, 1992.

Wessinger, Catherine L. *Annie Besant and Progressive Messianism*. Lewiston, NY: Edwin Mellen Press, 1988.

Bradlaugh, Charles

Charles Bradlaugh (1833–1891), politician, writer, editor, and social reformer, was one of the foremost spokespersons for atheism in Victorian Britain. His many essays and pamphlets, along with his dramatic performances on the debate stage and his sensational appearances in court, made him a celebrity in a time of fierce newspaper competition and larger-than-life personalities fit for an age of empire and revolution. With his companion and collaborator Annie Besant, he campaigned for women's rights and sought to raise awareness about birth control, a topic then still surrounded by strict moral taboos. His *Plea for Atheism* (1877) did much to advance the public's understanding of atheism as more than a denial or rejection of faith. Bradlaugh is best known as the first openly atheist member of the British Parliament.

Born in London, Bradlaugh received a diversified education that included formal schooling and experience in a variety of employments, including office work and military service. He never attended university. As a teenager, he was already an outspoken freethinker and critic of Christianity.

His career reflected the broad range of his interests, involving him in journalism, organizing, and public service. He founded the National Secular Society in 1866 and coedited with Besant the Society's free-thought newspaper, the *National Reformer*. Separated from his wife, Bradlaugh established a partnership with Besant, who had separated from her Anglican minister husband while launching her own career as radical author and activist. Like Besant, Bradlaugh supported women's suffrage, labor reform, and Irish home rule. He never, however, shared her commitment to socialism. His political orientation was the tradition of liberal individualism. Besant's later attraction to Theosophy may have corresponded to some extent with Bradlaugh's longtime interest in spiritualism. His attendance at séances and acquaintance with spiritualist literature remind twenty-first-century readers that nineteenth-century skeptics applied their skepticism to the mainstream science and medicine of their day as well as to traditional religion.

Bradlaugh's daughter Hypatia Bradlaugh Bonner, science educator and founder of the United Kingdom's Rationalist Peace Society, published a two-volume biography of her father in the early twentieth century. According to her, two major controversies defined Bradlaugh's career. The first was the decision to publish with Besant a pamphlet on birth control written decades earlier by the American physician Charles Knowlton. The work's 1877 appearance in the *National Reformer* landed the couple in court on charges of obscenity and placed them center stage in one of the sensational trials of the century. Bradlaugh and Besant were found guilty and sentenced to six months of severe imprisonment but never served time, due to a technical error in the proceedings. In the prosecution against Besant, the courts were more successful, judging her unfit to be a mother and granting her estranged husband custody of their child.

The second controversy concerned Bradlaugh's service in the House of Commons. Elected to represent his district in 1880, he was repeatedly blocked from joining the legislature by powerful parties opposed to his outright unbelief. At one point he was even incarcerated for refusing to vacate the parliamentary chambers. A key issue in the six-year dispute was his unwillingness to swear the traditional oath of allegiance. Finally allowed to take his seat in 1886, Bradlaugh was instrumental in passing legislation that permitted nonconformists and unbelievers to assume public office without harassment and to offer affirmations of honesty and integrity in place of oaths rooted in premodern convictions about theism and the moral force of God language.

Bradlaugh's brand of atheism reflected the Enlightenment's legacy of rational skepticism and moral critique of the historical record of Christianity. Like many Victorians, he was a lifelong Bible reader, displaying a high degree of biblical literacy and keen appreciation for the poetry and prose of the 1611 King James translation. His debates with leading Christian representatives, Protestant and Catholic, were major social occasions—sometimes stretching over several nights.

Bradlaugh's writings addressed a wide assortment of religious, philosophical, and political topics. His special contributions to atheist literature include his emphasis on what he saw as the social benefits of unbelief and the proper definition of atheism itself. The progressive causes of antislavery, religious toleration, science education, women's rights, labor unionism, and anti-imperialism, he argued, had all been advanced by the erosion of religious belief and the rise of relativism, not by religion's defense or propagation. Humanity was "a real gainer" from humanist skepticism, he declared.

Regarding the meaning of atheism, he offered important testimony from the dimension of personal experience—something many atheists in the twenty-first century have attempted to do. Atheism, as understood by the atheist, Bradlaugh maintained, is not a negation of or rebellion against something but rather the natural acceptance of a positive worldview. The real problem, he asserted, is the meaning of the word *God*. As he put it, what the atheist really ought to say to the theist is this: "I know not what you mean by God; I am without idea of God; the word God is to me a sound conveying no clear or distinct affirmation."

See also: Besant, Annie

Further Reading

Arnstein, Walter L. *The Bradlaugh Case: Atheism, Sex, and Politics among the Victorians*. Columbia: University of Missouri Press, 1983.

Besant, Annie. *Charles Bradlaugh: A Character Sketch*. Chennai, India: Theosophical Publishing House, 1941.

Bradlaugh, Charles. *A Few Words about the Devil, and Other Biographical Sketches and Essays*. New York: A. K. Butts, 1874.

Larsen, Timothy. *A People of One Book: The Bible and the Victorians*. Oxford: Oxford University Press, 2011.

Manvell, Roger. *The Trial of Annie Besant and Charles Bradlaugh*. New York: Horizon Press, 1976.

Niblett, Bryan. *Dare to Stand Alone: The Story of Charles Bradlaugh*. Oxford: Kramedart, 2011.

Royle, Edward. *Victorian Infidels: The Origins of the British Secularist Movement, 1791–1866*. Manchester: Manchester University Press, 1974.

Smith, Warren S. *The London Heretics, 1870–1914*. New York: Dodd, Mead, 1968.

C

Cady Stanton, Elizabeth

Elizabeth Cady Stanton (1815–1902), American social theorist and activist, was one of the prime architects of modern first-wave feminism. Today, her decisive role in the struggle to win the vote for women in the United States is universally recognized. The range of her social engagement was immense, stretching from abolition of slavery and the temperance movement to dress reform and medical care attuned to the needs of women. Working in an era that afforded virtually no advanced educational opportunities for women, she was an innovative historian of women's experiences and a formidable critic of Christianity, publishing one of the nineteenth century's most distinctive books of religious criticism: *The Woman's Bible* (1895, 1898).

A native of upstate New York, Cady Stanton attended grammar school in her hometown of Johnstown and the female seminary, a secondary school for young women, in nearby Troy. Despite her intellectual talents, legal sex discrimination barred her from following her brother and male associates to college. Instead, she studied informally in the law office of her politician and judge father and privately with a local minister. The Reformed tradition of Protestant Christianity informed her family's understanding of religion, and a new wave of evangelical revivals, often tinged with concern for social justice, was rapidly changing the religious landscape of the antebellum America she knew. In her autobiography *Eighty Years and More* (1898), Cady Stanton described her rejection of religious faith, largely due to the churches' defense of gender inequality, and her eventual adoption of reason and science as the trustworthy guides for the responsible search for truth.

In her twenties, she launched her career as a visionary leader in radical social reform. Her unconventional marriage with journalist and abolitionist

Henry B. Stanton—best symbolized by the elimination of the woman's traditional vow to "obey" from the text of the wedding ceremony—was a sign of things to come. Her attendance at the 1840 World Anti-Slavery Convention in London, which included only male speakers on the conference program, convinced her that chattel slavery and the suppression of women were two forms of one oppressive system. The experience propelled her—and colleagues Lucretia Mott and Susan B. Anthony—into action. The result was the historic 1848 Woman's Rights Convention in Seneca Falls, New York, the formal beginning of the modern feminist movement.

For the rest of her career, Cady Stanton served as writer, editor, orator, strategist, and symbol for the campaign for the legal, political, social, educational, financial, sexual, and spiritual rights of women. She founded the National Woman Suffrage Association, fighting for the basic rights of women in a democratic society, but did not live to witness the ratification of the Nineteenth Amendment to the U.S. Constitution in 1920, which recognized the right of all citizens to vote, regardless of sex. As the principal scholar and philosopher of the movement, Cady Stanton composed the Declaration of Sentiments that set the agenda for the Seneca Falls assembly. She edited the women's rights newspaper *Revolution* (1868–1870) and contributed three volumes to the six-volume, multiauthored *History of Woman Suffrage* (1881–1922). Her special concerns, aside from full involvement in the political process, included contentious topics such as divorce laws, child custody, and property rights. Today, historians acknowledge the survival of racist attitudes among Cady Stanton and other white leaders of the movement, despite their agitation for freedom and equality.

Like many other reformers, especially those whose houses have been declared National Historic Landmarks, Cady Stanton has suffered a significant degree of domestication in modern memory. Her radical religious thought is little known to members of the public who hail her part in women's history. Historians of religion, even those dedicated to feminist theories and methods, tend to ignore her or dismiss her as an amateur in the age of Ludwig Feuerbach, Karl Marx, and Friedrich Nietzsche—as if "professional philosopher" were a role available to any woman in the nineteenth century.

The Woman's Bible, published in two volumes, executes a thoroughgoing rereading of the Jewish and Christian scriptures from a perspective beginning with unqualified recognition of women's dignity and intelligence and laced with unquestioning rejection of patriarchal institutions and attitudes—something never before seen in the history of Western culture. The text offers free-flowing and freethinking commentary on most of the books of the Bible as well as the Jewish Kabbalah. All the contributors were women, and each entry was signed with the author's initials. Cady Stanton was the primary author, initiator, and organizer of the project; her spirited sections concluded with "ECS." The book appeared in a period when a new class of liberal and modernist biblical critics was publishing studies questioning the Bible's divine status, truth claims, and historical reliability, treating the Bible not as an untouchable sacred text but as a set of ancient books with enormous global influence. None could match *The Woman's Bible* for the audacity of its aims and the uniqueness of its point of departure.

Cady Stanton's personal views on religion are found in her autobiography, letters, editorials, speeches, and pamphlets. She publicly denied the Virgin Birth and the divinity of Jesus, whom she called the "great leading Radical of his time." While some early feminists attempted to bolster their countercultural propositions with themes of equality and female heroism from the Bible, Cady Stanton judged Christianity to be the source of the problem. In her essay "Bible and Church Degrade Woman" (1898), she indicts the teachings and teachers of the Christian tradition for centuries of injustice against women—from the stunting of women's minds to the destruction of their bodies, including but not limited to crusades against outspoken women heretics and dissenters, and independently minded women dubbed and demonized as witches. She did acknowledge change over time, but not in essentials: "We do not burn the bodies of women today; but we humiliate them in a thousand ways, and chiefly by our theologies."

Cady Stanton did not employ terms such as *atheist* or *agnostic* to describe her position or outlook. When it came to the specific question of God's existence, she invoked the perennial problem of evil. The hard fact of the prolonged suffering of the human race, she said, prevented her from believing in a "tender loving fatherly intelligence" overseeing the world.

See also: Christianity, Atheism and Agnosticism in; Feminism, Atheism and Agnosticism and

Further Reading

Banner, Lois W. *Elizabeth Cady Stanton: A Radical for Woman's Rights*. Boston: Little, Brown, 1980.

Cady Stanton, Elizabeth. *Eighty Years and More: Reminiscences 1815–1897*. New York: Simon and Schuster, 2019.

Cady Stanton, Elizabeth. *Solitude of Self.* Ashfield, MA: Paris Press, 2001.

Cady Stanton, Elizabeth. *The Woman's Bible*. Boston: Northeastern University Press, 1993.

Davis, Sue. *The Political Thought of Elizabeth Cady Stanton: Women's Rights and the American Political Traditions*. New York: New York University Press, 2008.

DuBois, Ellen Carol, ed. *The Elizabeth Cady Stanton-Susan B. Anthony Reader: Correspondence, Writings, Speeches*. Boston: Northeastern University Press, 1992.

Ginzberg, Lori D. *Elizabeth Cady Stanton: An American Life*. New York: Hill and Wang, 2009.

Jacoby, Susan. *Freethinkers: A History of American Secularism*. New York: Holt, 2004.

Joshi, S. T. *Atheism: A Reader*. Amherst, NY: Prometheus Books, 2000.

Ruether, Rosemary Radford, and Rosemary Skinner Keller, eds. *Women and Religion in America*. 3 vols. San Francisco: Harper and Row, 1986.

Turner, James. *Without God, without Creed: The Origins of Unbelief in America*. Baltimore, MD: Johns Hopkins University Press, 1985.

Christianity, Atheism and Agnosticism in

Atheism and agnosticism are typically seen as opposites or competitors of Christianity. Their relationship with the Christian tradition is frequently portrayed in stark, adversarial terms. In reality, the relationship between Christianity and atheism and agnosticism is more complex and more intimate than it would appear on the surface. For centuries, Christianity, atheism, and agnosticism have been intricately intertwined. The atheism and agnosticism dismissed or condemned by traditional Christian apologists are in many ways actually products of the Christian experience.

Significant studies that have advanced the thesis of the Christian sources of modern atheism include: Michael Buckley's *At the Origins of Modern Atheism* (1987), his *Denying and Disclosing God* (2004), Gavin Hyman's *A Short History of Atheism* (2010), and Dominic Erdozain's *The Soul of Doubt: The Religious Roots of Unbelief from Luther to Marx* (2016). These books, along with works by Marcel Gauchet, Gianni Vattimo, and Michael Allen Gillespie, represent the ongoing scholarly quest for not only the historical and cultural relationship between Christianity and atheism but also the deep genetic relationships that tie the two realities together.

Today, a growing number of Christian thinkers and activists see atheists and agnostics as dialogue partners and allies for social justice. Of the over two billion individuals who identify as members of the global Christian community in the twenty-first century, an unknown number experience degrees of affinity with atheist or agnostic approaches to reality. An unknown number also self-identify in one way or another as Christian atheists or agnostics.

Christianity arose in the context of the Roman empire during the first century CE. Roman critics of the new movement perceived it as a threat to social order and the relative harmony of local and regional religions, all characterized by a shared worldview imagining a pantheon of deities intersecting with earthly life. Christianity's monotheist and missionary faith seemed dangerous and incomprehensible to many Roman observers. The New Testament writer Paul called the people who practiced the old religions of Asia Minor and the Mediterranean *athéoi* ("godless"): individuals, he thought, who needed salvation in his crucified Jewish Messiah. Ironically Roman pundits used the same term to describe the followers of Paul's newfangled gospel: people, they said, who did not honor the gods. New gods could be incorporated into the empire's sprawling piety, but one God sounded like no god. Before his execution according to imperial decree, the second-century bishop Polycarp was ordered to proclaim before his accusers, "Away with the atheists!"—meaning his fellow Christians. Despised Christians were incorporated into the ranks of august company: five hundred years earlier, in Athens, Socrates had been condemned to death as *atheos*.

For most Christians today, the tradition's ancient association with atheism, insofar as it is remembered at all, seems like an ill-told joke or a case of mistaken identity. Christian thought, though, has always been in a state of ferment. Belief generates new belief. It also engenders unbelief. The New Testament itself portrays a community animated by disagreement over first principles. From the beginning, there were disputes over what adherents believed and did not believe about key issues such as the identity of Jesus, the question of authority, and the way human beings know the truth. The proliferation of texts outside the New Testament canon—the gnostic gospels and letters—demonstrated the theological and geographical scope of the debate. The practice of excommunication, mutual condemnations for heresy, and the emerging divisions within the expanding multicultural church demonstrated how much was at issue.

The union of Christian faith and Greek philosophy intensified the debate. The gradual incorporation of pagan literature into the curriculum of Christian education had a similar effect. By the fourth century, Christian intellectual life had become a dynamic dialogue between faith and reason, infused with pre-Christian wisdom. Combined with the prophetic iconoclasm, critique of idolatry, and recognition of God's ultimate unknowability inherited from Judaism, the injection of a new kind of critical reason into Christian thought gave the processes of questioning, doubting, and even disbelieving important roles in the drama of the Christian mind.

In the Middle Ages, esoteric variants of Christianity, expressed in magic, astrology, alchemy, and other arcane disciplines, gave full rein to speculation and deviations from developing orthodoxies. Strains of unitarianism and universalism, going back to early Christianity, also served as gadflies in the tradition's intellectual life, divulging open questions in the allegedly settled doctrines of Christ's divine nature and the justice of eternal damnation. Christian mysticism, laced with themes such as the "cloud of unknowing," the "dark night of the soul," *agnosto theo* (the "unknown God"), and *deus absconditus* (the "hidden God"), pointed to uncharted regions of spiritual experience on the edges of official teaching.

Some medieval theologians experimented with the *via negativa*, a way of searching for truth through negation, saying only what God was not. They exposed the limitations of long-standing metaphors for God such as father, king, judge—and even as a person. For some theologians, God was reason itself. For others, God was inscrutable will. Many wondered how God could be both great and good. German mystic Meister Eckhart, a target of heresy hunters, spoke of God beyond God, a transcendent absolute beyond the reaches of logic and language.

In some cases, atheist and agnostic perspectives were given breathing room in the atmosphere of premodern Christian thought. In his *Summa Theologiae*, the thirteenth century's Thomas Aquinas, inspired by the wisdom he found in the pagan philosopher Aristotle, advanced as many arguments against theism as for it. He began his "five ways" of proving the existence of God with unexpected respect for unbelief: "It seems that God does not exist." In university debates during Aquinas's time, one scholar would be assigned the role of the *advocatus diaboli*, the devil's advocate, responsible for poking holes in arguments. At the height of the Middle Ages, unbelief, as an abstract yet plausible position, was a built-in countertheme of the Christian imagination.

Counterorthodox impulses within Christianity became more evident in the early modern period, thanks to a number of factors: the proliferation of sects during and after the Reformation, widespread dissemination of print material, dramatic increases in literacy and travel, and the observation of ordinary people that notorious heretics (Catholic and Protestant), if they survived the wrath of their fellow human beings, were not struck down by lightning. With modernized censorship and the Rome-sponsored Inquisition, the crackdown on heresy became more extreme. At the same time, heresy (from the Greek *hairein* = "to choose") became more democratized and more normal. Christianity was a matrix from which unlimited heresies flowed. Heresy stalkers—such as the seventeenth-century author of *A Catalogue of the Several Sects and Opinions in England and Other Nations with a Brief Rehearsal of Their False and Dangerous Tenets*—had a hard time keeping track of them all. Three centuries later, sociologist Peter Berger would describe the modern experience itself as an enactment of the "heretical imperative." Being modern, he said, meant sorting through and selecting one's own beliefs.

By Berger's century, doubt, dissent, and disbelief were prominent features of Christian experience. Nineteenth-century liberals sought to accommodate Christianity to the standards of people whom German theologian Friedrich Schleiermacher called its "cultured despisers," individuals who could not square traditional belief with newly cherished ideals of progress. Twentieth-century modernists experimented with non-supernatural variants of faith. Broadening scientific consciousness and shifting ethical standards contributed to a cultural climate in which once incontestable doctrines were widely and routinely questioned.

God in particular was a problem, and Christian intellectuals of the era addressed the problem from different angles. Many offered redefinitions. Alfred North Whitehead imagined a finite God, part of the cosmic evolutionary process. Paul Tillich, who saw atheism as a corrective to biblical literalism, called God the transpersonal Ground of Being. Mary Daly urged readers to go beyond the God of patriarchy. James Cone dismantled the Eurocentric assumptions that made the Hebrew-Greek God a problem in the first place. Gustavo Gutiérrez pointed to parallels between the God of the Exodus and Marxist visions of liberation. Simone Weil suggested that Christians could learn much from atheism. She perceived atheism as a protest against naive and offensive views of God, a purifying force for faith.

A dramatic form of Christian atheism appeared in the 1960s. The publication of Gabriel Vahanian's *The Death of God* (1961), John A. T. Robinson's *Honest to God* (1963), Paul Van Buren's *The Secular Meaning of the Gospel* (1963), Jürgen Moltmann's *Theology of Hope* (1964), Harvey Cox's *The Secular City* (1965), Leslie Weatherhead's *The Christian Agnostic* (1965), Daly's *The Church and the Second Sex* (1968), and Cone's *Black Theology and Black Power* (1969) made the decade as revolutionary theologically as it was culturally and politically. In a time of upheaval and hope, the theological avant-garde sought to translate the gospel into secular terms and side definitively with the oppressed. Many thinkers were inspired by the "religionless" Christianity set forth by Dietrich Bonhoeffer, a Lutheran theologian executed by the Nazis for his role in a plot to assassinate Hitler. A major current of the new direction in Christian thought was the departure from the prescientific idea of a God "up there" and "out there"—the very deity, according to Russia's Nikita Khrushchev in 1961, that the first cosmonaut had not seen in space.

Radical, or death-of-God, theology announced the startling news that God had died. Throughout the decade, it grabbed headlines in print and radio and television—especially the red and black "Is God Dead?" cover for *Time* magazine's 1966 Easter issue and that year's August issue of *Playboy*. The controversial movement was principally associated with Thomas J. J. Altizer's *The Gospel of Christian Atheism* (1966) and essays he published with William Hamilton, both prominent professors in American Protestantism's educational establishment. Together they imagined a Christianity without God—a feature, according to Altizer, of the unorthodox Christian epic tradition stretching from Dante, John Milton, and William Blake to Herman Melville, Friedrich Nietzsche, and James Joyce.

The message of the death of God resonated with a generation of Christians who could no longer endorse the God of conventional faith. German theologian Dorothee Söllee's *Atheistically Believing in God* (1968), attracting European young people energized by Marxist principles, delivered an attack on what she called "Christofascism." Today, radical theology continues in the scholarship of Mark C. Taylor, author of *After God* (2007), and Lissa McCullough, author of *The Religious Philosophy of Simone Weil* (2014).

A complementary movement is the international Sea of Faith Network (https://www.sofn.org.uk), based in the United Kingdom. Advancing a nontheist version of Christianity, the network was inspired by the work of

Anglican priest and Cambridge scholar Don Cupitt, whose books *Taking Leave of God* (1981) and *After God* (1997) referred to traditional Christianity as the "Old Testament" of contemporary Christian thought. The network organizes annual conferences and publishes the journal *Sofia*. It takes its name from Matthew Arnold's 1867 poem "Dover Beach." One of the best expressions of the Victorian crisis of faith, the poem portrays the "Sea of Faith," once round and full at high tide, as now known only by its "melancholy, long, withdrawing roar." Cupitt's 1984 six-part BBC series, also called *The Sea of Faith*, introduced millions of viewers to a vision of Christianity that was rich in psychological insight and moral imagination but not grounded in belief in a literal deity. Christianity, home today to millions of fervent believers, is also home to atheists and agnostics of varying profiles, overt and covert, some relieved, some reluctant.

See also: Feuerbach, Ludwig; Islam, Atheism and Agnosticism in; Judaism, Atheism and Agnosticism in; Proofs for God, Atheist and Agnostic Critiques of

Further Reading

Altizer, Thomas J. J. *The Gospel of Christian Atheism*. Philadelphia: Westminster Press, 1966.

Altizer, Thomas J. J. *Living the Death of God: A Theological Memoir*. Albany: State University of New York Press, 2006.

Altizer, Thomas J. J., and William Hamilton. *Radical Theology and the Death of God*. Indianapolis: Bobbs-Merrill, 1966.

Berger, Peter L. *The Heretical Imperative: Contemporary Possibilities of Religious Affirmation*. Garden City, NY: Anchor Press/Doubleday, 1980.

Bloch, Ernst. *Atheism in Christianity: The Religion of the Exodus and the Kingdom*. Trans. J. T. McSwann. London: Verso, 2009.

Buckley, Michael J. *At the Origins of Modern Atheism*. New Haven, CT: Yale University Press, 1987.

Buckley, Michael J. *Denying and Disclosing God: The Ambiguous Progress of Modern Atheism*. New Haven, CT: Yale University Press, 2004.

Christie-Murray, David. *A History of Heresy*. Oxford: Oxford University Press, 1976.

Church, F. Forrester, ed. *The Essential Tillich: An Anthology of the Writings of Paul Tillich*. New York: Collier Books, 1987.

Cox, Harvey. *The Secular City: Secularization and Urbanization in Theological Perspective*. New York: Macmillan, 1966.

Cupitt, Don. *After God: The Future of Religion*. New York: Harper, 1997.

Cupitt, Don. *The Sea of Faith.* Cambridge: Cambridge University Press, 1988.

Cupitt, Don. *Taking Leave of God.* New York: Crossroad, 1981.

De Lubac, Henri. *The Drama of Atheist Humanism.* Trans. Anne Englund Nash, Edith M. Riley, and Mark Sebanc. 7th ed. San Francisco: Ignatius Press, 1983.

Erdozain, Dominic. *The Soul of Doubt: The Religious Roots of Unbelief from Luther to Marx.* Oxford: Oxford University Press, 2016.

Feuerbach, Ludwig. *The Essence of Christianity.* Trans. George Eliot. New York: Harper and Row, 1957.

Geering, Lloyd. *Christianity without God.* Santa Rosa, CA: Polebridge Press, 2002.

Goodin, David. *An Agnostic in the Fellowship of Christ: The Ethical Mysticism of Albert Schweitzer.* Lanham, MD: Lexington Books/Fortress Academic, 2019.

Hecht, Jennifer Michael. *Doubt: A History.* San Francisco: HarperSanFrancisco, 2003.

Hooks, Sidney. "The Atheism of Paul Tillich." In *Religious Experience and Truth: A Symposium.* Ed. Sidney Hook, pp. 59–64. New York: New York University Press, 1961.

Hyman, Gavin. *A Short History of Atheism.* London: I. B. Tauris, 2010.

Küng, Hans. *Does God Exist? An Answer for Today.* Trans. Edward Quinn. Garden City, NY: Doubleday, 1980.

McCullough, Lissa, and Brian Schroeder, eds. *Thinking Through the Death of God: A Critical Companion to Thomas J. J. Altizer.* Albany: State University of New York Press, 2004.

Perez-Esclarin, Antonio. *Atheism and Liberation.* Trans. John Drury. Maryknoll, NY: Orbis Books, 1978.

Pinnock, Sarah K., ed. *The Theology of Dorothee Söllee.* Harrisburg, PA: Trinity Press International, 2003.

Robinson, John A. T. *Honest to God.* Louisville, KY: Westminster John Knox Press, 2002.

Rodkey, Christopher D., and Jordan E. Miller, eds. *The Palgrave Handbook of Radical Theology.* London: Palgrave Macmillan, 2018.

Weatherhead, Leslie. *The Christian Agnostic.* Nashville, TN: Abingdon Press, 1990.

Christina, Greta

Greta Christina (b. 1961) is a leading atheist blogger, author, editor, and culture critic. She is well known in atheist and humanist networks across the United States and is a speaker in demand on the secular lecture circuit.

She has received the American Humanist Association's LGBTQ Humanist Award, Foundation Beyond Belief's Team Honored Hero Award, and the Secular Student Alliance Ambassador Award. In 2020, she was named one of the "50 Top Atheists in the World Today" by TheBestSchools.org. A member of the LGBTQ+ community, Christina identifies as pansexual and polyamorous. Her work in fiction and nonfiction has earned her a respected place in atheist, feminist, and literary circles.

Christina was born in Chicago and graduated from Reed College in Portland, Oregon. Since the late 1980s, she has built a career as a freelance writer and activist. She participated in New Age spirituality for a time and self-described as an agnostic before identifying as an atheist in the early twenty-first century.

Christina has contributed to the *Skeptical Inquirer* and *Humanist* magazines and serves on the advisory board for the Secular Student Alliance and the board of directors for Foundation Beyond Belief, the American secular community's premier humanitarian organization. A popular choice on the speakers bureau of the Center for Inquiry, she spoke at the Reason Rally in 2012 and is regularly featured on the program at Skepticon, the largest annual conference for atheists, agnostics, and freethinkers in the United States. Topics she addresses in her public speaking include diversity in the atheist community, activism burnout, and what atheists can learn from LGBTQ+ experiences. The cofounder of the feminist and progressive media site The Orbit (https://the-orbit.net), Christina advocates for socially engaged atheism.

Christina's books focus on practical issues related to becoming and being atheist in contemporary culture: *Why Are You Atheists So Angry?* (2012), *Coming Out Atheist* (2014), and *The Way of the Heathen: Practicing Atheism in Everyday Life* (2016). With wit and incisive social commentary, she confronts intolerance within the atheist movement and emphasizes the need for atheists to be in solidarity with other marginalized groups in society. Her intellectual signature is the advancement of life-affirming atheist morality. Her book *Comforting Thoughts about Death that Have Nothing to Do with God* (2014) examines the rarely investigated question of atheist views of death.

In addition to her work on atheism, Christina writes on the contested subject of sex positivity, defending the value of free and consensual sex, arguing for the legitimacy of antisexist pornographic art, and celebrating what she calls sexual transcendence. Her sex fiction has appeared in *Ms.*, *Penthouse*, *On Our Backs* (the first erotica magazine in the United States established by women for a lesbian audience), and anthologies such as *Three Kinds of Asking for It* (2005), edited by Susie Bright. Christina is the author of *Bending: Dirty Kinky Stories about Pain, Power, Religion, Unicorns and More* (2015), the coauthor of *My Favorite Lesbian Stories from Best American Erotica* (2016), and the editor of *Paying for It: A Guide by Sex Workers for Their Clients* (2015) and the *Best Erotic Comics* series for Last Gasp publishers. Christina is also cofounder of Godless Perverts, a nonprofit community organization in San Francisco promoting a positive approach to sexuality in a safe, healthy, and inclusive environment, best known for its annual Impurity Ball benefit dance.

See also: Feminism, Atheism and Agnosticism and; LGBTQ+ Persons, Atheist and Agnostic; Organizations, Atheist and Agnostic; Reason Rally; Skepticon

Further Reading

Christina, Greta. *Bending: Dirty Kinky Stories about Pain, Power, Religion, Unicorns and More*. Durham, NC: Pitchstone, 2015.

Christina, Greta. *Comforting Thoughts about Death that Have Nothing to Do with God*. Durham, NC: Pitchstone, 2015.

Christina, Greta. *Coming Out Atheist: How to Do It, How to Help Each Other, and Why*. Durham, NC: Pitchstone, 2014.

Christina, Greta, ed. *Paying for It: A Guide by Sex Workers for Their Clients*. Emeryville, CA: Greenery Press, 2015.

Christina, Greta. *The Way of the Heathen: Practicing Atheism in Everyday Life*. Durham, NC: Pitchstone, 2016.

Christina, Greta. *Why Are You Atheists So Angry? 99 Things that Piss Off the Godless*. Durham, NC: Pitchstone, 2012.

D

Darrow, Clarence

Clarence Darrow (1857–1938) is one of the most famous lawyers in U.S. history. He is also one of the nation's best-known agnostics—for many, the country's iconic agnostic. Darrow was a legendary defense attorney in his own day and a stubborn apologist for civil liberties. He gained a reputation for brilliance with the hardest and most sensational of cases. Above all, Darrow excelled in courtroom oratory—the riveting and rambling sort of discourse that, while continuing to inspire to this day, evokes images of a bygone era of jurisprudence set in the presence of all-male and all-white colleagues, rolltop desks, tobacco products, and attention spans honed to follow hours-long closing arguments and evangelical revival sermons. As skillful a writer as he was a speaker, Darrow published several books, stories, and essays, many of which recommended the virtues of skepticism in the age that gave birth to fundamentalism. His participation in the 1925 Scopes trial in Dayton, Tennessee, earned for him a permanent place in American myth.

Darrow was a child of Victorian America's Midwest, the region that produced architect Frank Lloyd Wright, social reformer Jane Addams, and poet and Lincoln biographer Carl Sandburg. His father studied for the Unitarian ministry at Meadville Theological Seminary but later turned to furniture making and undertaking. Darrow's home atmosphere in northeastern Ohio was infused with an undogmatic humanism and the village skepticism brand of freethinking still being propagated by the nation's "Great Agnostic," Robert Ingersoll. Darrow's experience in higher education was limited to a year at Allegheny College and a handful of courses at the University of Michigan. He was one of the last great American lawyers to pass the bar without a degree or formal law school training.

Darrow's career evolved slowly and at first without apparent direction. He practiced civil and labor law for several years but eventually gravitated toward criminal law. He became increasingly opposed to big business and the overstandardization of life that accompanied the growth of Gilded Age consumer culture. His political sympathies leaned toward near-anarchist libertarianism and away from majoritarian democracy. Naturally intellectual without being bookish, he was especially adept at applying insights from the new social sciences in his legal work. Before Darrow, few courtroom defenders had argued on sociological or psychological grounds. None had been so effective—and so disturbing, some said—in denying free will. Making Chicago his home, he assembled a group of professionals and university professors for regular multidisciplinary discussions treating topics from biology to theology. Some of his most memorable clients included Eugene Prendergast, who assassinated Chicago's mayor; socialist labor leader Eugene V. Debs; and Chicago's notorious teenage killers Nathan Leopold and Richard Loeb, depicted in the press as adolescent readers of Friedrich Nietzsche obsessed with the gratuitous act of crime.

Darrow's self-declared agnosticism was especially noticeable in the context of a culture marked by shifting loyalties within American Protestantism. The United States had long functioned as an unofficially Protestant nation, and the ethos of Protestant Christianity was dominant everywhere, from schoolhouse to White House. In Darrow's day, U.S. Protestants were increasingly divided into two opposing camps: liberalism or modernism, as exhibited by his friends at the University of Chicago Divinity School, and fundamentalism, promoted by a new set of upstart schools, denominations, and publishing houses. Modernism attempted to foster a non-supernatural Christianity accommodated to the changing ideas of modernity, especially in light of what many were calling Charles Darwin's second scientific revolution. Darrow recruited several of modernism's leading exponents to be his advisers at the Scopes trial. Fundamentalism, named in 1920 by Philadelphia Baptist leader Curtis Lee Laws, was an aggressive reaction to the modernist impulse. It sought to defend the relevance of the so-called fundamentals of Christian doctrine in terms borrowed from pre-Darwinian science, a worldview convinced of the harmony of reason and revelation and the divine design of the universe. Antievolution scientific creationism, still a major factor in twenty-first-century American culture, was a fruit of the new fundamentalist movement.

The widening gulf between modernists and fundamentalists set the stage for Darrow's greatest courtroom performance. Responding to pressure from new fundamentalist advocacy organizations, Tennessee became the third state in the country to ban evolution in public schools. The newly formed American Civil Liberties Union (ACLU) was looking for a test case to challenge the law's constitutionality, and the opportunity came when John T. Scopes, high school physics and math teacher and football coach in Dayton, was convinced by local civic boosters to volunteer as a defendant—in order, they said, to put their town's progressive credentials on the map. The World's Christian Fundamentals Association, based in Minneapolis, secured for the prosecution the services of the "Great Commoner" William Jennings Bryan, three-time presidential candidate, former U.S. secretary of state, majoritarian, beloved Protestant lay teacher, and author of *Orthodox Christianity versus Modernism* (1923). Darrow, fresh from the Leopold-Loeb affair, offered his services to the defense free of charge—a first in his career.

What resulted has been described as a combination of trial of the century, showdown of religion versus science, and Bible-thumping burlesque—portrayed with only partial accuracy in the fictionalized account called *Inherit the Wind*, both the 1955 play and the 1960 film. The first trial ever broadcast on radio, the eight-day Scopes trial, beset by sweltering summer heat and fears that the Rhea County courthouse floor would collapse under the weight of all principals and spectators, was transformed by the sprawling journalist corps into an epic contest between North and South, urban and rural, highbrow and lowbrow. The Baltimore *Evening Sun*'s sardonic H. L. Mencken, a Darrow intimate and author of the first English-language book on Nietzsche, gave the event the name the history books remember: the "Monkey Trial."

Darrow, never fully trusted by the ACLU or the instigators of the trial, seized the opportunity to prophesy against his familiar enemies: ignorance, fanaticism, censorship, and "the fires that have been lighted in America to kindle religious bigotry and hate." The testimony of his modernist experts, however, was ruled inadmissible by the court. His decision to call Bryan as a witness for the defense, grilling him for two hours on the intricacies of biblical interpretation, remains one of the greatest surprise moves in the annals of American courtroom drama.

After the trial, Darrow continued to write and speak widely, publishing fiction and nonfiction titles such as *Crime, Its Cause and Treatment* (1925), *An Agnostic's Anthology* (1929; with Wallace Rice), and his autobiography, *The Story of My Life* (1932). To many, his agnosticism was never distinguishable from atheism, and he exerted little effort to clarify the matter. His moral convictions remained resolute to the end: unflagging advocacy for the rights of the individual against the majority, unswerving commitment to the interrogation of all inherited opinions, and eternal opposition to arguments defending the moral justifications for capital punishment.

See also: Darwin, Charles; Ingersoll, Robert Green

Further Reading

Darrow, Clarence. *The Story of My Life*. New York: Da Capo Press, 1996.

Darrow, Clarence. *Why I Am an Agnostic and Other Essays*. Amherst, NY: Prometheus Books, 1995.

Hutchison, William R. *The Modernist Impulse in American Protestantism*. Durham, NC: Duke University Press, 1992.

Larson, Edward J. *Summer for the Gods: The Scopes Trial and America's Continuing Debate over Science and Religion*. Cambridge, MA: Harvard University Press, 1998.

Larson, Edward J., and Jack Marshall, eds. *The Essential Words and Writings of Clarence Darrow*. New York: Modern Library, 2007.

Marsden, George M. *Fundamentalism and American Culture*. 2nd ed. New York: Oxford University Press, 2006.

Moran, Jeffrey P. *The Scopes Trial: A Brief History with Documents*. Boston: Bedford/St. Martin's, 2002.

Numbers, Ronald L. *The Creationists: The Evolution of Scientific Creationism*. Berkeley: University of California Press, 1993.

Scopes, John T., and James Presley. *Center of the Storm: Memoirs of John T. Scopes*. New York: Holt, Rinehart and Winston, 1967.

Stone, Irving. *Clarence Darrow for the Defense*. Garden City, NY: Doubleday, 1941.

Darwin, Charles

Charles Darwin (1809–1882) occupies a place in history shared by few other people. He has been described as a scientific revolutionary, a British national treasure, an eminent Victorian, and the author of a second Enlightenment, defining the difference between early and later phases of modernity. He is a symbol as well as an individual. University students celebrate his birthday. Beetles and finches are named after him. So are islands, mountains, and a city in Australia. Religious fundamentalists, outraged by what they see as the modern world's assault on timeless truth, blame him for the incoherence of their world. Few who contest his ideas, however, have read his books. Fans, too, are relatively unacquainted with his output. Scientists who revere his name have trouble identifying even a fraction of his twenty titles.

Darwin fits awkwardly into popular versions of the history of science and of atheism and agnosticism. His life as a financially independent "gentleman naturalist" would be unrecognizable to a scientist working in academia, industry, or government today. The care with which he guarded his shifting religious views hardly aligns with his reputation as a modern doctor of suspicion. Even evolution was not an original component of his thought. Darwin was a person and product of his time. He benefited from Britain's imperial conquest and, despite his antislavery sentiments, reflected its colonial and racist attitudes. Evolution, or development as an explanatory concept in biology, predated him. His physician father read about it in the eighteenth-century French naturalists Georges-Louis Leclerc (Comte de Buffon) and Jean-Baptiste Lamarck. Darwin's achievement was the way he capitalized on his environment and experience, creatively synthesized vast amounts of information in his capacious mind, courageously allowed his curiosity to pursue its interests without hindrance, followed evidence wherever it led, and published his conclusions not for a scientific elite but for the educated public.

Born into an upper-middle-class family with roots in both the Anglican and Unitarian traditions, Darwin received the standard education designed for young men of his social class and presumed future. He took a love of plants and animals with him to the University of Edinburgh and then Christ's College, Cambridge. Each institution, however, became the scene for a career declined—first medicine, then ministry. Weak in mathematics, he strengthened his grasp of zoology and botany and developed considerable aptitude for writing. His books belong as much to the history of literature as the history of science.

The major turning point in Darwin's life came when he served as naturalist on the HMS *Beagle*, a refitted warship commissioned by the royal admiralty to conduct shoreline surveys of South America. Darwin was twenty-two years old when he set sail, and the British empire, well into its third century, was claiming as part of its global reach the Falkland Islands, off the coast of Argentina. *The Voyage of the Beagle* (1839), Darwin's first book, narrates his transition from naive collector of specimens to seasoned investigator of nature's riddles. Before he circulated his full-scale theory of biological change, he experienced his own personal evolution. The five-year excursion across the Atlantic, Pacific, and Indian Oceans allowed him to gain firsthand acquaintance with an immense array of animal and plant species previously unknown to him or his teachers. The cumulative effect of half a decade at sea provided Darwin with a massive set of data and a host of unanswered questions. He spent the rest of his life on land trying to put the two together.

Darwin advanced his mature theory of evolution in *On the Origin of Species* (1859), his best-known publication and a landmark in the history of ideas. His most important contributions include the concept of natural selection (the way in which advantageous biological variations benefit the persistence of species in their particular environments) and the more daring idea of the emergence of new species out of that process. Darwin applied these findings to his own species in *The Descent of Man* (1871), placing human beings fully within the framework of evolutionary change and uncertainty. Both books exerted a tremendous impact on modern life and thought. Once linked with new discoveries in genetics and geology, evolution became the cardinal principle of all scientific work in the late modern world. In *The Influence of Darwin on Philosophy* (1910), American educator John Dewey made the case that modern philosophy could not move forward without a full embrace of Darwin's thought.

Hostility to Darwin arose especially in the twentieth century. For some people of faith, he was the face of forces threatening cherished ideals of biblical authority, human uniqueness, and the relevance of religion. Fundamentalism, scientific creationism, and the intelligent-design movement have striven for decades to discredit his ideas and deflect his influence. Disparate attitudes toward Darwin in U.S. popular culture, first revealed during the contentious 1925 Scopes antievolution trial in Dayton, Tennessee, continue to shape public policy in the present day.

Not all religious communities have opposed Darwin and his ideas. Visionaries such as French Jesuit priest and paleontologist Teilhard de Chardin represent varied attempts to accommodate faith to the facts of evolutionary science. Some religious thinkers have constructed new theologies based on an evolutionary worldview. The process philosophy of British philosopher-mathematician Alfred North Whitehead, onetime collaborator with atheist thinker Bertrand Russell, imagined a finite, transpersonal God evolving along with the rest of the cosmos.

Since the late nineteenth century, Darwinism itself has evolved—with a wildly expanding family tree. The broad phenomenon called social Darwinism, applying Herbert Spencer's notion of "survival of the fittest" to modern social problems, has long been a factor in debates over ethnicity, war, immigration, public health, humanitarianism, the modern nation-state, and the history of Indigenous peoples, languages, and cultures. For contemporary professionals in mainstream science, Darwin is an initiator more than a guide. The historical Darwin remains obscure. Progressive, twenty-first-century science enthusiasts reading *The Descent of Man* have difficulty reconciling their icon with the author captive to Eurocentric assumptions of white and male superiority.

Darwin will forever be linked to the crisis of faith that marked the Victorian age. The expansion of Enlightenment skepticism, the encounter with the world's religious traditions, and the dramatic increase of human technical skill all conspired to make the nineteenth a century of doubt for the Western mind. A special role in this transformation was played by the rise of biblical criticism, scholarship that approached the Bible as a set of humanly produced texts, mixing history and myth, no different in essence from other ancient books.

In his private writings, Darwin applied his naturalist's eye to his own dissipating beliefs in God and miracles, comparing his gradual loss of faith to the process of becoming color-blind. He adopted for himself Thomas Henry Huxley's term *agnostic*. His religiously observant wife Emma referred to him as a materialist. Like many of his generation, Darwin saw the problem of suffering as the ultimate threat to religious belief. He could not square the traditional doctrine of God with the death of his ten-year-old daughter, Annie (an experience dramatized in Jon Amiel's 2009 film *Creation*). Over time, as Darwin's publications went through multiple editions, he regretted his references to creation and design. He never, however, ceased to marvel at the beauty of the flux of life. In the concluding section of *Origin*, contemplating a "tangled" river bank teeming with vegetation and beings with wings, scores of legs, and no legs, he celebrated the "grandeur in this view of life."

See also: Agnosticism; Dawkins, Richard; Huxleys, The; Russell, Bertrand

Further Reading

Bowlby, John. *Charles Darwin: A New Life*. New York: W. W. Norton, 1992.

Chadwick, Owen. *The Secularization of the European Mind in the 19th Century*. Cambridge: Cambridge University Press, 1975.

Darwin, Charles. *Autobiographies*. Ed. Michael Neve and Sharon Messenger. New York: Penguin Classics, 2002.

Darwin, Charles. *The Descent of Man*. New York: Penguin Classics, 2004.

Darwin, Charles. *On the Origin of Species*. Ed. William Bynum. New York: Penguin Classics, 2009.

Haught, John F. *God after Darwin: A Theology of Evolution*. Boulder, CO: Westview Press, 2000.

Jay, Elisabeth. *Faith and Doubt in Victorian Britain*. London: Macmillan, 1986.

Johnson, Paul. *Darwin: Portrait of a Genius*. New York: Viking, 2012.

Keynes, Randall. *Annie's Box: Darwin, His Daughter, and Human Evolution*. New York: Fourth Estate: 2001.

Loy, James D., and Kent M. Loy. *Emma Darwin: A Victorian Life*. Gainesville: University Press of Florida, 2010.

Dawkins, Richard

Richard Dawkins (b. 1941) is an evolutionary biologist, prolific writer, and public advocate-activist for science education and atheism. He, along with philosopher Daniel C. Dennett, neuroscientist Sam Harris, and journalist/literary critic Christopher Hitchens, provided leadership for New Atheism. Together, they won notoriety as the now legendary "four horsemen" of the early twenty-first-century resurgence of aggressive unbelief. Highly acclaimed for his distinguished scholarly career, Dawkins is today principally a popularizer of science and a well-known figure in popular culture himself, appearing frequently in documentaries and on television. He coined the word *meme* in his best-selling book *The Selfish Gene* (1976).

Dawkins was born far from the limelight of modern celebrity. He grew up in what is now the Republic of Kenya in a family associated with the British colonial service. He has even described himself as "all but born with a pith helmet on my head." One of the contemporary world's most notable critics of religion, he was raised as a nominal Anglican with virtually no firsthand knowledge of the dynamics of religious life in family or community. Nor did his education include any serious engagement with academic religious studies. In the first of his two autobiographies, *An Appetite for Wonder* (2013), he traced his atheism to a decisive teenage encounter with the thought of Charles Darwin—from that time on, Dawkins's "greatest scientific hero."

Dawkins received the conventional education reserved for privileged white males living in the British Empire's African colonies. His studies at Balliol College, Oxford, eventually led to a PhD in biology and an award-winning Oxford academic career. He was the inaugural holder of Oxford's Charles Simonyi Endowed Chair for the Public Understanding of Science and has delivered numerous lectures at colleges and universities around the world. The esteem with which his accomplishments have been held was demonstrated in 2004 by Balliol's creation of the Dawkins Prize to recognize outstanding scholarly achievement in the field of biology.

Over the course of his career, Dawkins has written nearly twenty books. *The Selfish Gene* (1976) earned him international renown in the field of gene-centered evolutionary theory. A series of other books—*The Extended Phenotype* (1982); *The Blind Watchmaker* (1986), attacking the claims and methods of intelligent design; *River Out of Eden* (1995); *Unweaving the Rainbow: Science, Delusion, and the Appetite for Wonder* (1998); and *A Devil's Chaplain* (2003)—established his reputation as a masterful science writer for the general educated reader. His blockbuster *The God Delusion* (2006), arguably the book that put New Atheism on the cultural map, has served for many as more manifesto than erudite argument. *Outgrowing God: A Beginner's Guide* (2019) covers similar ground for a new generation of readers. Essays and excerpts from Dawkins's works are now anthologized in collections of atheist texts, alongside classics by Darwin, John Stuart Mill, Emma Goldman, and Bertrand Russell.

The American Humanist Association named Dawkins Humanist of the Year in 1996. In 2003, the Atheist Alliance of America inaugurated the annual Richard Dawkins Award to honor individuals from various professions who promote reason, science, and secular values. Recipients of the award (now overseen by the Center for Inquiry in New York) have included Daniel C. Dennett, Ayaan Hirsi Ali, Christopher Hitchens, Susan Jacoby, and comedian/actor Ricky Gervais.

Throughout the twenty-first century, Dawkins has been a model of the scholar-activist, seeking, often through provocative means—notably his support for Ariane Sherine's Atheist Bus Campaign of 2008–2009 with its "There's Probably No God" ads—to raise awareness about what he sees as the dangers of supernatural thinking and the cultural promise of nonreligion. The Richard Dawkins Foundation for Reason and Science (www.richarddawkins

.net), launched in 2006 and now aligned with the Center for Inquiry, in the United States, pursues his goals of fostering at all levels of society greater scientific literacy and appreciation for a secular view of the world.

In 2011, Dawkins became embroiled in a controversy known to participants in some quarters of the global atheist community as "Elevatorgate." The controversy received its name after Rebecca Watson, science blogger and Skepchick.org founder, reported inappropriate behavior in a hotel elevator during the World Atheist Convention in Dublin, Ireland—just hours after she delivered a conference presentation on sexism in atheist circles. The incident is now part of the lore of contemporary atheism. Dawkins was not involved in the elevator encounter, but his subsequent publication of a letter to a fictional Muslim woman, mocking the concerns of Western women in light of the oppression faced by females in traditional Islamic countries, brought charges of both misogyny and Islamophobia. His later apology gave some indication of the durability of his reputation and the social climate of current organized atheism. Memes drawing attention to the affair circulate throughout cyberspace.

See also: Atheism, New; Dennett, Daniel C.; Harris, Sam; Hirsi Ali, Ayaan; Hitchens, Christopher; Jacoby, Susan; Organizations, Atheist and Agnostic

Further Reading

Dawkins, Richard. *An Appetite for Wonder: The Making of a Scientist.* New York: HarperCollins, 2013.
Dawkins, Richard. *The God Delusion.* Boston: Houghton Mifflin, 2008.
Dawkins, Richard. *Outgrowing God: A Beginner's Guide.* New York: Random House, 2019.
Dawkins, Richard, Daniel C. Dennett, Sam Harris, and Christopher Hitchens. *The Four Horsemen: The Conversation that Sparked an Atheist Revolution.* New York: Random House, 2019.

Deism

Deism is a distinctive view of God formed by ideas circulating in Western European countries and their colonies during the seventeenth and eighteenth centuries. Based on the Latin *deus* ("God"), the term serves as a flexible label for a cluster of beliefs shared by many of the prominent intellectuals of the Enlightenment era. Largely dependent upon the early modern concept of a mechanical universe, later discredited by Charles Darwin, Albert Einstein, and others, deism is often described by historians as more of a period philosophical position than a viable option for the present. Some individuals continue to embrace the term today, employing it to delineate perspectives falling on a spectrum between the theism of Christian orthodoxy and the varieties of atheism.

The core of deism is belief in a supreme creative force responsible for the creation, design, and methodical functioning of the universe. For the deist, God is understood to be an intelligence of infinite capability, the epitome and eternal source of rationality itself. During the Enlightenment, deists, often based in the cosmopolitan capitals of Europe, portrayed God as the archetype of architects. Freemasonry, a network of elite, male-only secret societies promoting Enlightenment political ideals, found its metaphysical supports in deism.

Seventeenth-century British aristocrat and writer Edward Herbert of Cherbury, identified as the unofficial founder of deism, centered the highly intellectual faith around a small set of basic convictions: the existence of an eternal creative mind, the harmony of the human mind with this deity, the priority of moral behavior over all other religious activities, and the existence of a moral order paralleling the natural order of the universe. Most deists spoke of their faith position as the religion of natural reason—an assortment of beliefs that every human being could endorse without revelation, prophets, saviors, miracles, or scriptures. Many imagined deism as the original religion of humanity. Seeing the abstract God of reason as superior to willful and personal deities of the world's many historical religions, deists referred to the divine in impersonal terms such as "Providence" or "Nature's God." Most promoted freedom of conscience and religious toleration. The language of deism permeates the foundational documents of the U.S. political system.

Early shapers of the deist mind in Britain included John Toland, author of *Christianity Not Mysterious* (1696); Anthony Collins, author of *Discourse of Freethinking* (1713); and Matthew Tindal, author of *Christianity as Old as the Creation* (1730). Virtually the entire roster of Enlightenment leaders in the English-speaking world affirmed or approximated deist notions. Some advocated for a natural theology, some for what they saw as a reasonable and dogma-free Christianity in tune with science and purged of supernaturalism. Christian opponents accused deists of harboring atheist sentiments.

In France, deism was represented by *philosophes* such as Voltaire, Jean-Jacques Rousseau, and the writers and editors of the *Encyclopédie* (1751–1772)—all critics of traditional Christianity and its alliances with the kingdoms of Europe. During the French Revolution, Maximilien Robespierre, mastermind of the Reign of Terror, established a Cult of the Supreme Being to replace the Revolution's earlier and short-lived Cult of Reason, the atheist festival that terminated the Christian calendar, established Temples of Reason throughout the country, and enshrined the Goddess of Reason—portrayed by revolutionary Sophie Momoro—in the Cathedral of Notre Dame in Paris. Robespierre's "Decree on the Supreme Being" (1794) declared deism the ceremonial civil religion of revolutionary France.

Thomas Paine, author of *Age of Reason* (1794, 1795, 1807), acted as a deist bridge linking Enlightenment Europe to revolutionary America. Key figures in the deist orbit in the British colonies and early U.S. culture included George Washington, Thomas Jefferson, Ethan Allen, and Elihu Palmer, founder of both New York's Deistical Society (1794) and the *Temple of Reason* newspaper (1800–1803). Benjamin Franklin called himself a "thorough deist."

Critics see in deism limitations similar to those aggravating classical Christian theism. As Voltaire himself noted in his poem on the devastating Lisbon earthquake of 1755, deism's responses to natural disaster are less than satisfying—a design flaw in intelligent design. As a variant of monotheism, deism also makes unwarranted assumptions about what humankind's natural religion might be. It mirrors the Eurocentric and bourgeois social location of its best-known proponents. Some of the most prominent American deists were lifelong investors in the global industry of African slavery.

Deism lives on today among a subset of intellectuals who identify with Enlightenment-era principles. Some have attempted to accommodate it to twenty-first-century science. Just before his death, British philosopher Antony Flew, whose *There Is a God* (2010) shocked the atheist world with news of his departure from unbelief, identified deism as his chosen approach to life. The World Union of Deists, based in the United States with representatives in some thirty countries, produces podcasts, manages an online library, and publishes the journal *Deism*. The bumper sticker for sale on its website (www.deism.com) sums up the message deists past and present could support: "God Gave Us Reason, Not Religion."

See also: Atheophobia; Flew, Antony; Media, Atheism and Agnosticism and the; Proofs for God, Atheist and Agnostic Critiques of

Further Reading

Franklin, Benjamin. *The Autobiography and Other Writings*. New York: Penguin Classics, 2003.

Holmes, David L. *The Faiths of the Founding Fathers*. New York: Oxford University Press, 2006.

Jacob, Margaret C. *The Secular Enlightenment*. Princeton, NJ: Princeton University Press, 2019.

Kramnick, Isaac, ed. *The Portable Enlightenment Reader*. New York: Penguin, 1995.

May, Henry F. *The Enlightenment in America*. New York: Oxford University Press, 1976.

Redman, Ben Ray, ed. *The Portable Voltaire*. New York: Penguin, 1977.

Dennett, Daniel C.

Daniel C. Dennett (b. 1942) is an American philosopher and interdisciplinary scholar. He teaches and writes in the areas of philosophy of mind, evolution, and artificial intelligence. The author of over ten books and hundreds of scholarly articles, he is active in debates shaping both philosophy and intellectual culture outside the academy. With biologist Richard Dawkins, neuroscientist Sam Harris, and journalist/literary critic Christopher Hitchens, he was one of the leaders of the early twenty-first-century New Atheist movement. With a solid reputation in the academy long before the 9/11 terrorist attacks in 2001, often seen as catalysts for New Atheism, Dennett brought a well-honed expertise in the philosophy of science to the New Atheist project.

Dennett grew up in Boston, the son of a teacher/editor and a U.S. diplomat specializing in the Middle East. He studied at Harvard and received a PhD in philosophy at Oxford. Since 1971, he has taught at Tufts University in Massachusetts, directing the institution's Center for Cognitive Studies. His first books—*Content and Consciousness* (1969), *Brainstorms* (1978), *Elbow Room* (1984), *The Intentional Stance* (1987), and *Consciousness Explained* (1991)—advanced cutting-edge work at the intersection of philosophy and science, focusing on the mystery of mind in embodied beings. *Darwin's Dangerous Idea* (1995), the sixth of his many books, established his place as a leader in the history and philosophy of science.

In his tenth book, *Breaking the Spell* (2006), his most significant contribution to New Atheism, Dennett offered a scientific appraisal of religion itself, describing the origins and development of religion as phenomena within the evolutionary process having nothing to do with supernatural forces. Belief in God or gods, according to Dennett, is a natural—if not logical—outcome of millennia of human experiences and choices.

Dennett's role in the New Atheist movement has been less combative than that of his fellow "horsemen." His engagement with Christian thinkers—such as scientist/theologian Alister McGrath and Alvin Plantinga, former president of the Society of Christian Philosophers—has led to more substantive dialogue than sensational debate. At the same time, his atheism is a fundamental stance, basic to his scholarship and worldview. His *Caught in the Pulpit: Leaving Belief Behind* (2015), coauthored with social scientist Linda LaScola, is a groundbreaking study of religious leaders who are closet unbelievers, bringing both new depth to New Atheist research and new clarity to the phenomenon of atheism within religious traditions. In 2004, Dennett was named Humanist of the Year by the American Humanist Association. He received the 2007 Richard Dawkins Award from Atheist Alliance of America. His essay on "Atheism and Evolution" in *The Cambridge Companion to Atheism* (2007) is the definitive summary of contemporary scholarship on the subjects.

See also: Atheism, New; Dawkins, Richard; Harris, Sam; Hitchens, Christopher; Humanist of the Year

Further Reading

Dennett, Daniel C. "Atheism and Evolution." In *The Cambridge Companion to Atheism*. Ed. Michael Martin, pp. 135–148. Cambridge: Cambridge University Press, 2007.

Dennett, Daniel C. *Breaking the Spell: Religion as a Natural Phenomenon*. New York: Viking Penguin, 2006.

Dennett, Daniel C. *Darwin's Dangerous Idea: Evolution and the Meaning of Life*. New York: Simon and Schuster, 1995.

Dennett, Daniel C., Richard Dawkins, Sam Harris, and Christopher Hitchens. *The Four Horsemen: The Conversation that Sparked an Atheist Revolution*. New York: Random House, 2019.

Dennett, Daniel C., and Linda LaScola. *Caught in the Pulpit: Leaving Belief Behind*. Durham, NC: Pitchstone, 2015.

Dennett, Daniel C., and Alvin Plantinga. *Science and Religion: Are They Compatible?* Oxford: Oxford University Press, 2010.

Stewart, Robert B., ed. *The Future of Atheism: Alister McGrath and Daniel Dennett in Dialogue*. Minneapolis, MN: Fortress Press, 2008.

Du Bois, W. E. B.

W. E. B. Du Bois (1868–1963) exerted a formative and formidable influence in U.S. intellectual history. A key figure especially in the development of twentieth-century African American thought, Du Bois set an early and high standard for critical scholarship and imaginative literature on the experiences of people of color in the United States. He published widely as historian and sociologist with the temperament of a philosopher-psychologist and is also recognized as a distinguished essayist, novelist, and editor. Well known as a critic of Booker T. Washington's accommodationist approach to Jim Crow segregation, which sought to appease white supremacy with calculated submission and self-reliance, Du Bois was the first U.S. intellectual to articulate a pan-African vision, promoting the global solidarity of people of African descent as a counterweight to American racism. In an age when virtually all African American leaders accepted faith as a supportive resource or pragmatic necessity, Du Bois charted a countercultural path toward a distinctively Black nonreligious humanism.

Du Bois was born and raised in western New England, with family roots running to African, French, Dutch, and Haitian ancestry. He graduated from public schools in majority white Great Barrington, Massachusetts, and displayed signs of precocious intellectual potential. After high school, he earned what would be his first college degree at Tennessee's Fisk University, a historically Black institution founded after the Civil War by the American Missionary Association, an antislavery, domestic missions and educational agency sponsored by northern Congregational churches. Du Bois completed a second bachelor's degree at Harvard, where he studied with the leading minds of America's philosophical golden age: pragmatist and pluralist William James and Catholic atheist George Santayana. After two years of specialized historical research at the University of Berlin, Du Bois returned to the United States to complete his doctoral studies at Harvard, writing his dissertation on the role of the United States in the international African slave trade. He was the first African American person to receive a PhD from Harvard.

Du Bois's career included scholarship, journalism, publishing, and social engagement. The unofficial dean of African American studies for his generation, he held teaching positions at Wilberforce University in Ohio and Atlanta University and published major studies of African American life in Philadelphia and in the South during Reconstruction. In the public sphere, he organized numerous international pan-African congresses, guided the U.S. Black civil rights initiative called the Niagara movement, and served as founding editor of *The Crisis*, the journal of the National Association for the Advancement of Colored People (NAACP). In addition to scholarly works, he wrote five novels, including a trilogy called *The Black Flame* (1957–1961), and many short stories, plays, and poems. In "A Litany of Atlanta," he broods over the 1906 Atlanta race riot, during which thousands of whites rampaged the city and left a Black death toll in double digits.

Du Bois's three autobiographies trace his transformation from reforming academic to radical scholar-activist. Moving far beyond his Harvard training, he increasingly incorporated Marxist principles into his analysis of racism, capitalism, and colonialism. He visited China and the Soviet Union, receiving the Lenin Peace Prize in 1959. Near the end of his career, he formally affiliated with the Communist Party and renounced his U.S. citizenship, emigrating to newly postcolonial Ghana and joining the country's thriving Black expatriate community already attracting writers and artists such as Richard Wright and Maya Angelou. Five thousand miles away from his birthplace, Du Bois died the night before Martin Luther King, Jr.'s March on Washington.

Du Bois's best-known work is *The Souls of Black Folk* (1903), a collection of essays acknowledged today as a great American treasure. In these pieces, each prefaced by a line of poetry and a musical quotation from an African American spiritual, Du Bois introduces a set of arresting themes that permeated his thought for decades. He defined the "color-line" forcefully separating people by race and ethnic background as the defining problem of the twentieth century. He used the image of the "Veil" as the sign of the deep psychological disparities distinguishing the world of oppressors from the largely hidden and conflicted world of the oppressed. And he identified the colonized mind of the person of color in a world of white domination as a disorienting form of "double-consciousness"— forcing people always to see themselves from the perspective of the demeaning, more powerful other. In these essays, Du Bois also advanced his trademark recommendation for the future of African American higher education: investment in the mentoring of what he called the population's "talented tenth"—a position that elicited charges of elitism.

In an especially powerful *Souls of Black Folk* essay, Du Bois offers an empathetic sociological portrait of the Black church, particularly its distinctive styles of preaching, music, and ecstatic experience. Du Bois believed that African American religion confirmed Marx's claim regarding the "opiate of the people," but he also had firsthand evidence of its potential as a resource for survival, creative expression, and revolt. Though raised in the genteel liberalism of the New England Congregational tradition, Du Bois watched his own faith gradually erode. It was, he said, a casualty of his experience of higher education. Questioning the tenets of Christianity during his Harvard years, he became a freethinker in Germany. In his U.S. academic appointments, at a time when piety was still a cultural expectation of professors, he shocked administrators by refusing to lead the student body in public prayer. A nine-paragraph "Credo," included in *Darkwater: Voices from Within the Veil* (1920), used the word *God* but emphasized social justice, the universality of the human experience, and Black solidarity. It was a postlude to his Christianity and a prelude to his Marxism. By midcentury, Du Bois professed a post-Christian agnosticism bordering on atheism. The evolution of his life and thought signaled a blossoming of African American humanist thought.

See also: Atheism and Agnosticism, African American; Hutchinson, Sikivu; Marx, Karl; Pinn, Anthony B.

Further Reading

Du Bois, W. E. B. *The Autobiography of W. E. B. Du Bois*. Oxford: Oxford University Press, 2007.

Du Bois, W. E. B. *Darkwater: Voices from Within the Veil*. New York: Harcourt, Brace, and Howe, 1920.

Du Bois, W. E. B. *The Souls of Black Folk*. New York: Penguin Classics, 1989.

Johnson, Brian L. *W. E. B. Du Bois: Toward Agnosticism, 1868–1934*. Lanham, MD: Rowman and Littlefield, 2008.

Kahn, Jonathon S. *Divine Discontent: The Religious Imagination of W. E. B. Du Bois*. Oxford: Oxford University Press, 2009.

Lewis, David Levering. *W. E. B. Du Bois: A Biography*. New York: Henry Holt, 2009.

Rabaka, Reiland. *Against Epistemic Apartheid: W. E. B. Du Bois and the Disciplinary Decadence of American Sociology*. Lanham, MD: Lexington Books, 2010.

Sundquist, E. J., ed. *The Oxford W. E. B. Du Bois Reader*. New York: Oxford University Press, 1996.

Zuckerman, Phil, ed. *Du Bois on Religion*. Walnut Creek, CA: AltaMira Press, 2000.

F

Feminism, Atheism and Agnosticism and

The critique of patriarchy and the critique of God go hand in hand for many people. Doubts about the claims of male superiority frequently accompany doubts about the claims of religious traditions, especially those that portray the universe's ultimate power as a father. Not all feminists are atheists or agnostics. Not all atheists and agnostics are feminists. All three ways of thinking and being, though, spring from a vision of life that sees empowerment, freedom, and self-determination as core components of authentic human personhood and community.

In Western culture, the first feminists and the first atheists and agnostics appeared on the historical stage at about the same time. Significant women leaders and thinkers were not unknown before the rise of modernity. Neither were religious skeptics—often labeled as blasphemers, heretics, apostates, or witches, before the words *atheist* and *agnostic* became standard. Public advocates for women's rights and the cause of free thought, however, were rare before the modern period. Individuals inclined toward such concerns did not enjoy the security, opportunity, and in some cases even the shared vocabulary to make a case for the equality and dignity of women and the value of religious nonconformity. Male authority in church and state was enshrined with an aura of permanency and surrounded by thick hedges of law, custom, and presumed divine sanction. With few exceptions, male authority controlled not only the pulpit but also the pen and printing press.

Today, the story of modern feminism is normally narrated in waves—the first running from the mid-nineteenth to the early twentieth centuries, the second arising in the 1960s, and subsequent waves following in succession around the end of the twentieth and the beginning of the twenty-first centuries. The origins of modern feminism, however, can be found as early as the seventeenth and eighteenth centuries, among apologists for women such as Margaret Fell Fox and George Fox, founders of the Quaker movement, and Enlightenment-era writers such as Mary Astell, Catharine Sawbridge Macaulay Graham, Judith Sargent Stevens Murray, Olympe de Gouges, and Mary Wollstonecraft. The relationship of these figures to modern atheism and agnosticism is unclear. None was known to be a professed unbeliever, but theirs was still an age of life-threatening intolerance and atheophobia. Seventeenth-century Quakers, male and female, were persecuted, jailed, and executed for promoting their dogma-free Christianity. The eighteenth-century writers, faced with a massive burden of inequity, focused not on freedom of belief but on education, marriage, divorce, and property. Wollstonecraft, author of *A Vindication of the Rights of Woman* (1792), was accused of atheism, a charge her enemies thought fitting in light of her radical politics and advocacy for sexual freedom. Her daughter Mary, author of *Frankenstein* (1818), married the poet Percy Bysshe Shelley, also a defender of free love and one of the first open atheists of modern times.

What is described as first-wave feminism was one dimension of what Unitarian minister Thomas Wentworth Higginson called the "Sisterhood of Reforms" in nineteenth-century America. U.S. reformers, with counterparts in other countries, targeted a wide gamut of social ills—from dueling and modern warfare to child labor and the inhumanity of prisons. Many attempted to create heavens on earth, experimenting with utopian communities far from urban industry. Others decried the way modernity was destroying human bodies. They called for diet reform, clothing reform, and anti-alcohol legislation. The two supreme causes in this family of reforms were the abolition of slavery and the advancement of women's rights.

The 1848 Woman's Rights Convention, held in Seneca Falls, New York, marked the formal beginning of the organized women's movement in the United States. Its Declaration of Sentiments, proclaiming "that all men and women are created equal," set the agenda for first-wave feminism, demanding equality in marriage, education, and employment; the right to own property and initiate divorce; and, most of all, women's suffrage or the right to participate in the political process. The passage of the Nineteenth Amendment to the U.S. Constitution in 1920, recognizing the right of all citizens (still excluding Native Americans) to vote regardless of sex, is often seen as the culmination of first-wave feminism.

Many actors in the first wave drew from religious inspiration, invoking the Bible and Christian doctrine to support gender equality. Coinciding with the rise of religious liberalism, the movement supplied momentum to forces affirming the right of women to speak in public and to serve as ordained ministers in Protestant denominations. Sojourner Truth's celebrated 1851 "Ain't I a Woman?" speech drew heavily from this fund of Christian values.

Other figures identified religion as one of patriarchy's principal props. Frederick Douglass, a signer of the Seneca Falls declaration, along with his collaborator, German-born Ottilie Assing, found inspiration in the Christian modernism and Christian atheism then streaming out of Europe, especially David Friedrich Strauss's *The Life of Jesus* (1835), locating the Jesus story largely in myth, and Ludwig Feuerbach's *The Essence of Christianity* (1841), describing God as a projection of human aspirations.

Elizabeth Cady Stanton, one of the organizers of the 1848 convention, was atheist or agnostic in all but name. Her *Woman's Bible* (1895, 1898) executed an unprecedented feminist rereading of the scriptures. Her "Bible and Church Degrade Woman" (1898) indicted the teachings and teachers of the Christian tradition for centuries of injustice against women. Human suffering, she said, was what kept her from belief in an omnipotent, loving God.

Polish native Ernestine Rose was one of the few openly atheist participants in the century's U.S. and UK feminist circles. With the publication of *My Path to Atheism* (1878), British activist Annie Besant, who explicitly added contraception to the movement's agenda, arguably became the best-known atheist feminist in the world. Philosopher John Stuart Mill, who released his defense of women's rights, *The Subjection of Woman*, in 1869, withheld his atheist writings from publication for fear of backlash from Victorian traditionalists.

Twentieth-century, second-wave feminism was a revival of the first wave's energy and an expansion of its vision. Like first-wave feminism, it functioned within a broad-based band of movements aiming for social change in the United States and around the world—including the civil rights movement for racial justice, the movement to end the Vietnam War, the countercultural youth movement, and the sexual revolution, breaking age-old gender roles and patterns of sexual practice grounded in patriarchal assumptions. Participants moved in a variety of directions. Some worked pragmatically, concentrating strictly on full equality in professional life. Others agitated for autonomy and freedom from oppression in every aspect of life, including the lives of lesbian, bisexual, queer, and transgender women. Among the key issues for the second wave were sexism in education and the workplace, reproductive rights, portrayals of female identity in the media, rediscovery of women's lost history, passage of an Equal Rights Amendment, and appreciation of women's experience as a realm of reality distinct from men's. Landmark events included the launching of the National Organization of Women (NOW) in 1966 and the legalizing of abortion in 1973.

Feminism's second wave occurred as U.S. religion was experiencing massive pluralization and tremendous theological ferment. Religious feminists pursued different objectives, just as feminists in civil society did. Reformers campaigned for greater representation of women in religious leadership positions and experimented with inclusive language and feminine images of God. Revolutionaries sought total transformation of their traditions, in doctrine and life, maintaining that feminism meant not only the end of male-dominated hierarchy but the end of hierarchy itself.

American philosopher-theologian Mary Daly's intellectual odyssey paralleled the evolution of second-wave feminism. In *The Church and the Second Sex* (1968), a Catholic homage to Simone de Beauvoir's *The Second Sex* (1949), she denounced centuries of misogyny in church teaching and called for female priests and bishops. Seven years later, after publishing *Beyond God the Father* (1973), she compared women seeking ordination in the church to African Americans seeking membership in the Ku Klux Klan. In 1971, as the first woman ever to preach in Harvard University's Memorial Church, she led a postsermon "exodus" of women from the chapel, declaring the final verdict on Christianity as irredeemably patriarchal.

During the highly charged time, feminists navigated their own individual spiritual migrations. Some left traditional religions but did not abandon religion. They formed new covenant communities and populated a new spiritual counterculture permeated with wisdom from Asian, New Age, Wiccan, and Indigenous sources. What they rejected, they said, were traditions anchored in masculine visions of the world, expressed in exclusivist notions of membership, mind-body dualism, and theologies of shame. What they hungered for was the spiritual equivalent of Virginia Woolf's *A Room of One's Own* (1929)—space to improvise not laws carved in stone but, as psychologist Naomi Goldenberg put it, creeds "written on water."

For many feminists, even such tentative creeds were too much. The liberation of women, they insisted, was about myth-busting, not mythmaking. For Beauvoir, author of *The Second Sex*, the second wave's manifesto and reference book, feminism and atheism were two sides of the same process leading to authenticity. Betty Friedan, one of the founders of NOW and author of *The Feminine Mystique* (1963), the book credited with the swelling of the second wave, was an agnostic—signer of the second Humanist Manifesto (1973) and recipient of the American Humanist Association's Humanist of the Year award in 1975. Writers of three best sellers from 1970, charting the course of the radical wing of the movement, took as their starting point the bankruptcy and irrelevance of religion. Germaine Greer, author of *The Female Eunuch*, Kate Millett, author of *Sexual Politics*, and Shulamith Firestone, author of *The Dialectic of Sex: The Case for Feminist Revolution*, founded prospects of a feminist future on the presumption of atheism.

Subsequent waves of feminism have brought greater diversification to what in the twenty-first century is a multicultural, multigender global movement. Feminism is not simply a means to an end but a lens through which reality can be continually rediscovered and reimagined—by all sorts of people. Interdisciplinary scholar and social activist bell hooks communicated the increasingly expansive vision of feminism in her 2000 book *Feminism Is for Everybody*.

Feminist influences on literature, the arts, history, philosophy, politics, law, medicine, psychology, religion, entertainment, sexuality, and family have been profound. Programs in women's studies, gender studies, and queer studies continue to transform teaching and scholarship. Their proponents often collaborate with allies in the academy to work toward the decolonization of education itself. Sexism, however, remains strong in certain sectors of society, including religion, one of its prime sources. The #MeToo movement, initiated by American activist Tarana Burke in 2006, and based on the testimony of countless abuse survivors, has revealed both the pervasive reality of sexual assault in the corporate world and the relative success of feminist consciousness in the legal system.

Three major innovations set new directions for the course of feminist theory and practice in the twenty-first century. Womanism, originally formulated by novelist and humanist Alice Walker, author of *The Color Purple* (1982), emphasizes the need to take seriously the distinctive set of challenges and experiences that shape the lives of African American feminists and all women of color. Intersectionality, a concept developed by law professor and critical race theorist Kimberlé Williams Crenshaw, draws attention to the complex overlapping of ethnic, gender, and class identities in a person's interactions with self, ancestry, community, and structures of power in society. Performativity, the centerpiece of philosopher Judith Butler's thought, highlights gender as an active, not static, dimension of embodied beings' lives—a socially constructed work of art in progress.

Atheism and agnosticism continue to weave in and out of the diverse story of modern feminism. New exodus experiences happen all the time, often sparked by intractable patriarchy within religious traditions. At the same time, unbelief is no unambiguous promised land. Sexist attitudes and actions persist in atheist and humanist networks. Some critics call contemporary atheism a boy's club. Prominent figures associated with New Atheism have been repeatedly accused of sexist bias and behavior.

In the United States, women remain generally more religious than men, and the varieties of religious feminism continue to multiply. According to the Pew Research Center, women constitute 43 percent of the country's religiously unaffiliated population (32 percent of self-identified atheists and 38 percent of agnostics). LGBTQ+ persons make up 41 percent of the unaffiliated (8 percent of atheists and 9 percent of agnostics). The extent to which feminist interests and commitments have influenced these identities is not clear. The number of atheist and agnostic feminists inside religious communities is unknown.

See also: Atheism, New; Atheism and Agnosticism, African American; Atheopaganism; Atheophobia; Beauvoir, Simone de; Besant, Annie; Cady Stanton, Elizabeth; Goldman, Emma; Hirsi Ali, Ayaan; Humanist Manifestos; Humanist of the Year; Hurston, Zora Neale; Hutchinson, Sikivu; Kristeva, Julia; LGBTQ+ Persons, Atheist and Agnostic; Media, Atheism and Agnosticism and the

Further Reading

Brewster, Melanie Elyse. "Atheism, Gender, and Sexuality." In *The Oxford Handbook of Atheism.* Ed. Stephen Bullivant and Michael Ruse, pp. 511–524. Oxford: Oxford University Press, 2013.

Butler, Judith. *Gender Trouble: Feminism and the Subversion of Identity.* New York: Routledge, 2007.

Cady Stanton, Elizabeth. *The Woman's Bible.* Boston: Northeastern University Press, 1993.

Collins, Patricia Hill. *Black Feminist Thought: Knowledge, Consciousness, and the Politics of Empowerment.* 2nd ed. London: Routledge, 2002.

Daly, Mary. *Beyond God the Father: Toward a Philosophy of Women's Liberation.* Boston: Beacon Press, 1985.

Daly, Mary. *The Church and the Second Sex*. Boston: Beacon Press, 1985.

Eisler, Riane. *The Chalice and the Blade: Our History, Our Future*. New York: HarperCollins, 1995.

Garst, Karen L., ed. *Women beyond Belief: Discovering Life without Religion*. Durham, NC: Pitchstone, 2016.

Gaylor, Annie, ed. *Women without Superstition: "No Gods—No Masters": The Collected Writings of Women Freethinkers of the Nineteenth and Twentieth Centuries*. Madison, WI: Freedom from Religion Foundation, 1997.

Goldenberg, Naomi. *Changing of the Gods: Feminism and the End of Traditional Religions*. Boston: Beacon Press, 1979.

Gorham, Candace R. M. *The Ebony Exodus Project: Why Some Black Women Are Walking Out on Religion—and Others Should Too*. Durham, NC: Pitchstone, 2013.

Hazleton, Lesley. *Agnostic: A Spirited Manifesto*. New York: Riverhead Books, 2016.

hooks, bell. *Feminism Is for Everybody: Passionate Politics*. London: Pluto Press, 2000.

Kindig, Jessie, with Sophia Giovannitti, Charlotte Heltai, and Rosie Warren, eds. *The Verso Book of Feminism: Revolutionary Words from Four Millennia of Rebellion*. Brooklyn, NY: Verso, 2020.

Mill, John Stuart. *On Liberty and the Subjection of Woman*. Ed. Alan Ryan. London: Penguin Classics, 2006.

Overall, Christine. "Feminism and Atheism." In *The Cambridge Companion to Atheism*. Ed. Michael Martin, pp. 233–249. Cambridge: Cambridge University Press, 2007.

Stone, Merlin. *When God Was a Woman: The Landmark Exploration of the Ancient Worship of the Great Goddess and the Eventual Suppression of Women's Rites*. New York: Houghton Mifflin Harcourt, 1976.

Walker, Alice. *In Search of Our Mothers' Gardens: Womanist Prose*. New York: Harvest, 1983.

Walters, Ronald G. *America's Reformers 1815–1860*. New York: Hill and Wang, 1983.

Wollstonecraft, Mary. *A Vindication of the Rights of Woman*. London: Penguin, 1992.

Feuerbach, Ludwig

Ludwig Feuerbach (1804–1872) was a pivotal figure in the exposition and defense of open atheism during a time of revolutionary transformation. His most important work, *The Essence of Christianity* (1841), published before *The Communist Manifesto* (1848), Charles Darwin's *The Origin of Species* (1859), and Friedrich Nietzsche's *The Gay Science* (1882), and nearly a century before Sigmund Freud's *The Future of an Illusion* (1927), is now recognized as a landmark of post-theist speculation and argumentation. Feuerbach was a rogue theologian in a state-supported church who exerted enormous influence on a generation rapidly rethinking both institutions. Theologian Hans Küng called him the "church father" of modern atheism.

Feuerbach was the product of a Germany charged with unprecedented political and cultural energy, advancing toward new national identity and assuming its self-declared role as intellectual leader of the Western world. In the wake of the French Revolution (1789–1799), the supreme symbol of colossal change from Russia to Haiti, a new class of intellectuals identified the critique of inherited ideas and institutions as the prime task of their vocation. Romantic views of evolution, socialism, and alternatives to Christianity swept through Europe's salons and seminar rooms.

A native of Bavaria, Feuerbach followed his sense of calling from the University of Heidelberg to the University of Berlin, from the discipline of theology to philosophy, and eventually from Christian faith to antitheism. He studied with G. W. F. Hegel, then the dominant force in European philosophy, whose idealized version of the Christian worldview sought to explain history's dynamic process to contemporary minds convinced they were experiencing the dawning of a new age. Feuerbach, however, was no mere or meek disciple. A radical leader among the so-called Young Hegelians, including the pre-*Manifesto* Karl Marx, he followed his master's philosophy of progress to what he thought was its logical conclusion. Hegel's secularized God guiding all of history, Feuerbach declared, was an invention of the human mind.

Feuerbach was not working in a vacuum. The German theological world as a whole was undergoing drastic alteration. Three centuries of Protestant innovation had crowded Christian doctrine with a previously unimaginable array of views and perspectives. Any lingering notion of static orthodoxy stretching back to the early church was severely compromised. The Enlightenment's challenge to defend belief on reason's grounds met with a seemingly unending series of responses, each in turn stimulating a set of new problems—and all making the existence of a personal, transcendent God harder and harder to prove and accept. The study of the religions of the world, ironically fueled by Europe's colonial impulse, fostered an expanding atmosphere of relativism, as citizens of Christian lands encountered flood stories, virgin births, golden rules, and dying-and-rising gods in the myths of other cultures.

The rise of biblical criticism especially signaled the end of Christian intellectual life as it had been known for centuries. Applying modern scientific methods to the study of ancient Hebrew and Greek scripture, so-called higher critics raised never-before-asked questions about the Bible's uniqueness, authenticity, reliability, and relevance. Publication of *The Life of Jesus, Critically Examined* (1835) by German theologian David Friedrich Strauss, assigning much of the Jesus story to early Christian imagination, sent shock waves through the academic establishment and the reading public. Its translation by Victorian Britain's freethinking novelist George Eliot spread the startling new ideas throughout the English-speaking world.

Feuerbach teased out the implications of Hegel's thought and his own thought in this lively context and over the course of an exceptionally productive career. His first books included *Thoughts on Death and Immortality* (1830); two volumes on the *History of Modern Philosophy* (1833 and 1837); *Abelard and Heloise* (1843); *Pierre Bayle* (1838), a sympathetic study of the seventeenth-century French Protestant skeptic (and, according to some interpreters, closet atheist); and *On Philosophy and Christianity* (1839). In the last years of his life, as an independent scholar, Feuerbach published *Principles of Philosophy of the Future* (1843), *The Essence of Faith according to Luther* (1844), *Lectures on the Essence of Religion* (1851), *Theogony According to the Sources of Classical, Hebrew and Christian Antiquity* (1857), and *God, Freedom, and Immortality* (1866).

Feuerbach's most important book was *The Essence of Christianity*, arguably the nineteenth century's most radical piece of theological scholarship—also translated by England's Eliot. In this book of twenty-seven chapters, Feuerbach focused on the uniquely human character of religion and the uniquely interior and natural sources of religion. Before Feuerbach, Martin Luther had located religion not in cognitive apprehension or intellectual certainty but in an act of the heart called faith or trust. In *Religion: Speeches to its Cultured Despisers* (1799), Friedrich Schleiermacher, often referred to as the founder of liberal Christianity, traced religion to a psychological or experiential source: the sense of absolute dependence. After Feuerbach, numerous thinkers worldwide would seek the origins of religious belief and behavior solely in nature, without reference to the supernatural—in psychological need, genetics, chemistry, even climate. Feuerbach was the turning point. His identification of God as the projection of human aspirations—"wishes of the heart"—onto a screen of cosmic proportions detached Western speculation about God from both the apparatus of Christian reflection and Enlightenment rationalism's obsession with the question of God's existence . Atheism, he said, is the "secret of religion," but it is a special sort of secret. For Feuerbach, theology (*theos* + *logos*, words about God) was in reality anthropology, words about humanity. God, in peculiar imitation of Christian dogma, is not human but humanity itself.

Feuerbach's impact on Nietzsche and Freud and their followers was direct and deeply felt. In his lifetime, however, his influence on social, political, and economic thought was particularly forceful. One of Marx's earliest books, *Theses on Feuerbach* (written in 1845), identified his fellow Young Hegelian as a catalyst for his critique of capitalism and his view of religion as social alienation. Marx's collaborator Friedrich Engels published a massive summary statement near the end of his life: *Ludwig Feuerbach and the End of Classical German Philosophy* (1888). Marx said Feuerbach gave socialism a solid philosophical foundation. He was, Marx concluded, the "true conqueror of the old philosophy."

See also: Christianity, Atheism and Agnosticism in; Freud, Sigmund; Marx, Karl; Nietzsche, Friedrich

Further Reading

Caldwell, Peter C. *Love, Death and Revolution in Central Europe: Ludwig Feuerbach, Moses Hess, Louise Dittmar, Richard Wagner*. New York: St. Martin's Press, 2009.

Feuerbach, Ludwig. *The Essence of Christianity*. Trans. George Eliot. New York: Harper and Row, 1957.

Harvey, Van A. *Feuerbach and the Interpretation of Religion*. Cambridge: Cambridge University Press, 1995.

Küng, Hans. *Does God Exist? An Answer for Today*. Trans. Edward Quinn. Garden City, NY: Doubleday, 1980.

Flew, Antony

Antony Flew (1923–2010) was an eminent British philosopher, known to virtually all students of philosophy during the second half of the twentieth century. He held a number of academic appointments in the United

Kingdom and North America, including a long tenure at the University of Reading, in England. Flew was best known as a leading exponent of the English-language analytic school of philosophy, minimizing rationalism and idealism and emphasizing the complex functions of language and the significance of empirical experience. His argument for the "presumption of atheism," shifting the burden of proof from nontheism to theism, permanently transformed the ongoing debate between belief and unbelief.

Flew was the son of a Methodist minister and New Testament tutor who taught at a pastoral training school in Cambridge. He attended a Methodist boarding school but, as he mentioned in a brief autobiographical sketch, never shared the devotional sentiments of his family members or coreligionists. By the time he was fifteen years old, he had rejected his parents' faith but continued to emulate, as he said, his father's commitment to high standards in intellectual pursuits. At Oxford University, Flew made public his nonbelief in God and life after death. As a postgraduate student, he worked with Gilbert Ryle, another product of a ministerial home and author of the essay "Systematically Misleading Expressions" (1932). Like Ryle, Flew was greatly influenced by the iconoclast Viennese thinker Ludwig Wittgenstein. Under Wittgenstein's unofficial, and legendarily brilliant but chaotic, leadership, British philosophy abandoned both metaphysics and the legacy of public rationalism, exemplified so memorably in Bertrand Russell's application of disciplined philosophical inquiry to social issues of education, sex, war, and economic inequality. For the next half century, the English-speaking philosophical academy confined itself to technical problems of language, especially the precise meaning and usage of words. An extreme form of this movement, called logical positivism and illustrated in the work of A. J. Ayer, declared God's existence or nonexistence to be a question that could never be answered—not for lack of evidence, but because the question itself is nonsensical.

Flew, and other advocates of linguistic or ordinary language philosophy, took a strict but generally more moderate approach in the new philosophical climate. He maintained that the question of God was coherent enough to be debated and potentially answered. As a student, he first made a name for himself in the context of Oxford's Socratic Club, a fashionable salon for believers and skeptics in the 1940s and '50s, presided over by the literary scholar and Christian apologist C. S. Lewis. Flew's paper on "Theology and Falsification," delivered before the group in 1950, established the terms for determining proper verification of faith claims and became a landmark in the modern philosophy of religion. Always interested in parapsychology, he wrote his first book on *A New Approach to Psychical Research* (1953).

Over the course of his career, Flew increasingly became a spokesperson and symbol for a rigorously argued atheism, laced with a brainy sense of humor. He signed the second Humanist Manifesto, delivered the 1991 Prometheus Lectures in the United States on the fundamentals of unbelief, and participated in numerous high-profile debates with celebrated Christian theists, some attracting audiences numbering in the thousands. His *God and Philosophy* (1966), a classic critique of Christian theism, has gone through numerous revisions through the years. *The Presumption of Atheism* (1976), respected by intellectuals all across the atheism-theism spectrum, is still the standard presentation of the thesis that atheism, or nontheism, represents the natural or normative state of the human mind. Belief in God, not nonbelief, Flew maintained, is the stance that requires justification.

Near the end of his life, just as New Atheism was gaining momentum, Flew shocked the intellectual world by announcing he had come to accept the existence of God, or a god. In *There Is a God* (2007), with the sensationalist subtitle *How the World's Most Notorious Atheist Changed His Mind*, he rehearsed the steps that led him to such an unanticipated reversal of opinion. It was a journey of reason, not faith, he explained. The God he affirmed was the impersonal God of Aristotle, the God of deism, an "infinitely intelligent Mind," not the allegedly all-loving personal deity of Christian doctrine who hears and answers prayer, conducts the redemption of the world through Jesus Christ, and assigns souls eternally to heaven and hell. The book concentrates principally on the questions of the origins of being itself—why there is something and not nothing—and the rationally understandable operation of the universe. Today, the book is the center of an unresolved controversy. Some readers mistake Flew's change of mind for a near-deathbed reversion to the faith of his forebears. Critics suspect intellectual malpractice on the part of his coauthor, conservative Roman Catholic apologist Roy Abraham Varghese. Questions about the integrity of the text remained unanswered at the time of Flew's death.

See also: Deism; Humanist Manifestos; Russell, Bertrand

Further Reading

Flew, Antony. *Atheistic Humanism*. Buffalo, NY: Prometheus Books, 1993.
Flew, Antony. *God and Philosophy*. New York: Harcourt, Brace and World, 1966.

Flew, Antony. *An Introduction to Western Philosophy: Ideas and Arguments from Plato to Popper.* London: Thames and Hudson, 1989.

Flew, Antony. *The Presumption of Atheism.* New York: Harper and Row, 1976.

Flew, Antony, and Terry L. Miethe. *Does God Exist?* San Francisco: HarperSanFrancisco, 1992.

Flew, Antony, with Roy Abraham Varghese. *There Is a God: How the World's Most Notorious Atheist Changed His Mind.* New York: HarperOne, 2007.

Freud, Sigmund

Sigmund Freud (1856–1939), prolific writer and founder of psychoanalysis, was one of the most original thinkers of the twentieth century. His ideas have exerted an enormous impact on virtually every dimension of modern experience—from medicine and sexual identity and behavior to art, literature, education, and religion. His bold and controversial theories revolutionized long-held notions of human development and the sources and purposes of culture. They remain influential today. Freud is especially significant because of his contributions to the secularization of Western society. To be modern, as many observers have suggested, is to be Freudian or post-Freudian. As a self-described "godless Jew," Freud provides an excellent example of a distinctive kind of atheism in the modern world.

Born in what is now the Czech Republic, Freud spent most of his life in Vienna, a vibrant center for creative intellectual and artistic expression in the Hapsburg Empire during the early twentieth century. He was raised in a semiobservant, middle-class Jewish home. Though he cultivated a strong sense of Jewish identity and retained a lifelong interest in the Bible and Jewish thought, he abandoned traditional belief and practice as a young adult. His premier biographer Ernest Jones spoke of him as "always an unrepentant atheist." Freud's life coincided with the rise of modern history's most virulent form of antisemitism. In the last months of his life, fleeing Nazi persecution, he joined Europe's flood of Jewish refugees and emigrated with his wife and adult daughter Anna, a well-known psychoanalyst and writer in her own right, establishing a home in suburban London. Nazi students burned his books. Four of his five sisters died in concentration camps.

Freud's education and diverse set of interests led to an unconventional professional career. After obtaining his medical degree from the

University of Vienna, he steered away from traditional health-care institutions and customary patterns of research and teaching, pursuing most of his work in private practice, serving individuals suffering from neurological disorders. Shaped by the ideals of the Enlightenment and the insights of Charles Darwin, he advocated the primacy of reason, the principle of empirical observation, and the paradigm of biological evolution. At the same time, a strong humanist impulse drove him beyond the natural sciences toward a wide gamut of subjects in cultural studies. He defended the legitimate place of speculation in intellectual life and published for a broad audience of educated nonspecialists. Throughout his career, he was the target of criticism issuing from both representatives of the mainstream science of his day and defenders of traditional religious and moral values.

Freud's contributions to the understanding of human experience can be reduced to two main achievements: developing a new dynamic view of the operations of the human mind and designing a special method to expose and track those processes—all within the context of a naturalist worldview, free from notions of God, sin, and the afterlife. Freud never wrote a systematic summary of his thought. His seminal convictions can be found in works such as *The Interpretation of Dreams* (1900), *The Psychopathology of Everyday Life* (1904), *Three Essays on the Theory of Sexuality* (1905), *Beyond the Pleasure Principle* (1920), and *The Ego and the Id* (1923). Here his first readers encountered an expansive view of humanity's inner life, concentrating especially on the relationship between the conscious self and the forgotten or stifled drives and desires of the unconscious mind. These books, filled with innovative concepts, such as libido, repression, innate bisexuality, the Oedipus complex, and transference, permanently altered the thought and vocabulary of people in the modern world. Challenging the assumptions of long-standing religious systems and the all-too-simplified myth of Enlightenment rationality, they inaugurated a new therapeutic age in Western history.

Freud's distinctive method is best captured in the image of his much-celebrated couch, now on display at the Freud Museum in London. Early in his career he briefly experimented with hypnotism but soon settled on the famous talking cure as the cornerstone of psychoanalytic procedure. Seated behind the individual reclining on the couch, he invited the patient to speak of dreams and memories and, through uncensored and spontaneous free association, to bring into focus hidden or denied aspects of deeper psychic life. Primarily a humanist approach to the challenges of life, revealing confidence in the power of introspection, Freud's conversational practice bypassed established medical technique and was, as he put it, "a cure through love."

Criticism of Freud is vast, varied, and often vehement. The entire twentieth century represented not only an extended appropriation of Freud but an ongoing argument with him as well. Early challenges, initiated by disciples such as Alfred Adler and Carl Jung, have spawned a legion of others. Feminist assessments have found Freud's views of women, especially women's sexuality, unsubstantiated and in conflict with his own therapeutic aims. Scholars from Melanie Klein and Karen Horney to Juliet Mitchell and Julia Kristeva have demonstrated how Freud perpetuated unscientific patriarchal assumptions and seriously misread what he called the "riddle of femininity." His disturbing and unexplained dismissal of women's testimonies of molestation, interpreting them instead as evidence of infantile sexual fantasies, continues to impede and misdirect important research on abuse. Edward Said's *Freud and the Non-European* (2003) critiques the Eurocentric orientation of psychoanalysis.

Freud's views on God and religion can best be seen in the classics produced during his final period. In *The Question of Lay Analysis* (1926) and *An Autobiographical Study* (1935), he spoke of his work in medical science as a "detour" from lifelong interests in history, literature, and culture. Freud returned to these subjects in what are his most adventurous and audacious books: *Totem and Taboo* (1913), *The Future of an Illusion* (1927), *Civilization and Its Discontents* (1930), and *Moses and Monotheism* (1939). Like other atheists of the time, he decried the negative impact of religion on human experience but spoke sparingly of its crimes and expended little energy criticizing traditional creeds. He was most interested in offering a naturalist explanation of religion's psychological origins and its function in the history of culture, drawing parallels between religion and the many defense mechanisms formulated by individuals to deal with the mysterious forces of their unconscious life.

For ages, Judaism had feared idolatry, the making of substitutes for God. For the "godless Jew" Freud, God is the ultimate idol, not so much an error as an illusion—the supreme self-deception—and religion the universal neurosis. Like all wishful thinking, he concluded, the construct "God" prevents people from recognizing the reality of their place in the world and taking responsibility for the course of their lives.

See also: Darwin, Charles; Kristeva, Julia

Further Reading

Bettelheim, Bruno. *Freud and Man's Soul*. New York: Alfred A. Knopf, 1983.

Freud, Sigmund. *An Autobiographical Study*. Trans. James Strachey. New York: W. W. Norton, 1963.

Freud, Sigmund. *Civilization and Its Discontents*. Trans. James Strachey. New York: W. W. Norton, 1961.

Freud, Sigmund. *The Future of an Illusion*. Trans. James Strachey. New York: W. W. Norton, 1989.

Freud, Sigmund. *Moses and Monotheism*. Trans. Katherine Jones. New York: Vintage Books, 1967.

Freud, Sigmund. *Totem and Taboo*. Trans. James Strachey. New York: W. W. Norton, 1950.

Gay, Peter. *A Godless Jew: Freud, Atheism, and the Making of Psychoanalysis*. New Haven, CT: Yale University Press, 1987.

Jones, Ernest. *The Life and Work of Sigmund Freud*. 3 vols. New York: Basic Books, 1963.

Mitchell, Juliet. *Psychoanalysis and Feminism: A Radical Reassessment of Freudian Psychoanalysis*. New York: Basic Books, 2000.

Phillips, Adam. *Becoming Freud: The Making of a Psychoanalyst*. New Haven, CT: Yale University Press, 2014.

Roudinesco, Élisabeth. *Freud in His Time and Ours*. Trans. Catherine Porter. Cambridge, MA: Harvard University Press, 2016.

Said, Edward. *Freud and the Non-European*. London: Verso, 2003.

Storr, Anthony. *Freud: A Very Short Introduction*. Oxford: Oxford University Press, 2001.

Friendly Atheist, The

The Friendly Atheist is the moniker by which American media personality and atheist spokesperson Hemant Mehta (b. 1983) is best known. The founder and host of *The Friendly Atheist* blog and weekly podcast, he is an author, public speaker, social commentator, and advocate for intellectual freedom, separation of church and state, and humanist service to society. One of the featured speakers at the Washington, DC, Reason Rally in 2012, he is a leading figure in the transformation of the atheist voice and presence in twenty-first-century culture.

Before he became the Friendly Atheist, Mehta was a secondary school math teacher. Born in Chicago, he received his undergraduate degree in mathematics and biology from the University of Illinois at Chicago and a master's degree in math education from DePaul University. His family of origin has its roots in the Jain tradition, whose ancient Indian founder Mahavira (599–527 BCE) advanced a path to individual fulfillment without recourse to worship of deities. Mehta dates his secular atheist outlook to his teenage years. He gained notoriety as the "eBay atheist" in 2006, when he auctioned his willing attendance to the church of the highest bidder. Proceeds from the experience were donated to the Secular Student Alliance, the nationwide support organization for nonreligious high school and college students.

Mehta's blog is one of the most popular faith channels on Patheos, the interfaith and multifaith religion and spirituality online media company launched in 2009 by Colorado-based technology entrepreneurs Leo and Cathie Brunnick. His three books, two published by Patheos Press, capture the best of his online commentaries: *I Sold My Soul on eBay* (2007), *The Young Atheist's Survival Guide* (2012), and *The Friendly Atheist: Thoughts on the Role of Religion in Politics and Media* (2013). Mehta also writes for the *Washington Post*'s "On Faith" column and produces *The Atheist Voice* YouTube series. In all of his writings and public appearances, he addresses issues of public policy and cultural diversity with a distinctively dialogical and amiable style. He is active in leadership and fundraising roles with nonreligious human rights groups such as the Secular Student Alliance and the humanist charitable organization Foundation Beyond Belief.

See also: Media, Atheism and Agnosticism and the; Reason Rally

Further Reading

Mehta, Hemant. *The Friendly Atheist: Thoughts on the Role of Religion in Politics and Media.* Englewood, CO: Patheos Press, 2013.

Mehta, Hemant. *I Sold My Soul on eBay: Viewing Faith through an Atheist's Eyes.* Colorado Springs, CO: WaterBrook Press, 2007.

Mehta, Hemant. *The Young Atheist's Survival Guide: Helping Secular Students Thrive.* Englewood, CO: Patheos Press, 2012.

G

Goldman, Emma

Emma Goldman (1869–1940) was an outspoken and embattled social activist, the leader of an alternative to first-wave feminism, and mother of the anarchist movement in the United States. Her lifetime spans the decades of an intense period in modern history marked by rapid social change and unprecedented ferment in social thought and political agitation. Women, workers, immigrants, the jobless, and other marginalized individuals and groups toiled in a variety of ways to resist and overcome the injustices of unregulated industrialism, aggressive capitalism, and the rule of wealth and privilege in league with sexism, racism, and traditional religious ideals. An unbeliever with Jewish ancestry, known to friends and opponents as Red Emma, Goldman committed her life to the spread of the anarchist message and its refutation of long-held beliefs in the authority of God and the state.

Born in prerevolutionary Russia (modern-day Lithuania), Goldman emigrated to the United States as a teenager, escaping both the social repression of the czarist regime and the domestic violence of a dysfunctional family. She gained firsthand knowledge of America's Gilded Age economic exploitation as a low-wage employee in the garment industry. Over the course of her life, she supported herself as a seamstress, a nurse, a cook, a writer, an editor, a lecturer, a theatrical agent, and, for a brief period, an admittedly ineffective and uninspired prostitute.

Gifted in several languages (including German and Yiddish), she supplemented an inadequate early education with voracious reading in philosophy, literature, and political theory and with equally ravenous discussions with leaders in the burgeoning leftist communities of the urban Northeast and upper Midwest. She continued her self-education during a year in jail, convicted of inciting a riot after encouraging unemployed laborers to take bread to feed their families, and completed her formal training in Vienna with degrees in nursing and midwifery, attending lectures by the young, not-yet-famous Sigmund Freud. In her autobiography, she traced the roots of her radicalism to the 1887 execution of anarchists accused of murdering police in the bloody aftermath of the Chicago Haymarket strike.

By the beginning of the twentieth century, Goldman enjoyed an international reputation as a magnetic orator on the political lecture circuit and an original thinker in anarchist circles. She had many admirers and notable rivals but few true colleagues. Her rejection of utopian and gradualist reform schemes alienated her from many fellow progressives. Her unrepentant individualism distanced her from potential allies in organized labor. Her dismissal of electoral politics created barriers between her and suffragist feminists. Her advocacy of birth control and free love and her unqualified acceptance of homosexuality cemented her notoriety among defenders of the status quo. More than anything, Goldman's refusal to renounce violence and her associations with violent actors in the 1892 Homestead strike and the 1901 assassination of President William McKinley defined her image in the public eye. Especially during the Red Scare of the 1920s and '30s, the U.S. government and mainstream media portrayed her as an enemy of the national interest and decency.

Goldman's most significant conflict with the established order occurred during World War I. Organizing the Free Speech League and the No-Conscription League, she denounced the war as a capitalist venture. She campaigned vigorously against censorship and the draft and defended the rights of conscientious objectors. Bucking militaristic public opinion, she orchestrated antipreparedness rallies in major American cities. Washington, citing wartime exigencies, responded to her and other critics with harsh legislative measures culminating in the Espionage Act (1917), the Alien Immigration Act (1917), the Sedition Act (1918), and the Anti-Anarchist Act (1918)—all of which sought to limit the volume and impact of dissent in American culture. At the height of U.S. involvement in the war, Goldman, along with scores of other anarchists, including her long-time companion and collaborator Alexander Berkman, was imprisoned and eventually deported to the Soviet Union. Nonconformist and foe of totalitarianism wherever she went, she even attempted to convince Vladimir Lenin of the value of unhindered freedom of speech. Aside from a ninety-day lecture tour crisscrossing the United States in 1934, she spent the rest of her life speaking and writing in Europe and Canada, interrupting her forced sabbatical to participate in the Spanish Civil War. A cluster of American artists and intellectuals, thanks to the efforts of poet Edna St. Vincent Millay, provided her with much-needed moral and financial support during these years.

Goldman is a perfect example of the literary activist, well known in the American radical tradition. Her insights are preserved in her magazine *Mother Earth* (1906–1917), her numerous pamphlets, and her four books: *Anarchism and Other Essays* (1911), *The Social Significance of the Modern Drama* (1914), *My Disillusionment in Russia* (1923), and *Living My Life* (1931). In all of her publications, she linked human liberation to atheism. Her pamphlet *The Philosophy of Atheism and the Failure of Christianity* (1916), frequently anthologized in collections of atheist classics, summarizes her vision. Unbelief came to her naturally. No crisis of faith or conscience punctuated her youth. Like many progressives of her generation, she placed religion in evolutionary context, viewing theism as rooted in the fear and ignorance of prehistorical humanity, as developing gradually into a tool of social control, indifferent to injustice, and as eventually declining into a spent force, fighting a rearguard battle against science. Still, in the modern period, religion represented a lucrative enterprise all too comparable to the international arms industry. Ultimately, for Goldman, atheism was no mere negation or escape. Release from the prolonged "nightmare of gods," it was also the supreme affirmation of human existence: the "eternal yea to life, purpose, and beauty."

See also: Feminism, Atheism and Agnosticism and; Marx, Karl

Further Reading

Chalberg, John C. *Emma Goldman: American Individualist*. 2nd ed. New York: Pearson, 2007.

Falk, Candace. *Love, Anarchy, and Emma Goldman*. New York: Holt, Rinehart and Winston, 1984.

Goldman, Emma. *Living My Life*. New York: Penguin, 2006.

Gornick, Vivian. *Emma Goldman: Revolution as a Way of Life*. New Haven, CT: Yale University Press, 2011.

Shulman, Alix Kates, ed. *Red Emma Speaks: An Emma Goldman Reader*. 3rd ed. New York: Open Road Media, 2012.

Ward, Colin. *Anarchism: A Very Short Introduction*. New York: Oxford University Press, 2004.

Wexler, Alice R. *Emma Goldman: An Intimate Life*. New York: Pantheon, 1984.

Harris, Sam

Sam Harris (b. 1967) is a neuroscientist, philosopher, podcast host, and internationally known writer and speaker. His work has appeared in the *New York Times*, the *Los Angeles Times*, the *Economist*, the London *Times*, and many other venues. With biologist Richard Dawkins, philosopher Daniel C. Dennett, and journalist Christopher Hitchens, he was one of the so-called four horsemen, the principal leaders of the early twenty-first-century New Atheism movement.

Raised in a nonreligious household in California, Harris studied philosophy at Stanford University and received his PhD in neuroscience from the University of California, Los Angeles, while the New Atheist movement was in its ascendency. His *New York Times* best seller *The End of Faith* (2004), winner of the 2005 PEN award for nonfiction, is an aggressive critique of the religious fundamentalism that fueled the September 11, 2001, terrorist attacks and a long line of atrocities before them. In many ways, it was a precursor to New Atheism. In *Letter to a Christian Nation* (2006), he sought to convince conservative U.S. Christians, as well as their moderate and liberal coreligionists, of the high degree of self-deception required to be both a Christian faithful to ancient scripture and a member of modern society benefiting from science. Harris has defined atheism as not another faith or worldview but simply the recognition of what is obvious.

After the death of Hitchens in 2011, and the subsequent conclusion or transformation of the New Atheist movement, Harris redefined his profile and redirected his agenda and activities. His books began to reflect an expanded range of topics: *Free Will* (2012), *Lying* (2013), *Waking Up: A Guide to Spirituality without Religion* (2014), and *Making Sense* (2020), a collection of some of his most popular podcasts. *Islam and the Future of Tolerance* (2015), a dialogue with the secular Muslim commentator Maajid Nawaz, developed into a documentary in 2018, built upon themes first explored in *The End of Faith*. Along with other New Atheist writers, Harris has been accused of racism, sexism, and Islamophobia—issues he addresses at length on his website (https://samharris.org).

In TED talks and his regular *Making Sense* podcasts, Harris defends the notion of moral responsibility without belief in God and the claim that science can tackle ethical questions. More interested in Asian traditions than any of the other original New Atheist figures, he has advocated for disciplined meditation practice, based principally on his extensive study of Tibetan models, and what he describes as spirituality without religion. Like many other Western intellectuals, Harris promotes a nonreligious appreciation of Buddhism's insights into and contributions to understandings of consciousness and concentration. He does not speak of a nonreligious appreciation of other religious heritages. His *Waking Up* app for electronic devices offers daily meditations and commentary on issues related to health, wellness, and mindfulness.

See also: Atheism, New; Dawkins, Richard; Dennett, Daniel C.; Hitchens, Christopher

Further Reading

Harris, Sam. *The End of Faith: Religion, Terror, and the Future of Religion.* New York: W. W. Norton, 2004.

Harris, Sam. *Free Will.* New York: Simon and Schuster, 2012.

Harris, Sam. *Letter to a Christian Nation.* New York: Vintage, 2008.

Harris, Sam. *Lying.* Opelousas, LA: Four Elephants Press, 2013.

Harris, Sam. *Making Sense: Conversations on Consciousness, Morality, and the Future of Humanity.* New York: Ecco, 2020.

Harris, Sam. *The Moral Landscape: How Science Can Determine Human Values.* New York: Free Press, 2010.

Harris, Sam. *Waking Up: A Guide to Spirituality without Religion.* New York: Simon and Schuster, 2014.

Harris, Sam, Richard Dawkins, Daniel C. Dennett, and Christopher Hitchens. *The Four Horsemen: The Conversation that Sparked an Atheist Revolution.* New York: Random House, 2019.

Harris, Sam, and Maajid Nawaz. *Islam and the Future of Tolerance: A Dialogue.* Cambridge, MA: Harvard University Press, 2019.

Hirsi Ali, Ayaan

Ayaan Hirsi Ali (b. 1969) is an award-winning human rights activist and best-selling author, well known for her indictment of Islam and the distinctive viewpoint she has contributed to global feminism's diversity. She has been especially dynamic as a champion of free speech since the murder of Dutch filmmaker Theo Van Gogh, her collaborator in the production of *Submission* (2004), an exposé of the repression of women in Muslim societies. Condemned by Islamic fundamentalists and chided by Western multiculturalists, Hirsi Ali has gained a unique, controversy-ridden reputation as an independent scholar in the contemporary marketplace of ideas. Recipient of the Simone de Beauvoir Prize and the Atheist Alliance of America's Richard Dawkins Award, both in 2008, she is today one of the world's foremost atheist speakers and writers.

Hirsi Ali has published riveting accounts of her life in two autobiographies: *Infidel* (originally published in Dutch, 2006) and *Nomad* (2010). Born in Mogadishu, Somalia, she grew up in a culture shaped by a mixture of premodern African traditions, exclusive variants of Islam, the legacy of Western colonialism, and modern African self-determination. Her father, educated at Columbia University in the United States, agitated for educational and political reform in independent Somalia and spent many years in the Soviet client state's prison system and many more in exile, leading the Somali Salvation Democratic Front in a number of African countries. Hirsi Ali, raised by her mother and grandmother, knew little of her father or the outside world. Her report about humans walking on the moon was rejected as nonsense at home. The family moved from Somalia to Saudi Arabia, then Ethiopia, and then Kenya, with Hirsi Ali attending sex-segregated Qur'an madrassahs and an English-language girls' school along the way. During high school, she became increasing interested in the Saudi-style puritan Wahhabi movement and was the first young woman in her school to wear a full hijab. Later she realized the movement was no return to tradition but an antimodernist protest fueled by oil wealth and Arab ambition.

The crucial moment in Hirsi Ali's childhood was the experience of excision or female circumcision, known more broadly as female genital mutilation (FGM). At the age of five, she was forcibly held by her grandmother and two other women, while a "strange man" with scissors cut off her inner labia and clitoris and sewed the remaining flesh together with a long blunt needle. On the same day, her younger sister received the same treatment, only hers was botched, requiring restitching. A pre-Islamic tradition still endorsed by many Muslims, FGM has been inflicted upon untold generations of girls. For Hirsi Ali, it became the sign of the demented side of religion and the first step of her long journey toward what her former coreligionists call apostasy.

As a young adult, Hirsi Ali fled an unwanted arranged marriage and attained refugee status and eventually citizenship in the Netherlands. She earned undergraduate and graduate degrees in political science at the University of Leiden and became deeply impressed with the efficiency and tolerance of nonreligious societies. She read the classic makers of the modern Western mind—including Baruch Spinoza, John Locke, Voltaire, Charles Darwin, Sigmund Freud, and Émile Durkheim—and became increasingly double minded herself. The little "shutter" that separated two parts of her brain, she said, snapped open after the terrorist attacks of September 11, 2001. The decisive step, ushering her into open, self-confessed atheism, was a reading of *Atheïstisch Manifest* (1995) by Dutch philosopher Herman Philipse. The murder of her friend Van Gogh by pistol- and knife-wielding Moroccan Muhammad Bouyeri was a chilling communication of what is at stake in being an ex-Muslim atheist.

Hirsi Ali's career has taken her from freelance translator to member of the Dutch Parliament to American public intellectual. Currently a fellow at Harvard University's John F. Kennedy School of Government, she has been associated with a number of think tanks and foundations, including her own AHA Foundation (www.theahafoundation.org), a nonprofit organization founded in 2007, to promote the rights of women within Islam. Aligning herself with the Western tradition of classical free-market liberalism, she is best associated with the freethinking wing of the contemporary neoconservative movement. In addition to her autobiographical writings, her books—*The Caged Virgin* (2008), *Heretic* (2015), and *Prey* (2020)—focus on the need for human rights reform in Islam. Leaders of the New Atheist movement have seen her as a comrade in arms.

Champions of Hirsi Ali have praised her candor, courage, and commitment to rationality and democratic values. Critics have accused her of misrepresenting traditional Islam and fostering Islamophobic intolerance. Some scholars suggest that she has appropriated the perspective of discredited Orientalism, perpetuating stereotypes grounded in an outdated and morally indefensible colonial perspective. Her call for an Islamic Enlightenment parallel to the West's, they say, demonstrates a failure to reckon with the sources of colonialism in the early modern Age of Reason. Liberal Muslims claim that she has ignored their long-standing efforts. On another front, a controversy in Europe has centered around charges that she attained asylum in Holland using a false name and birth date. No one can argue with the way Ayaan Hirsi Ali has brought new prominence to the cause of international women's rights and of women in contemporary atheism.

See also: Atheism, New; Feminism, Atheism and Agnosticism and; Islam, Atheism and Agnosticism in

Further Reading

Hirsi Ali, Ayaan. *The Caged Virgin: An Emancipation Proclamation for Women and Islam*. New York: Atria, 2008.

Hirsi Ali, Ayaan. *Heretic: Why Islam Needs a Reformation Now*. New York: Harper, 2015.

Hirsi Ali, Ayaan. *Infidel*. New York: Atria, 2008.

Hirsi Ali, Ayaan. *Nomad: From Islam to America, A Personal Journey through the Clash of Civilizations*. New York: Atria, 2010.

Hirsi Ali, Ayaan. *Prey: Immigration, Islam, and the Erosion of Women's Rights*. New York: Harper, 2020.

Hitchens, Christopher

Christopher Hitchens (1949–2011), prolific journalist and social critic, published over twenty books and scores of essays on a wide variety of topics—from politics and literature to his personal experience of water-boarding torture. Recognized as an impeccable prose stylist, he also gained a reputation as a stimulating conversationalist, a peerless public speaker, and a consummate contrarian. Evolutionary biologist Richard Dawkins hailed him as the "greatest orator of our time." Author of the best-selling *god is not Great* (2007) and compiler of *The Portable Atheist* (2007), Hitchens was one of the principal initiators of the movement known as New Atheism.

Raised in the British middle class, Hitchens was the elder son of a former Royal Navy commander father and a talented, exuberant mother, whose suicide during his young adult years profoundly affected his outlook and sense of identity. He progressed through the traditional boarding-school system and flourished in the environment of Balliol College, Oxford—not so much as a would-be specialist but as a public intellectual in the making. In his memoir *Hitch-22* (2011), he speaks of the true writer's "promiscuous mandate" to be interested in all things. During his 1960s university experience, a natural in the Oxford Union culture of debate, he inaugurated what would be a lifetime pattern of drafting his mastery of the English canon—and the writing craft—into the service of broad-ranging commentary on the political, social, and economic forces dramatically, and sometimes violently, reshaping the world.

Hitchens was always part artist, part activist, part provocateur. For the better part of two decades, he followed the cause of democratic socialism to hot spots around the world—from Cuba and Czechoslovakia to Libya and Iraq—exposing the evils and idiocies of Western imperialism and right-wing dictatorships. By the end of the twentieth century, as the world changed, so did he. Disillusioned by what he believed to be the liberal West's ineffective response to Islamic extremism, he became more sympathetic to the claims of political realism and entered the "culture wars" then embroiling U.S. society. In 2007, he became a U.S. citizen, while retaining his British citizenship.

As columnist, foreign correspondent, and university professor, Hitchens wrote engaging books characterized by effortless eloquence and a trademark irreverent wit. He was a virtuoso of the shrewd, edgy essay. His work appeared regularly in magazines such as the *New Statesman*, *The Nation*, *Vanity Fair*, *World Affairs*, *Slate*, and the *Atlantic Monthly*, covering everything, as *The Quotable Hitchens* (2011) says, from alcohol to Zionism. He mingled with heads of state and celebrated friendships with stars in the literary firmament. He admired figures such as Thomas Paine and George Orwell but subjected idols of the Left and the Right—Henry Kissinger, Bill Clinton, Billy Graham, the British royals, and others—to merciless critique. His polemical squib against the then near-saint Mother Teresa, memorably titled *The Missionary Position* (1995), set a new standard in the tradition of humanist iconoclasm.

After the terrorist attacks of September 11, 2001, Hitchens's lifelong atheism became an increasingly important feature of his public profile. He was quickly recognized as a leading voice—arguably the most poetic—in what became known as the New Atheism movement: one of the "four horsemen" of an atheist resurgence, along with Dawkins, neuroscientist Sam Harris, and philosopher Daniel C. Dennett. Drawing from his rich experience as inveterate globetrotter, incurable bon vivant, and keen observer of human foibles, Hitchens contributed great flair and verve to the mounting of a distinctively twenty-first-century case against religion. In 2011, the Atheist Alliance of America honored him with its Richard Dawkins Award.

god is not Great—the lowercase *g* is intentional—is a spirited world tour of the absurdities and atrocities that have been part of religion's legacy throughout human history. In flawless prose, laced with autobiographical insights, Hitchens scrutinizes creeds and codes from a lavish spectrum of faiths—especially the Abrahamic traditions of Judaism, Christianity, and Islam—and finds all of them intellectually defective or morally depraved. Individuals surveyed represent for Hitchens a sampling of the world's hucksters, fakirs, and frauds, and the groups mentioned he sees as history's most duped and devilish populations. From his perspective, the record of religion, from prehistory to the present, is a long and not surprising story alternating between sad forms of deception and crushing forms of intimidation.

Hitchens concludes *god is not Great* with a call for a new Enlightenment, an Age of Reason recalibrated for the twenty-first century. His *Portable Atheism*, a five-hundred-page anthology of atheist literature, provides a roster of writers who, in their own times, issued calls for a candid verdict on religion's role in society, genuine tolerance for unpopular ideas, and appreciation for doubt and experiment in the intellectual life. Lucretius (c. 99–55 BCE) is the book's only figure from the ancient world and one of the few poets. Skeptics and heretics from the Enlightenment and Victorian periods, including David Hume, Percy Bysshe Shelley, and John Stuart Mill, are well represented. Twentieth-century writers, such as Emma Goldman, Bertrand Russell, and Carl Sagan, serve as the backbone for the collection.

Critics have noted that Hitchens's chorus of freethinkers is composed overwhelmingly of privileged white men from the Western world, some of whom have sketchy records on race and colonialism. Hitchens himself fielded criticisms of classism and sexism. Feminist and atheist writer Sikivu Hutchinson minced no words when she decried his "elite white alpha dog world." Some scholars, including nonreligious experts on religion, have observed that Hitchens seemed unaware of the sophisticated work in religious and theological studies regularly produced in the contemporary academy, including his own alma mater. Others have suggested that he placed too much stress on religion as a set of ideas (caricaturing religion as "philosophy with the questions left out"), ignoring religion's enormous impact on world art and music. Progressive people of faith have expressed dismay over Hitchens's almost exclusive focus on prescientific founders and unreflective modern believers, wondering why he dismissed the impressive ranks of religious folk who have advanced peace and social justice from spiritual motives or produced so much of the literature he loved so well.

Detractors turn into reluctant admirers when they encounter *Mortality* (2011), the essays Hitchens published when he was suffering from terminal esophageal cancer at age sixty-one. Here he showed a curious and incredulous world how a convinced atheist might deal with life's ultimate challenge. This unbeliever, affably tolerant of the calls for prayer and conversion that issued from anonymous foes and former debate opponents, faced death the way he faced life: with grace, charm, courage, incredible powers of introspection, and a sense of humor adversaries could only envy.

See also: Atheism, New; Dawkins, Richard; Dennett, Daniel C.; Harris, Sam

Further Reading

Hitchens, Christopher. *Arguably: Essays by Christopher Hitchens*. New York: Twelve, 2011.

Hitchens, Christopher. *god is not Great: How Religion Poisons Everything*. New York: Twelve, 2007.

Hitchens, Christopher. *Hitch 22: A Memoir*. New York: Twelve, 2011.

Hitchens, Christopher. *Letters to a Young Contrarian*. New York: Basic Books, 2001.

Hitchens, Christopher. *The Missionary Position: Mother Teresa in Theory and Practice*. London: Verso, 1995.

Hitchens, Christopher. *Mortality*. New York: Twelve, 2012.

Hitchens, Christopher, ed. *The Portable Atheist: Essential Readings for the Nonbeliever*. Philadelphia: Da Capo, 2007.

Hitchens, Christopher, Richard Dawkins, Sam Harris, and Daniel C. Dennett. *The Four Horsemen: The Conversation that Sparked an Atheist Revolution*. New York: Random House, 2019.

Hutchinson, Sikivu. *Moral Combat: Black Atheists, Gender Politics, and the Values Wars*. Los Angeles: Infidel Books, 2011.

Mann, Windsor, ed. *The Quotable Hitchens: From Alcohol to Zionism*. Cambridge, MA: Da Capo Press, 2011.

Humanism

Humanism is a rich philosophy of life—more properly, a set of interconnected philosophies of life—absorbed with and celebrating all things human. Humanism has appeared in many different forms throughout history and around the globe. A humanist may endorse theism, atheism, agnosticism, or any number of other religious and nonreligious points of view. Humanists may be organized and socially engaged or individualist and aloof. They may be conservative or liberal. What unites all who gravitate toward the name is not an ideology but an inclination of life displaying at least three basic characteristics: curiosity about the mystery of the human condition, delight in the astonishing array of human accomplishments, and concern for the achievement of genuine human fulfillment. With warm appreciation for things of this world at the heart of the perspective, humanists of all stripes find common ground with Terence, the ancient Roman playwright who said, "Nothing human is alien to me."

Ancient versions of humanism emphasized the cultivation of the mind, the relevance of artistic expression, an outward-facing practical orientation of life, and a judicious disregard for deities and overly zealous religious establishments. During China's Zhou dynasty in the first millennium BCE, Confucius's *jun-zi*, or "superior person," independent of gods and generals, embodied a new model of the self-governing individual whose learning served society and whose command of both action and contemplation was an emblem of the near-infinite range of possibilities embedded within the finitude of human experience. Two centuries later, Greek drama presented unvarnished portraits of human heroism and spiritual yearning, and the perfection of the art of sculpture during the Hellenistic age, unfettered by doctrines of shame, honored the grace and dignity of the human person by glorifying the unadorned human body. Hebrew thought of the biblical period, otherwise obsessed with divine authority and nursing notions of sin, advanced the humanist ideal with its own tribute to human beings, "a little lower" than the angels.

Medieval Christian humanism, drawing from Jewish, classical, and Islamic sources, explored the cultural and psychological implications of the cardinal belief that humanity is, as the Bible put it, made in the image of God. These ramifications were embodied especially in the new institution called the university, whose leading feature was its commitment to universality. Founded on the conviction that the proper object of study for the human mind was the full range of learning, the medieval university did not confine its curriculum to sacred subjects of scripture, dogma, and pious speculation. The intellectual consensus of Europe's age of faith recognized the pagan classics as models for refined and elevating literature. In the *Summa Theologiae* of Thomas Aquinas, the exalted role of "the Philosopher" was played by Aristotle, and the principal guide in *The Divine Comedy*, Dante's fanciful journey through the afterlife, was Virgil, author of the epic *Aeneid*—neither of whom could be counted as a Christian believer.

The original meaning of the "humanities" reflected this breadth of vision. The *studia humanitatis* did not denote a restricted set of nonscientific fields (as it does in today's academy) but rather the study of all things within the human frame of reference: literature, philosophy, arts, law, mathematics, medicine, and nature—everything, that is, distinct from divinity, or the study of God. Every scholarly discipline was called a science (from the Latin *scientia*, "knowledge"). Theology was portrayed as queen of the sciences, but every path of learning, even the most worldly, had its place and integrity.

As the university evolved, so did humanism and its exemplars. Those who first bore the name "humanist" were the intellectuals and artists of the Renaissance period. Their slogan, *ad fontes* ("to the sources"), stirred a rebirth of interest in classical languages and the art of Europe's pre-Christian heritage, thanks in large part to greater contact with the literary treasures of the Arab world. What historian Lisa Jardine calls the Renaissance humanists' "classroom without walls" made internationalism and cosmopolitanism identifying marks of the highest levels of their version of Western intellectual culture. Their efforts, valuing the natural and temporal on their own terms, not simply as foils of the supernatural and eternal, laid the mental groundwork for the making of modern secular society. Erasmus's *In Praise of Folly* (1514) and other works on peace and religious reform emphasized, with withering satire, the priority of morality and humane empathy over doctrinal and ritual correctness. Thomas More's *Utopia* (1516), centuries before John Lennon and Yoko Ono, imagined a happy world without religion.

Forms of humanism recognizable to observers today took shape in the early modern West, as decades of Reformation-era religious violence discredited church authority and sparked calls for separation of church and state and greater intellectual freedom and toleration. What historians still call the Enlightenment or Age of Reason (labels conspicuous for their self-congratulatory tone) fostered the conditions necessary for upheavals in science, economics, philosophy, social organization, and politics—all the factors that make modern experience identifiably modern. Some political revolutions led to regicide, an unthinkable act in the Middle Ages. In the universities, the queen of the sciences was deposed, if not banished. On the frontispiece of the *Encyclopédie* (1751–1772), the era's supreme literary monument to unfettered reason produced by Denis Diderot and other greats of the French Enlightenment, a scantily veiled Truth stands radiant and regnant over subservient Theology. In heroic couplets, Alexander Pope proclaimed the thesis of modern humanism: "the proper study of mankind is man" [*sic*]. Mary Wollstonecraft, exposing one of the many limitations of the emerging worldview, simultaneously expanded and challenged Enlightenment thought with *A Vindication of the Rights of Woman* (1792).

Modern and contemporary humanism, religious and secular, rises from this dense and fertile historical and cultural milieu. Liberal and modernist forms of religion in the West, especially in the nineteenth and early twentieth centuries, attempted to accommodate traditional teachings, practices, and institutions to the increasingly dominant values and assumptions of modern culture—over time creating forms of Christianity and Judaism less and less dependent upon literal belief in the Bible and the reality of supernatural powers. Some innovators attempted to unmask and moderate or eradicate the sexism and racism they detected at the core of Abrahamic religious traditions. A special role in this process was played by three important factors: (1) the rise of biblical criticism, scholarship that approached the Bible as a set of humanly produced texts, mixing history and myth, no different in essence from other ancient books; (2) the challenge of Charles Darwin's theory of evolution and post-Darwinian science; and (3) the encounter of Western monotheist faiths with the traditional religions of Africa, Asia, Australia, and the Americas—an encounter ironically made possible by the expanding reach of Western imperialism and colonialism.

Religious humanism paralleled these trends but differed, and continues to differ, from these liberalizing and modernizing efforts in several respects. Religious humanism significantly redefines *God* or eliminates it altogether. Religious humanists who retain the word speak in terms of an impersonal or transpersonal force permeating all of life or the spirit of humanity as a whole. God serves as shorthand for the ideal of human existence, the source and summit of all human values and aspirations. Nontheist religious humanists, seeing no reason to remain tied to the vocabulary of premodern worldviews, advocate for religion without God. The recognition of dimensions of life or life itself as sacred, they maintain, does not require reference to or endorsement of the God idea, personal or impersonal, transcendent or immanent. Virtually all religious humanists, theist and nontheist, have followed a universalist path, cutting allegiances to the creeds, scriptures, rites, histories, calendars, and collective identities of particular traditions—in many cases the traditions that have nurtured their own earlier spiritual formation and spurred them toward humanism.

Early classics in religious humanism include Julian Huxley's *Religion without Revelation* (1927), Charles Francis Potter's *Humanism: A New Religion* (1930), the first Humanist Manifesto (1933), and John Dewey's *A Common Faith* (1934). A century ago, the Unitarian and Universalist traditions served as havens for various types of religious humanism. Since the 1962 merger of the groups in the United States, the Unitarian Universalist movement has continued to be one of the principal environments for vibrant religious humanist exploration and expression. Humanistic Judaism, exemplified in the work of North American rabbi Sherwin T. Wine, signer of Humanist Manifesto II (1973) and author of *Judaism beyond God* (1995), represents the successful incorporation of the religious humanist spirit into the fabric of a particular religious tradition.

Religious humanism values reason, science, intellectual freedom, social and moral progress, the dignity of each human being, and, in the words of John Dewey, not "religion" but the "religious"—a dimension of experience, within the bounds of nature, that includes the enrichment of the human spirit through love, joy, creativity, and the expansion of consciousness. Nonreligious or secular humanists share the same set of essential principles but balk at the category of "religious," finding it a useless carryover from an outdated worldview. They seek and support a definitive break with the supernatural mindset and the acceleration and extension of the secularization process. The deepest dimensions of human experience—awe, imagination, commitment, and hope—necessitate, they say, no gesture of reverence or nostalgia toward religious ideas or instincts.

Secular humanism gained notoriety during the rise of the U.S. New Religious Right in the 1970s and '80s. Philosopher and publishing entrepreneur Paul Kurtz, author of *A Secular Humanist Declaration* (originally published in 1980), became a prominent spokesperson for the perspective. After Ayatollah Khomeini's 1979–1980 Islamic Revolution in Iran, many secular humanists saw Christian and Muslim neofundamentalisms as twin threats to human freedom and progress. The second and third Humanist

Manifestos (1973 and 2003) signaled a determined departure from religious humanism. Today, many nonreligious individuals self-identify as humanists because of lingering negative stereotypes associated with atheism and agnosticism. Ironically, secular humanism is sometimes recognized by proponents and outside observers as a religion. Some colleges and universities support humanist chaplaincies. Some include humanist student organizations among their campus religious groups. *The Good Book: A Humanist Bible* (2011), by atheist philosopher A. C. Grayling, arranges wisdom from humanist writers from different historical periods and cultures in a scripture-like chapter-and-verse format.

The demographics of humanism are daunting. Humanists of all kinds are difficult to count and can fall through the cracks of census data and religious identity surveys and opinion polls. Religious humanists exist inside an untold number of religious bodies worldwide, from Buddhism to Wicca. They often prize and protect relative anonymity to avoid harassment or expulsion. Unaffiliated religious humanists and many secular humanists frequently pursue their interests in relative isolation. Atheopagans, humanist pagans, and self-designated atheist witches sometimes live and work in the blurry boundary land between secularity and spirituality, religious and nonreligious. The important scholarship of Anthony B. Pinn, editor of *By These Hands: A Documentary History of African American Humanism* (2001), has given greater visibility to U.S. Black humanists, historically excluded from both the African American religious enclave and the traditionally white-dominated humanist establishment.

Since the twentieth century, humanist organizations have been gradually proliferating and building a base of statistical data. The American Humanist Association is reported to have thirty-two thousand members in the United States and supports four subdivisions: Black Humanist Alliance, Feminist Humanist Alliance, Latinx Humanist Alliance, and LGBTQ Humanist Alliance. The Society for Humanistic Judaism has ten thousand members. Humanists International represents over 180 humanist organizations. Estimates of the global humanist population, often blurring the various categories of atheism, agnosticism, nonreligion, and liberal religion, are notoriously unreliable.

Whatever their numerical status, humanists are currently active in literature, education, the arts, entertainment, politics, business, science, humanitarian causes, and advocacy for women's rights, LGBTQ+ rights, reproductive rights, racial justice, environmentalism, and other social reform efforts. For centuries, humanists have been viewed with suspicion by guardians of religious establishments and single-idea totalitarian regimes. Critics have focused on humanism's alleged elitism and its penchant for scientism, a perceived tendency to overemphasize the intellectual dimension of life, especially the role and methods of the natural sciences. Animal rights activists and transhumanists find in all forms of humanism an unexamined and unwarranted speciesism, or the presumption of human uniqueness.

See also: Amsterdam Declarations; Atheopaganism; Humanist Manifestos; Humanist of the Year; Kurtz, Paul

Further Reading

Copson, Andrew, and A. C. Grayling, eds. *The Wiley Blackwell Handbook of Humanism*. Oxford: John Wiley and Sons, 2015.

Flew, Antony. *Atheistic Humanism*. Buffalo, NY: Prometheus Books, 1993.

Franklin, R. William, and Joseph M. Shaw. *The Case for Christian Humanism*. Grand Rapids, MI: Eerdmans, 1991.

Gibbons, Kendyl L. R., and William R. Murry, eds. *Humanist Voices in Unitarian Universalism*. Boston: Skinner House Books, 2017.

Grayling, A. C. *The Good Book: A Humanist Bible*. New York: Walker, 2011.

Grayling, A. C. *Meditations for the Humanist: Ethics for a Secular Age*. Oxford: Oxford University Press, 2002.

Green, Mark A. *Atheopaganism: An Earth-Honoring Path Rooted in Science*. Santa Rosa, CA: Green Dragon, 2019.

Hutchison, William R. *The Modernist Impulse in American Protestantism*. Durham, NC: Duke University Press, 1992.

Jardine, Lisa. *Erasmus, Man of Letters*. Princeton, NJ: Princeton University Press, 1993.

Kurtz, Paul. *Humanist Manifesto 2000: A Call for a New Planetary Humanism*. Amherst, NY: Prometheus Books, 2000.

Kurtz, Paul, ed. *Humanist Manifestos I and II*. Buffalo, NY: Prometheus Books, 1973.

Kurtz, Paul. *A Secular Humanist Declaration*. Buffalo, NY: Prometheus Books, 1983. Originally published in 1980.

Law, Stephen. *Humanism: A Very Short Introduction*. Oxford: Oxford University Press, 2011.

Modras, Ronald. *Ignatian Humanism: A Dynamic Spirituality for the 21st Century*. Chicago: Loyola Press, 2004.

Murry, William R. *Reason and Reverence: Religious Humanism for the 21st Century*. Boston: Skinner House Books, 2006.

Norman, Robert. *On Humanism*. London: Routledge, 2004.

Olds, Mason. *American Religious Humanism*. Rev. ed. Minneapolis: Fellowship of Religious Humanists, 1996.

Pinn, Anthony B. *African American Humanist Principles: Living and Thinking Like the Children of Nimrod*. New York: Palgrave MacMillan, 2004.

Pinn, Anthony B., ed. *By These Hands: A Documentary History of African American Humanism*. New York: New York University, 2001.

Pinn, Anthony B. *The End of God-Talk: An African American Humanist Theology*. Oxford: Oxford University Press, 2012.

Pinn, Anthony B. *What Is Humanism and Why Does It Matter?* London: Routledge, 2014.

Wine, Sherwin T. *Humanistic Judaism*. Buffalo, NY: Prometheus Books, 1978.

Wine, Sherwin T. *Judaism beyond God: A Radical New Way to Be Jewish*. Hoboken, NJ: KTAV, 1996.

Humanist Manifestos

Three important documents bear the title Humanist Manifesto. Two were written in the twentieth century, one in the twenty-first. Each represents a milestone in the development of the concept of humanism. Each was drafted by a team of writers and sanctioned by a larger set of signers. Each defines humanism in its own way and seeks to distinguish humanism from other philosophical options. Each recommends humanism as the most appropriate intellectual framework for understanding human experience and for charting a satisfactory future for human beings in the context of evolving natural and social worlds. All three of the manifestos attempt to communicate for their respective generations the relevance of humanism as both a distinctive and much-needed perspective or worldview and as an energizing way of life. Today the manifestos are recognized as classics in the expanding literature of humanism, broadly conceived.

The first Humanist Manifesto, known as Humanist Manifesto I, appeared in 1933. It grew out of conversations taking place within the Humanist Fellowship of Unitarian faculty and students at the University of Chicago. Raymond Bennet Bragg and other nontheist leaders in the tradition, then known as the most liberal Protestant denomination in the United States, had been experimenting for a number of years with *humanist* as a label for their post-Christian faith. As discussions expanded beyond the Midwest and outside Unitarianism, the idea of a common statement surfaced and gained support. Based on drafts by University of Chicago professor Roy Wood Sellers, the statement took the form of a public manifesto and was published in the Humanist Fellowship's magazine, the *New Humanist*.

Four pages in length and organized in nineteen paragraphs, the Humanist Manifesto argued that the time had come for a sea change in religious consciousness and moral behavior. The rise of science, the maturation of the democratic process, and the expansion of human awareness of the universe through improvements in education and technology, the writers maintained, called for comparable adjustments in religion. Unlike the manifestos to follow, Humanist Manifesto I made the case for a specifically religious humanism—in tune with modern convictions and free from the restraints of premodern creeds and codes.

Humanist Manifesto I addressed fifteen points or theses. They include affirmation of the uncreated status of the universe, all things belonging to the full human experience, the scientific method and mindset, a cooperative social and economic order, the place of humanity in the flux and flow of nature, and the never-ending quest for the good life. Ideas and behaviors rejected include traditional theism, the notion of the supernatural, the distinction between sacred and secular, the dualism of mind and body, consumerism, and any system of religion that does not foster human creativity and joy.

Thirty-four scholars, writers, clergy, and editors, nearly half of whom were Unitarians, signed the document. Notable endorsers included Unitarian minister Charles Francis Potter, advisor to Clarence Darrow during the 1925 Scopes trial and author of *Humanism: A New Religion* (1930), and Columbia University philosophers John Herman Randall and John Dewey. Often identified as an important contributor to the manifesto, Dewey expanded the argument for religion beyond church and dogma in his *A Common Faith*, published a year later.

Forty years after the original manifesto, a second Humanist Manifesto, three times as long, was issued by another group of signers, three times as big. Between Humanist Manifesto I and Humanist Manifesto II (1973), World War II had changed the world, and the Cold War was changing the nature of war and augmenting its threat to all life on the planet. Along with the civil rights movement in the United States, the rise of new, independent, postcolonial nations around the world, and the global spread of a cultural revolution challenging long-held views on race, sex, citizenship, and happiness, these circumstances created a context requiring a new statement of humanist values.

While the first manifesto yearned for a world aligned with the principles of modern science, Humanist Manifesto II acknowledged that science could be the agent of grave evil. Humanist Manifesto II, no longer tolerant of religious humanism, presented a vision of humanism at once chastened and emboldened. It was humbled by the recognition of the failure of the historical process to deliver fully the dreams of progress spawned by the Enlightenment and by the acknowledgment of the fact that the abandonment of theism itself does not necessarily lead to the improvement of human life. It was inspired by social changes that made individual-based ethics, reproductive freedom, participatory democracy, racial harmony, and international cooperation genuine and desirable possibilities for the present and near future. Though distancing itself from the religious humanism of Humanist Manifesto I, it nevertheless referred to the humanist vision as a "living and growing faith."

The principal architects of Humanist Manifesto II were Edwin Wilson, former executive director of the American Humanist Association, and Paul Kurtz, longtime editor of *The Humanist* and founder of Prometheus Books, America's premier publishing house dedicated to disseminating works of atheism, agnosticism, philosophy, and science. Signers, numbering over one hundred and representing the United States, Canada, and European countries, included biochemist and prolific writer Isaac Asimov; analytic philosopher Antony Flew; behaviorist psychologist B. F. Skinner; Mordecai Kaplan, founder of Reconstructionist Judaism; and Sherwin Wine, founder of Humanistic Judaism. Additional signers included Joseph Fletcher, atheist Episcopal priest and author of *Situation Ethics* (1966); Betty Friedan, author of *The Feminine Mystique* (1963) and founder of the National Organization for Women (NOW); and Julian Huxley, author of *Religion without Revelation* (1927) and former head of the United Nations Educational Scientific and Cultural Organization (UNESCO).

Humanist Manifesto III, entitled "Humanism and Its Aspirations," appeared in 2003. The shortest of the three documents, it featured nearly one hundred signatories, including Oxford biologist and future New Atheist Richard Dawkins; Arun Gandhi, grandson of Mohandas K. Gandhi; filmmaker Oliver Stone; novelist Kurt Vonnegut; twenty-two Nobel laureates; and the only individual who had also signed Manifestos I and II: Unitarian Universalist minister Lester Mondale, author of *The Unitarian Way of Life* (1943).

The breadth of its vision, the skillful balance of its interests, and the clarity and concision of its prose make "Humanism and Its Aspirations" arguably the most effective of the three manifestos. Defining humanism as a "lifestance" shaped by reason, compassion, and experience, it affirms the rights, responsibilities, and dignity of the human person in society while giving equal attention to humanity's biological placement and moral role in the planetary ecosystem. Less concerned with the burden of the religious past, it portrays wonder, awe, and joy as natural dimensions of the human existence. It is the only manifesto to mention death.

The Humanist Manifestos, an open canon of humanist testimony, have been promoted and propagated by the descendant of the Humanist Fellowship: the American Humanist Association (AHA), organized in 1941. The title "Humanist Manifesto" is now a trademark of the AHA. All three manifestos were products of English-speaking North American culture. Despite the growing diversity of the supporting bodies, the figures associated with the documents' creation and circulation have been predominantly white and male, virtually all products of the Western educational establishment. Critics, even those sympathetic with the texts' aims and convictions, have maintained that the universalism informing the texts minimizes the importance of ethnicity, class, and gender. The words *feminist* and *feminism* do not appear in any of the documents. None addresses issues of animal rights, earth justice, transhumanism, or artificial intelligence. Secular humanists find the manifestos too accommodating to religion. Landmarks in the history of a unique and significant point of view, the manifestos represent the assets, limitations, and growing edges of the unfinished project called humanism.

See also: Amsterdam Declarations; Atheism, New; Darrow, Clarence; Flew, Antony; Humanism; Huxleys, The; Kurtz, Paul

Further Reading

Gibbons, Kendyl L. R., and William R. Murry, eds. *Humanist Voices in Unitarian Universalism.* Boston: Skinner House Books, 2017.

Kurtz, Paul. *Humanist Manifesto 2000: A Call for a New Planetary Humanism.* Amherst, NY: Prometheus Books, 2000.

Kurtz, Paul, ed. *Humanist Manifestos I and II.* Buffalo, NY: Prometheus Books, 1973.

Kurtz, Paul. *A Secular Humanist Declaration.* Buffalo, NY: Prometheus Books, 1983.

Law, Stephen. *Humanism: A Very Short Introduction.* Oxford: Oxford University Press, 2011.

Olds, Mason. *American Religious Humanism*. Rev. ed. Minneapolis, MN: Fellowship of Religious Humanists, 1996.

Schulz, William F. *Making the Manifesto: The Birth of Religious Humanism*. Boston: Skinner House, 2002.

Wilson, Edwin H. *The Genesis of a Humanist Manifesto*. Amherst, NY: Humanist Press, 1995.

Humanist of the Year

Humanist of the Year is an annual award of distinction bestowed by the American Humanist Association (AHA). Founded in 1941, the Washington, DC–based nonprofit is the most prominent humanist education, support, and advocacy organization in the United States. The Humanist of the Year award recognizes an individual notable for the exemplification and promotion of humanist values, broadly defined. Nominations are solicited from the Association's membership, and final decisions are made by a selection committee appointed by the group's board of directors.

The award was inaugurated in 1953 and has been conferred without interruption into the twenty-first century. It is publicly bestowed at the AHA Annual Conference, which features a keynote address delivered by the recipient. Full texts of the award speeches are subsequently published in the AHA's *Humanist* magazine.

Humanists of the Year have included people from a variety of national and cultural backgrounds, the majority of whom have come from North America. Honorees represent a wide range of professions and vocations—from science and scholarship to social activism, art, literature, politics, entertainment, and business. The AHA's first Humanist of the Year was University of Chicago physiologist Anton J. Carlson, one of the signers of the original 1933 Humanist Manifesto. The 2020 award went to Jared Huffman, at the time the only openly humanist member of the U.S. Congress, founder of the Congressional Freethought Caucus. Women recipients include birth-control educator Margaret Sanger, feminist leaders Betty Friedan and Gloria Steinem, and writers Margaret Atwood, Joyce Carol Oates, and Alice Walker. The full list of awardees is a roll call of eminent thinkers and activists who have advanced the goals of intellectual freedom and secular society throughout the twentieth and early twenty-first centuries. The AHA also presents five other annual awards: the Isaac

Asimov Science Award, the Humanist Arts Award, the LGBTQ Humanist Award, the Humanist Media Award, and the Lifetime Achievement Award. Other organizations that confer an annual Humanist of the Year award include Harvard University's Humanist Chaplaincy and the Council of Australian Humanist Societies. The Unitarian Universalist (UU) Humanist Association honors a UU Person of the Year.

See also: Dawkins, Richard; Dennett, Daniel C.; Feminism, Atheism and Agnosticism and; Humanism; Humanist Manifestos; Huxleys, The; Organizations, Atheist and Agnostic; Rushdie, Salman

Hurston, Zora Neale

Zora Neale Hurston (1891–1960) was a gifted novelist, playwright, essayist, short-story writer, and anthropologist. *Their Eyes Were Watching God* (1937), cited by Pulitzer Prize–winning author Alice Walker as the most influential book in her intellectual development, is frequently identified as the first feminist novel published by an African American author. Largely overlooked during her multifaceted career, Hurston is today honored as an unrepeatable act in the U.S. literary experience and one of the most significant contributors to the heritage of Black humanist thought.

The daughter of a schoolteacher and a bivocational Baptist preacher, Hurston was born in Alabama and raised in Florida. Her life span coincided with that of Jim Crow racial segregation, but her early years in Eatonville, Florida, the first incorporated Black township in the United States, allowed her to observe firsthand African American leadership and self-determination. Family setbacks, however, interrupted her education. She worked her way through high school, nearly a decade older than her fellow students, and graduated from Howard University and Barnard College, where she studied with the highly esteemed German American anthropologist Franz Boas, internationally known for his theory of cultural relativism. After several years of work in education, music, and theater, in the 1930s Hurston pursued doctoral studies in anthropology at Columbia. Over the course of her life, she worked for the Federal Writers Project and served as a story consultant for the film industry in Hollywood. She received a Guggenheim Fellowship, Howard University's distinguished alumni award, and an honorary doctorate from Morgan State College (now University).

Despite her remarkable accomplishments in literature and scholarship, Hurston died impoverished and was buried in an unmarked grave. Thanks to an ongoing revival of interest in her life and legacy, her achievements in fiction and drama, including her major contributions to the famed Harlem Renaissance movement, are now a matter of record in American cultural history. Critics and fans rank her novels *Jonah's Gourd Vine* (1934), *Moses, Man of the Mountain* (1941), and *Seraph on the Suwanee* (1948), along with *Their Eyes Were Watching God*, as classic examples of the best of the twentieth-century artistic imagination.

Hurston's field research in anthropology and folklore is still underappreciated in academic circles. She studied hoodoo and vernacular spiritual healing rites in the U.S. South, Jamaica, Haiti, and Honduras, and published her original findings in learned journals, popular magazines, and two nonfiction books, *Mules and Men* (1935) and *Tell My Horse* (1938). Her intimate acquaintance with the world of charismatic religious leadership and ecstatic ritual performance is dramatically apparent in the vivid portraits of Black church life that enrich her novels and stories.

Hurston grew up in an insular culture saturated with religious faith and fervor—the "faith of the fathers" that W. E. B. Du Bois characterized in *The Souls of Black Folk* (1903) as a potent mix of preacher, music, and frenzy. Her own views on religion, frequently anthologized in print and electronic humanist collections, are best found in the chapter titled "Religion" in her autobiography *Dust Tracks on the Road* (1942). Describing herself as a person "born with God in the house," she narrates the evolution of a mind marked by both the erosion of belief and deep empathy for those who cannot cease to believe. Like many of her generation, she was assailed by questions and doubts, especially during her college years. The cultural relativism of her mentor and her chosen field of specialization, coupled with her temporary exile from the South, arguably played a considerable role as well. Hurston said hers was a worldview grounded in matter, "ever changing, ever moving, but never lost," yet not an ideology hostile to what many call spirit. As she put it, she neither prayed nor professed a creed but, due to an uncommon marriage of courage and respect, never denied the consolation others find in those "words around a wish."

The ongoing Hurston renaissance is a literary cottage industry, engaging experts and committed enthusiasts. It dates back to a 1975 *Ms.* magazine article by Walker, recognized herself nearly two decades later as the American Humanist Association's Humanist of the Year. Searching for the site of Hurston's earthly remains in the untended grounds of Fort Pierce,

Florida's Garden of Heavenly Rest, Walker rediscovered a preeminent, though thwarted, predecessor and an unexpected humanist ancestor.

See also: Atheism and Agnosticism, African American; Du Bois, W. E. B.; Humanism; Hutchinson, Sikivu; Pinn, Anthony B.

Further Reading

Boyd, Valerie. *Wrapped in Rainbows: The Life of Zora Neale Hurston.* New York: Scribner, 2011.

Du Bois, W. E. B. *The Souls of Black Folk.* New York: Penguin Classics, 1989.

Hemenway, Robert E. *Zora Neale Hurston: A Literary Biography.* Urbana: University of Illinois Press, 1980.

Hurston, Zora Neale. *Dust Tracks on the Road: An Autobiography.* New York: HarperCollins, 1996.

Hurston, Zora Neale. *Jonah's Gourd Vine.* New York: Harper Perennial, 1990.

Hurston, Zora Neale. *Moses, Man of the Mountain.* New York: Harper Perennial, 2009.

Hurston, Zora Neale. *Mules and Men.* New York: HarperCollins, 2009.

Hurston, Zora Neale. *Seraph on the Suwanee.* New York: Harper Perennial, 2008.

Hurston, Zora Neale. *Tell My Horse: Voodoo and Life in Haiti and Jamaica.* New York: Harper Perennial, 1990.

Hurston, Zora Neale. *Their Eyes Were Watching God.* Urbana: University of Illinois Press, 1978.

Schweitzer, Bernard. *Hating God: The Untold Story of Misotheism.* Oxford: Oxford University Press, 2010.

Walker, Alice, ed. *I Love Myself When I am Laughing . . . and Then again When I Am Looking Mean and Impressive: A Zora Neale Hurston Reader.* New York: Feminist Press of the City University of New York, 1979.

Walker, Alice. *In Search of Our Mothers' Gardens: Womanist Prose.* New York: Harvest, 1983.

Hutchinson, Sikivu

Sikivu Hutchinson (b. 1969) is an award-winning humanities scholar, critical theorist, educator, novelist, playwright, and feminist social critic. An advocate for the rights of LGBTQ+ people and nonreligious people of color, she has published unparalleled analyses of U.S. racial injustice, the African American religious establishment, and the dominance of white male elites in contemporary atheist, humanist, and secular movements.

Especially notable for her support of freethinking organizers and agitators in the Black community, Hutchinson is a provocative contributor to conversations about the intersectionality of race, religion, and gender in twenty-first-century American culture.

Hutchinson received her PhD in performance studies from New York University and has been active in theater and film since the release of her *White Nights, Black Paradise* (2015), a novel/play on Jim Jones's Peoples Temple and the 1978 Jonestown mass suicide/mass murder that left over nine hundred people dead. Her science fiction play *NARCOLEPSY, INC.* (2018), about a gender-nonconforming African American woman scientist in a Reagan-era capitalist theocracy, debuted as an acclaimed web series in 2019. Her three best-known works of nonfiction—*Moral Combat* (2011), *Godless Americana* (2013), and *Humanists in the Hood* (2020)—address the lived experiences of atheists and agnostics of color facing the double challenge of the Black church's legacy of social conservatism and the enduring effects of the Religious Right's impact on U.S. politics and domestic policy.

Moral Combat introduced Hutchinson to activists and allies in the nonreligious community and to journalists covering the unprecedented rise of unbelief in America. The distinctive concerns animating the study have continued to permeate her subsequent publications and public presentations: the unique and uneasy place of atheists and agnostics in the African American community, the oppressive social and economic legacy of white-dominated Christianity in the American experience, and the ways in which the Black church has been complicit in the perpetuation of popular Christianity's antagonism toward intellectual freedom and sexual self-determination. Hutchinson principally focuses on the rarely acknowledged trials facing the person of color who questions, doubts, or rejects the religious and supernatural worldview still infusing many minority communities across the nation. Her reliance upon the heritage of African American humanism—from Frederick Douglass and W. E. B. Du Bois to the writers of the Harlem Renaissance, Alice Walker, and a new generation of secular Black college students—grants her current-affairs scholarship a broad sense of historical perspective.

Hutchinson has gained notoriety for her critique of classism and sexism in the New Atheist movement. She argues that the highly publicized case against Christianity advanced by Richard Dawkins, Daniel C. Dennett, Sam Harris, Christopher Hitchens, and others has been ineffective in reaching Black and brown people, especially women of color. It overemphasizes the Christian tradition's alleged resistance to science and fails to confront the religion's record of racism, sexism, homophobia, and colonialism. Any criticism of Christianity, she maintains, that begins with abstract questions of belief and not down-to-earth experiences of injustice betrays a perspective of white male privilege, out of touch with reality, curiously mirroring the churches' historic bent toward otherworldliness.

Hutchinson is active as a blogger, media commentator, university instructor, and conference speaker. She is founder of Black Skeptics of Los Angeles and the Women's Leadership Project, cofounder of the People of Color Beyond Faith network, editor of the blog blackfemlens.org, and a senior fellow of the Institute for Humanist Studies. In 2013, Secular Woman Inc. named her Secular Woman of the Year. She received the 2015 Humanist Innovator Award from the nonprofit Foundation Beyond Belief, the 2016 Backbone Award from the Secular Student Alliance, and, along with Ijeoma Oluo and Mandisa Thomas, the Humanist Chaplaincy at Harvard's 2020 Humanist of the Year Award. The 2012 African Americans for Humanism national billboard campaign, featuring images of Hutchinson and novelist/folklorist Zora Neale Hurston side by side, was an extraordinary tribute to her extraordinary career.

See also: Atheism and Agnosticism, African American; Atheism, New; Du Bois, W. E. B.; Feminism, Atheism and Agnosticism and; Hurston, Zora Neale; Pinn, Anthony B.

Further Reading

Hutchinson, Sikivu. *Godless Americana: Race and Religious Rebels*. Los Angeles: Infidel Books, 2013.

Hutchinson, Sikivu. *Humanists in the Hood: Unapologetically Black, Feminist, and Heretical*. Durham, NC: Pitchstone, 2020.

Hutchinson, Sikivu. *Moral Combat: Black Atheists, Gender Politics, and the Values Wars*. Los Angeles: Infidel Books, 2011.

Hutchinson, Sikivu. *Rock 'n' Roll Heretic: The Life and Times of Rory Tharpe*. Los Angeles: Infidel Books, 2018.

Hutchinson, Sikivu. *White Nights, Black Paradise*. Los Angeles: Infidel Books, 2015.

Huxleys, The

The Huxleys were a prominent family in British intellectual and literary life during the nineteenth and twentieth centuries. A family of talented and creative scientists, philosophers, novelists, and intellectual adventurers, they were deeply involved in the cultural debates of their respective generations and enormously effective in shaping public opinion. Three members of the family made notable contributions to the history of modern atheism and agnosticism: Thomas Henry Huxley, crusader for the theory of evolution and inventor of the term *agnostic*, and two of his grandsons—Julian Huxley, biologist, educator, public intellectual, and signer of the second Humanist Manifesto (1973), and Aldous Huxley, whose internationally acclaimed novels, essays, and screenplays made him an incomparable force in twentieth-century literature and culture.

Thomas Henry Huxley (1825–1895) is best known to history as "Darwin's Bulldog," a moniker he earned or gave himself promoting Charles Darwin's provocative new theories after the 1859 publication of *On the Origin of Species*. Sixteen years younger than Darwin, he pursued a career that was, in broad stokes, strikingly similar to Darwin's. Both inaugurated their adult lives with a multiyear sea voyage in the Southern Hemisphere; both inhabited the Victorian role of "gentleman naturalist," a foreign concept to present-day, university-trained professional scientists; and both stimulated intellectual controversy and sparked a new way of thinking about science, its meaning, and its place in society. Both also functioned as catalysts in the breakdown of Britain's nineteenth-century Christian consensus.

Like Darwin, Huxley participated in a Royal Navy transoceanic coastal survey project. On board the HMS *Rattlesnake* in the South Pacific, he served on the medical staff and conducted extensive studies of marine life from 1846 to 1850. For the rest of his life, he was recognized as one of Britain's outstanding experts in comparative anatomy. He taught natural history (today, natural science) and published numerous articles in professional medical and scientific journals. He wrote one of the first positive reviews of Darwin's *Origin*, and his *Evidence as to Man's Place in Nature* (1863) arguably prepared the way for Darwin's *Descent of Man* (1871). As a steadfast proponent for the theory of evolution, Huxley participated in written and public debates, most notably with the Anglican Bishop of Oxford, Samuel Wilberforce—a contest that, according to popular legend, Huxley won handily.

Huxley occupies a special place in the history of skepticism and unbelief due to his introduction of *agnostic* and *agnosticism* into the modern lexicon. Ironically, he coined the terms because of his impatience with ideological labels. As he indicated in his 1889 essay "Agnosticism," he did not intend to name a position on the spectrum of responses to the question of God. Agnosticism, he said, represented a more general approach to all questions facing human beings—that is, not itself an answer, and certainly not a creed or a flight into indecision, but a disciplined way of thinking through problems, a posture of openness before the unknown and possibly unknowable. For Huxley, the true agnostic was one who put faith in the light of reason as far as it would go and respected the questions reason could not fully illuminate.

In the estimation of the next generation, Huxley, like Darwin, was a giant in the ranks of eminent Victorians. His son Leonard, at the turn of the century, memorialized him with a two-volume *Life and Letters of T. H. Huxley* (1900). His eldest grandchild Julian followed his iconic grandfather into a distinguished science career and, as an internationally known public figure, addressed similar issues of faith and doubt and imagination.

Julian Huxley (1887–1975) studied at Eton College and Balliol College, Oxford. He specialized in zoology, sharing his grandfather's interest in sea creatures, and excelled in the study of birds. He taught at Oxford and King's College and also briefly in the United States. He brought forward-looking leadership to the London Zoo, modernizing the august institution. His chief contributions to science were his many eloquent and accessible books for a broad inquiring readership: *Evolution: The Modern Synthesis* (1942), *Evolutionary Ethics* (1943), *Evolution as a Process* (1954), and *Charles Darwin and His World* (1965). As founding director-general of the United Nations Educational Scientific and Cultural Organization (UNESCO), he brought his evolutionary vision to bear on global issues of social and intellectual progress. He was a champion for birth control and supported the decriminalization of homosexuality. Though he supported some forms of eugenics in Britain, he condemned Nazi racism and its corruption of scientific integrity.

Regarding questions of belief, he identified with scientific humanism and, in good family tradition, the idea he dubbed with his own neologism: *transhumanism*—a mental picture of what humans could become in future phases of evolution. Though he did not share the French Jesuit paleontologist's commitment to Christianity, he applauded Pierre Teilhard de Chardin's attempts to combine Catholic faith and evolutionary theory, especially as seen in the priest-scientist's *The Phenomenon of Man* (1959). Julian communicated his own philosophy in *Religion without Revelation* (1927), an experiment in the fusion of science and spirituality without recourse to God, scripture, or the supernatural. The American Humanist Association named him Humanist of the Year in 1962, and the British

Humanist Association made him its first president. He was one of the founders of the International Humanist and Ethical Union, now Humanists International. Throughout his long life, he embodied the ideal behind his grandfather's most famous addition to the English language: a mind open to change and wonder.

Julian's youngest brother, Aldous Huxley (1894–1963), also made an impressive impact on the development of atheism and agnosticism. He, too, was educated at Eton and at Balliol, Oxford, and demonstrated exceptional intellectual capability early on. Though sharing the family interest in science, he concentrated in English literature, forgoing a medical career largely due to the debilitating eye disease he suffered as a teenager, a harrowing experience that left him visually challenged for the rest of his life.

His extraordinary literary success is well known. A partial list of his novels alone evokes virtually the entire history of twentieth-century literature: *Crome Yellow* (1921), *Point Counter Point* (1928), *Brave New World* (1932), *Eyeless in Gaza* (1936), and *The Devils of Loudun* (1952), to name fewer than half. In his fiction, poetry, plays, screenplays, and essays, Aldous Huxley offered a candid portrait of the promise and perils of modern science, the ferocious beauty and erotic madness of modern society, the obscenity of modern war, the horror of the impending ecological crisis, and the metaphysical homelessness of the modern soul. A severe critic of what he identified as modernity's twin dangers of overpopulation and overorganization (in government, business, industry, and education), he was a prophet of constructive nonviolence in a century of endless war. He edited a one-of-a-kind *Encyclopedia of Pacifism* (1937). When applying for U.S. citizenship during the Cold War, a goal he eventually abandoned, he insisted that his refusal to bear arms for the country was based on philosophical, not religious, grounds.

His philosophical path led him to destinations his grandfather could have never foreseen. Like so many of his generation, Aldous Huxley was an exile from the pieties and certainties of the Western religious legacy and from what a character in *Brave New World* refers to as the "thing called God." At the same time, he found meaning in the world's mystical traditions, especially modern variants of undogmatic Hindu wisdom, which were only then beginning to take root in the Western world. These pursuits he coupled with an interest in the spiritual potential of psychedelic drugs mescaline and LSD. *The Perennial Philosophy* (1945) and *The Doors of Perception* (1954) became unofficial scriptures of the emerging youth counterculture—with singer/songwriter Jim Morrison borrowing part of the second title (which Huxley himself had appropriated from William Blake's *The Marriage of Heaven and Hell*) for the name of his legendary 1960s rock band.

The press once dubbed Aldous Huxley "the man who hates God." His, by his own admission, was an unscripted, reverent agnosticism. The honest voyager of the unknown, he said in "Variations on a Philosopher" (1950), must not set out convinced that it is already known or known to be wholly unknowable. He called himself an agnostic who aspired to be a gnostic.

See also: Agnosticism; Darwin, Charles; Humanist Manifestos; Humanist of the Year; Organizations, Atheist and Agnostic

Further Reading

Bedford, Sybille. *Aldous Huxley: A Biography*. New York: Alfred A. Knopf; Harper and Row, 1974.

Bibby, Cyril. *Scientist Extraordinary: The Life and Scientific Work of Thomas Henry Huxley, 1825–1895*. New York: St. Martin's Press, 1972.

Castell, Alburey, ed. *Thomas Henry Huxley: Selections from the Essays of T. H. Huxley*. New York: Appleton-Century-Crofts, 1948.

Clark, Ronald W. *The Huxleys*. New York: McGraw-Hill, 1968.

Huxley, Aldous. *Brave New World*. New York: Harper Perennial, 2006.

Huxley, Aldous. *Themes and Variations*. London: Chatto and Windus, 1950.

Huxley, Julian. *Religion without Revelation*. Westport, CT: Greenwood Press, 1979.

Waters, C. Kenneth, and Albert Van Helden, eds. *Julian Huxley: Biologist and Statesman of Science*. College Station, TX: Texas A&M University Press, 2010.

I

Ingersoll, Robert Green

The name Robert Green Ingersoll (1833–1899), lawyer, politician, and public speaker, has long been synonymous with a distinctively nineteenth-century tradition of American free thought. A member of neither the academy nor the literary guild, he occupied a position in U.S. intellectual culture in the gap between serious writer and eccentric crank—which, for over a century, has left his reputation in limbo between half-hearted respect and near ridicule. His contemporaries confirmed his unique standing with memorable but affably dismissive nicknames—most of which live on into the present, thanks to his empathetic biographers and visitors to the Robert Green Ingersoll Birthplace Museum in Dresden, New York: Great Agnostic, American Infidel, Immortal Infidel, Pagan Politician, and Professional Atheist. Ingersoll's blend of homespun skepticism and high-flung oratory makes him a bridge figure between the urbanity of the Enlightenment *philosophe* and the twenty-first-century god-free individual whose nonreligion has little or no relation to Christian faith or Victorian doubt.

Born in the Finger Lakes region of upstate New York, Ingersoll grew up in an age of religious revivals, competing sects, and mounting utopian fervor. His Presbyterian minister father moved the family several times, perhaps due to antagonism toward his abolitionist sympathies, still unpopular in many parts of the North. Like Abraham Lincoln, Ingersoll was self-educated, becoming a lifelong lover of books and the spoken word, especially Shakespeare and the Scottish romantic poet Robert Burns. He passed the Illinois bar when he was twenty-one years old. During the Civil War, Ingersoll served as colonel in a voluntary U.S. cavalry regiment until his capture by Confederate forces. He entered politics, aligning with the new Republican Party, was elected state attorney for Illinois, but lost his later bid for the governorship. The height of his political career was his much-publicized "Plumed Knight" speech at the 1876 Republican presidential convention in Cincinnati.

Ingersoll was notable for his success as a traveling lecturer, promoting intellectual freedom, religious skepticism, and strict separation of church and state at a time when the Protestant ethos dominated U.S. culture, especially politics and the public schools. He made a name for himself as a cross-country orator, mocking discrepancies in the Bible, exposing religion's shameless moral record, arguing for acceptance of the then-new Darwinian science, debating high-profile Christian clergy, and defending the honor of Thomas Paine, Revolutionary-era author of *Common Sense* (1776), *Rights of Man* (1791–1792), and *Age of Reason* (1794, 1795, 1807)—the man Theodore Roosevelt called a "filthy little atheist." Though he garnered many adversaries, some who claimed he died by suicide or pleading for a priest, his audiences always applauded his stirring and patriotic rhetoric and generously enriched his handlers and hosts.

Ingersoll's most famous speeches, now collected in the twelve volumes of his *Complete Works*, included "The Gods," "Heretics and Heresies," "Sabbath Superstition," and "Some Mistakes of Moses." He helped to popularize Thomas Henry Huxley's new word, *agnostic*, in America but insisted he made no distinction between atheism and agnosticism. He campaigned for the rights of women, African Americans, immigrants, laborers, and spouses seeking divorce. He also devoted much energy to opposing the Gilded Age's rising xenophobia, blasphemy laws, and the new federal Comstock obscenity and chastity laws that threatened both the advance of safe and reliable birth control and the poetry of Walt Whitman, another of Ingersoll's heroes.

Biographer and free-thought advocate Susan Jacoby identifies Ingersoll's three main achievements and underscores their enduring relevance for the twenty-first century: emphasizing the true meaning of science as an open-ended exercise in candid curiosity, confronting the repressive nature of religion without restraint or apology, and cultivating a living memory of the daring forerunners of modern unbelief. Ingersoll was saddled with a reputation as one of America's archetypal oddballs and was eclipsed by the later rise of Clarence Darrow—recognized after the 1925 Scopes trial as the nation's dissenter in chief. Ingersoll stands out as a crucial figure in a period of rapid social change, when the country needed a creative and winsome communicator who could translate new progressive ideas into the language of ordinary people.

See also: Agnosticism; Darrow, Clarence; Darwin, Charles; Huxleys, The; Jacoby, Susan

Further Reading

Greeley, Roger E. *Ingersoll: Immortal Infidel*. Buffalo, NY: Prometheus Books, 1977.

Ingersoll, Robert Green. *The Complete Works of Robert G. Ingersoll*. 12 vols. New York: Dresden, 1901.

Jacoby, Susan. *Freethinkers: A History of American Secularism*. New York: Holt, 2004.

Jacoby, Susan. *The Great Agnostic: Robert Ingersoll and American Freethought*. New Haven, CT: Yale University Press, 2013.

Larson, Orvin. *American Infidel: Robert G. Ingersoll*. Madison, WI: Freedom from Religion Foundation. 1993.

Plummer, Mark A. *Robert G. Ingersoll: Peoria's Pagan Politician*. Macomb: Western Illinois Monograph Series, 1984.

Smith, Frank. *Robert G. Ingersoll: A Life*. Buffalo, NY: Prometheus Books, 1991.

Turner, James. *Without God, without Creed: The Origins of Unbelief in America*. Baltimore, MD: Johns Hopkins University Press, 1985.

"In God We Trust"

"In God We Trust" is the official motto of the United States. It appears on all forms of U.S. currency and on the nation's Great Seal. The phrase is also the official motto of the state of Florida, a number of local governments, and a variety of state and municipal government agencies across the country. Since 2014, it has appeared on the State Seal of Mississippi. In various locales, with official sanction, "In God We Trust" is displayed on the facades of government buildings, the walls of public school classrooms, police and fire department vehicles, and automobile license plates. In 1956, the phrase became the authorized motto of the United States, displacing the earlier, unofficial *e pluribus unum* ("out of many, one").

The phrase's status in American culture has been largely dependent upon war and wartime national consciousness. It first appeared on U.S. coins during Abraham Lincoln's second term as president in the context of the final year of the American Civil War. In response to a campaign organized by northern Protestant clergy and churchgoers at the beginning of the war, seeking to enshrine the word *God* more prominently in public discourse, Secretary of the Treasury Salmon P. Chase issued a call for project proposals from the U.S. Mint in 1861. Three years later, Congress passed the Coinage Act, and the selected phrase "In God We Trust" was incorporated into a new design for the two-cent coin. Before the war's end, a wide range of gold and silver coins included the four-word phrase. By contrast, coins minted by the Confederate states featured an image of the Roman goddess Minerva but did not employ the word *God*. After 1938, "In God We Trust" was engraved on all U.S. coins, in both the North and South.

The phrase became the nation's official motto during the Cold War of the twentieth century. Interest in raising the profile of the phrase was fueled by surging anticommunism in U.S. society and a post–World War II revival of religious sentiment. The religious revival of the late 1940s and '50s is often seen as the high-water mark of the Protestant ethos in the American experience. Prayer and the reading of the Protestant King James Bible were conspicuous parts of public life and the culture of public schools. Churchgoing was fashionable and explicitly encouraged by government leaders. The National Advertising Council inundated the press with popular "Back to God" and "Back to Church" slogans.

The era also witnessed the increased usage of the term *Judeo-Christian* to describe the shared religious and moral heritage of the American people. Sociologist Will Herberg's *Protestant, Catholic, Jew* (1955) portrayed the three religious traditions as the three main ways to enact American identity. Radio and television religious broadcasting brought new celebrity faith leaders from these traditions to an expanding faith-friendly media audience. A new line of mass-market spiritual self-help books did too. Rabbi Joshua Liebman's *Peace of Mind* (1946), Catholic bishop Fulton J. Sheen's *Peace of Soul* (1949), evangelical preacher Billy Graham's *Peace with God* (1952), and mainline Protestant spokesperson Norman Vincent Peale's *The Power of Positive Thinking* (1952) attracted millions of middle-class readers seeking solace and assurance at the beginning of the Cold War's international arms race.

The legislation to recognize "In God We Trust" as the national motto was initiated by Charles Edward Bennett, a World War II veteran, Democratic congressman from Florida, and opponent of federal desegregation efforts in the South. The resolution received unanimous support in both chambers of Congress and was signed into law by President Dwight D. Eisenhower, a supporter of the nationwide religious revival. Two years earlier, the war hero president had approved adding "under God" to the Pledge of Allegiance. After 1956, "In God We Trust" appeared for the first time on all denominations of the nation's paper currency.

Since its acceptance, the national motto has received multiple challenges in the courts. Significant challenges include *Aronow v. United States* (1970), *O'Hair v. Blumenthal* (1978), *Lynch v. Donnelly* (1984), and the 2013 case launched by the Freedom from Religion Foundation, based in Madison, Wisconsin. All have argued that the motto violates the First Amendment of the U.S. Constitution prohibiting the establishment of religion. All legal challenges have been unsuccessful. Defenders of the motto contend that the phrase does not represent official support for any religion or mandate belief in a deity. Judicial advocates have spoken of the nation's motto as a unique form of secular ceremonial language consistent with separation of church and state and freedom of conscience. Critics maintain that the courts have seriously misunderstood the function of symbolic language, especially the rhetorical force entailed within the word *God*.

Scholars see the motto as a prime example of what sociologist Robert Bellah, borrowing from Jean-Jacques Rousseau, called America's Civil Religion, the mix of national myth and ritual, separate from the traditional and transplanted religions of the country's pluralistic landscape, that is on display in presidential rhetoric, civil holiday celebrations, federal monuments, and state funerals. Coined in time of war, the motto "In God We Trust" is a crucial sign of the ongoing battle over the complex and evolving relationship between religion and politics in U.S. society.

See also: Atheophobia; O'Hair, Madalyn Murray; "Under God"

Further Reading

Bellah, Robert N. *Beyond Belief: Essays on Religion in a Post-Traditional World.* Berkeley: University of California Press, 1991.

Bellah, Robert N. *The Broken Covenant: American Civil Religion in Time of Trial.* 2nd ed. Chicago: University of Chicago Press, 1992.

Ellwood, Robert S. *1950: Crossroads of American Religious Life.* Louisville, KY: Westminster John Knox Press, 2000.

Ellwood, Robert S. *The Fifties Spiritual Marketplace: American Religion in a Decade of Conflict.* New Brunswick, NJ: Rutgers University Press, 1997.

Kruse, Kevin M. *One Nation under God: How Corporate America Invented Christian America.* New York: Basic Books, 2015.

Warburton, Nigel. *Free Speech: A Very Short Introduction.* Oxford: Oxford University Press, 2009.

Islam, Atheism and Agnosticism in

Atheism and agnosticism are growing features of life and thought in the global Muslim community. Like Judaism and Christianity, Islam encompasses a broad spectrum of belief along with a wide range of types of doubt and disbelief, some visible, some invisible. Islam recognizes no centralized teaching authority and no systematic interpretation of scripture or doctrine. The *Shahadah*, the basic confession of faith recited by devout practitioners every day, makes a simple declaration of faith in one God, the same God professed by Jews and Christians: "There is no God but God." As in other Abrahamic traditions, however, Islamic monotheism constitutes a field, not a point—an expansive space for reflection on life's ultimate meaning and purpose. One boundary of this three-sided plane touches polytheism (envisioning many forms of the sacred). Another touches pantheism (seeing one divine presence in all things). Still another boundary marks the line where theism and atheism meet—where it is difficult to differentiate the absolute transcendence of a formless God from what seems like the absence or nonexistence of God. For the approximately 1.8 billion Muslims around the world, atheism and agnosticism are minority positions, often endangered, but in some cases real options.

Since the time of Muhammad (570–632), the Muslim community has cultivated many ways to balance fear of unbelief or misbelief with respect for the role of reason and imagination in human life. Like premodern Jews and Christians, premodern Muslims rarely encountered anything close to full and open disavowal of God. The unbelievers mentioned in the Qur'an were mainly pagans who did not accept Muhammad's message of one God, or Jews or Christians who did not acknowledge Muhammad's claim to be the final prophet of that God. The Qur'an, early Islamic teachers, and the Hadith (records of the sayings and deeds of Muhammad) did, however, confront the threats of idolatry, heresy, blasphemy, and apostasy (defined as defection from the faith). The Qur'an condemns those who have "gone from belief to disbelief" (9.66). In cultures where Islam has been dominant, punishments for public or flagrant unbelief, especially apostasy, have included arrest, torture, banishment, and death.

Despite the fear of nonconforming belief ingrained within all variants of the monotheist worldview, several factors in the Islamic tradition have encouraged diversity of belief and stimulated debate on the topic of God: the prohibition against images of God, the emphasis on the utter transcendence of God, the appreciation for the integrity of human reason, the rationalist *kalām* method of theological disputation (based on unlimited questioning), and the tradition of the ninety-nine names of God—one of which is *al-Batin*, the "Hidden One." In many ways, these elements have fostered both suspicion of overly simplistic creeds and support for the attempt to think critically about the unthinkable. Multiple heresies and rival lineages have enlivened Muslim intellectual life, and numerous philosophers and mystics have pushed against the limits of orthodox teaching, concluding that the mystery they called God is ultimately opaque. The boldest thinkers crossed into what would later be called agnosticism, at times even approaching the edges of atheism.

Two of the greatest minds in the historic Islamic intellectual tradition, both physician-philosophers, argued for the legitimate role of questioning within the life of faith and the right of reason to operate without theological restraint. The eleventh-century Ibn Sina, known to the West as Avicenna, and the twelfth-century Ibn Rushd, also known by the Latin name Averroës, affirmed the responsibility of human reason to penetrate fearlessly into the cloud of the unknown. Their position on the eternity of creation, eliminating the question of the universe's origins, destabilized the conventional idea of a creator. The poet Al-Ma'ari (d. 1058), a severe critic of injustice and hypocrisy in all religion, is sometimes described as Islam's best-known closet atheist. Two medieval schools of thought, the Dahri, asserting the eternity of matter, and the Mutazilites, freethinkers, were both accused of atheism. The case of the Sufi poet Al-Hallaj, executed in 922 for allegedly claiming to be God, exposes the confusion with which traditional Islam contemplated the blurry line distinguishing pantheism from atheism.

In the modern period, atheism and agnosticism have appeared more openly in Islamic experience. Europe's Enlightenment skepticism challenged Islam just as it did Judaism and Christianity. The process of secularization was slower in Muslim cultures, though, partly due to the absence of a campaign for religious tolerance or separation of religion and politics preceding the critical reexamination of belief in light of modern science. The big difference was the angle at which the Abrahamic traditions encountered the emerging modern worldview. Jews and Christians saw modern values as natural, though sometimes troubling, outgrowths of their shared heritage. Muslims experienced modernity as a Western export, foreign cultural cargo associated with technological brilliance and unimaginable wealth but also linked to a record of crusader and colonial aggression. Both conservative and liberal Muslims have argued with the West's

Enlightenment legacy. Traditionalists have long seen democracy, feminism, capitalism, Marxism, and post-Darwinian science as carriers of Western irreligion. Liberals trace the roots of Islamophobia and Orientalism, minimizing Islam's contributions to world civilization, to the Enlightenment's view of European superiority.

For many Muslims today, modernization of Islam means Westernization of Islam. High-profile autobiographies, such as Ayaan Hirsi Ali's *Infidel* (2013), equate the erosion of belief with conversion to Western political and social ideals. Progressive Muslims often feel torn between their aims and their cultural identities. Some reformers have called for a distinctively Muslim Enlightenment, drawing from values deeply rooted in African and Asian cultures. The terrorist attacks of September 11, 2001, have had a double effect: turning some Muslims toward nonreligion and turning others toward rediscovery of tradition.

Academic study of atheism and agnosticism in Islam is only in its beginning stages. Most observers agree that the concept of ex-Muslim atheist or agnostic currently has greater traction in the popular imagination than the notion of Muslim atheist or agnostic. Organizations such as Ex-Muslims of North America (www.exmna.org) offer support and advocacy for individuals transitioning from Sharia law to secularism. A realistic estimate of the number of unbelievers within contemporary Islam is virtually impossible to attain. Atheophobia remains strong within many sectors of the international Muslim community. Muslim humanists and freethinkers around the globe face threats from multiple sources.

See also: Atheophobia; Christianity, Atheism and Agnosticism in; Hirsi Ali, Ayaan; Judaism, Atheism and Agnosticism in; Proofs for God, Atheist and Agnostic Critiques of; Rushdie, Salman

Further Reading

Benchems, Ahmed. "Invisible Atheists." *New Republic*, April 23, 2015.

Harris, Sam, and Maajid Nawaz. *Islam and the Future of Tolerance*. Cambridge, MA: Harvard University Press, 2019.

Hirsi Ali, Ayaan. *The Caged Virgin: An Emancipation Proclamation for Women and Islam*. New York: Atria, 2008.

Hirsi Ali, Ayaan. *Infidel*. New York: Atria, 2013.

Rahman, Fazlur. *Islam and Modernity: Transformation of an Intellectual Tradition*. Chicago: University of Chicago Press, 1982.

Rizvi, Ali A. *The Atheist Muslim: A Journey from Religion to Reason.* New York: St. Martin's Press, 2016.

Strousma, Sarah. *Freethinkers of Medieval Islam.* Leiden, Netherlands: E. J. Brill, 1999.

Wadi, Adam. *Atheism for Muslims: A Guide to Questioning Islam, Religion, and God for a Better Future.* N.p.: Independently Published, 2017.

Whitaker, Brian. *Arabs without God.* London: Zed Books, 2015.

J

Jacoby, Susan

Susan Jacoby (b. 1945) is an American writer and independent scholar, a distinguished advocate for intellectual freedom and secular government. The recipient of numerous grants and awards, she has won particular distinction for the literary quality of her journalism and the timeliness of her historical studies for the general reader. Her "Spirited Atheist" column for the *Washington Post*, which ran from 2010 to 2012, provided an unprecedented platform for a positive and forthright message of nonreligion's value in the public square. Her best-selling *The Age of American Unreason* (2008), updated in the era of the Donald Trump administration as *The Age of American Unreason in a Culture of Lies* (2018), forcefully communicates her overriding concerns about the decline of intellectual life and the erosion of civil liberties in U.S. society. Recipient of the Atheist Alliance of America's 2010 Richard Dawkins Award and a fellow of the nonprofit secular think tank Center for Inquiry, Jacoby is hailed as one of the clearest and most coherent voices in contemporary atheism.

Raised in a Catholic home in New York, Jacoby discovered in young adulthood the Jewish ancestry of her father. Her book *Half-Jew: A Daughter's Search for Her Family's Buried Past* (2000) re-creates the course of that path of self-discovery. Jacoby graduated from Michigan State University and commenced her writing career as a reporter for the *Washington Post*. In the late 1960s and early '70s, her work as a correspondent in the Soviet Union led to the publication of her first two books: *Moscow Conversations* (1972) and *Inside Soviet Schools* (1974). Since then, her articles, essays, and reviews have appeared in newspapers and journals such as the *New York Times*, the *Los Angeles Times*, *The Nation*, and *Mother Jones*. Subsequent books have covered topics ranging from immigration and baseball to the history of the concept of revenge.

Since 2000, Jacoby has been active in raising awareness about the vitality and varieties of secularity and intellectual nonconformity in a United States profoundly shaped by religious faith and desires. Two of her books have made especially notable contributions toward a serious recovery of the lost or suppressed story of unbelief at the heart of the U.S. experience: *Freethinkers: A History of American Secularism* (2004) and *The Great Agnostic: Robert Ingersoll and American Freethought* (2013). In broad strokes, *Freethinkers* narrates the full sweep of dissent and skepticism in national life, from Thomas Jefferson's much-alleged atheism to the so-called New Atheists and Nones of the twenty-first century. Jacoby has no patience for typecast freethinkers: eccentric crackpots and feckless naysayers. She pays careful attention to the positive role progressive nonbelievers have played in the founding and maintenance of the country's core institutions and in the advancement of social reform campaigns at crucial turning points in the nation's development, highlighting abolitionism, feminism, and the twentieth-century civil rights movement. The historical reconstruction of American atheism and agnosticism is still in its infancy. Its current state of health owes much to Jacoby's conscientious scholarship.

In her biography of the "Great Agnostic," Jacoby successfully rescues nineteenth-century lawyer and lecturer Robert Ingersoll from his "niche fame" as the nation's archetypical oddball. A native of upstate New York, Ingersoll—dubbed "Injuresoul" by his challengers—made a name for himself as a cross-country orator, mocking discrepancies in the Bible, exposing religion's shameless moral record, arguing for acceptance of the then-new Darwinian science, and defending the honor of his personal hero Thomas Paine, author of *Common Sense* (1776), *Rights of Man* (1791–1792), and *Age of Reason* (1794, 1795, 1807)—the man Theodore Roosevelt called a "filthy little atheist." Jacoby identifies Ingersoll's three main achievements and underscores their enduring relevance for the present moment: emphasizing the true meaning of science as an open-ended exercise in candid curiosity, confronting the repressive nature of religion without restraint or apology, and cultivating a living memory of the daring forerunners of modern unbelief.

Richard Dawkins and other leaders of the New Atheist movement have praised Jacoby's extensive achievements, seeing her as the great atheist chronicler of American free thought's often forgotten heritage. Jacoby, however, has reminded them just how dangerous and discomforting a true historian can be. In her "Letter to the 'New' Atheists," the inverted commas around the word *new* speak volumes. Set aside elements of Revolutionary-era jargon and Victorian eloquence, she says, and the New Atheist message differs little from that of previous unbelieving generations. Jacoby maintains that all parties engaged in the contemporary exchange of ideas, religious and irreligious, will profit from immersion in the neglected history of atheism and agnosticism, especially if they want to reclaim the true origins and intentions of their shared democratic values. A champion of freedom of conscience, like many other secular thinkers, she is distinct in her efforts to link future progress to a fascinating, usable past.

See also: Atheism, New; Ingersoll, Robert Green

Further Reading

Jacoby, Susan. *The Age of American Unreason in a Culture of Lies*. New York: Vintage Books, 2018.

Jacoby, Susan. *Freethinkers: A History of American Secularism*. New York: Holt, 2004.

Jacoby, Susan. *The Great Agnostic: Robert Ingersoll and American Freethought*. New Haven, CT: Yale University Press, 2013.

Jacoby, Susan. *Half-Jew: A Daughter's Search for Her Family's Buried Past*. New York: Scribner, 2000.

Jacoby, Susan. *Strange Gods: A Secular History of Conversion*. New York: Pantheon: 2016.

Judaism, Atheism and Agnosticism in

Atheism and agnosticism are significant factors shaping contemporary Jewish life and thought. The worldwide Jewish population presently hovers around fifteen million, with the greatest numbers of Jews living in North America, France, Great Britain, and Israel. Judaism recognizes no magisterial teaching office or governing authority and possesses no central organizational structure. It embraces a wide range of options for belief and behavior and honors many different expressions of religious and cultural identity. About half of the international Jewish population admits some affinity with at least one variant of nonreligion—sometimes characterized as humanism or skepticism or secularism, sometimes measured by degrees of nonpractice. Recent studies suggest that a small but significant percentage of that portion of the global Jewish community explicitly identifies as both Jewish and atheist. In the United States, 17 percent of Jews currently self-describe as atheists. Today, atheism and agnosticism represent two of the many ways of being Jewish.

Judaism has traditionally been associated with rigorous monotheism, popularly understood to mean both belief in one God and belief that there is only one God to believe in. The long record of Judaism's coming to terms with God and concepts of God, however, reveals a more complicated story. Historical, literary, and archaeological studies of the last two hundred years have shown that modern models of monotheism, often static and largely influenced by Christianity, Islam, or particular schools of philosophy, do not fully reflect the fluid nature of Judaism's distinctive ideas about God—ideas, often born in experiences of anguish, that have developed over the course of centuries and that continue to evolve. Scholars in contemporary Jewish studies point out that certain types of doctrines about God or gods do not constitute the core of Jewish identity anyway. Judaism's basic principle of practice over belief, deed over creed, sets the stage for a tradition, often seen as the paragon of theism, that appreciates and even generates forms of atheism and agnosticism.

Historians divide the development of the Jewish tradition into three main periods: (1) ancient or biblical Judaism, stretching from roughly 2000 BCE to 70 CE, the date of the Roman empire's destruction of the second temple in Jerusalem; (2) classical or rabbinic Judaism, during which forms of Jewish life and thought survived, and in some cases flourished, in the context of medieval Christian or Muslim cultures; and (3) modern Judaism, which since the era of the French Revolution has entailed the diversification of Jewish existence into a broad spectrum of traditional and nontraditional forms of belief, practice, and self-definition. Modern Orthodox Judaism represents a continuation of classical Judaism in the post-Enlightenment world. Reform, Reconstructionist, Humanistic, and secular Judaisms exemplify the various ways in which Jewish life and thought have been accommodated to modern and postmodern sensibilities. Conservative Judaism occupies an imprecisely defined middle ground between the preservation of premodern values and the liberal and progressive re-definitions of Jewish life and thought.

The Jewish tradition's most ancient views of God, as portrayed in the Hebrew Bible or Tanak, the scriptures of ancient Israel composed of Torah (Law), Nevi'im (Prophets), and Ketuvim (Writings), depict a formidable divine will associated with both the forces of nature and extraordinary events in history. The God of the Jewish Bible is best known as the liberator of enslaved Hebrews and the founder of the ancient people of Israel, designated in the texts as a nation called to be holy. Understood as invisible but acutely personal, the deity is identified by many names, including Elohim (the plural of *god*), Adonai (Lord), and the uncanny YHWH or Yahweh (thought to be related to the Hebrew for *being* or *becoming*), a name so sacred that a taboo outlawed its utterance. Some modern English-speaking Jews, retaining the spirit of reverence for the divine name, write the word *God* as *G-d*.

Running through the Bible is the contrast between this God and the pantheon of other ancient Near Eastern deities, described alternately as rival or false gods. Early Israelite theology was henotheist, not strictly monotheist. It reflected a quasi-exclusive attachment to a particular deity rather than an abstract belief in a lone transcendent God. Over time, with the universalizing influence of great literary prophets such as Isaiah and Jeremiah in the first millennium BCE, a form of cosmic monotheism emerged. Its imposing vision was destined to have tremendous moral and psychological impact on vast segments of humanity. Sigmund Freud called the prophets' God the prototype of the world's superego.

The Bible narrates numerous theophanies (appearances of God), but it also speaks of God's inaccessibility, inscrutability, and disturbing absence and silence. The Bible's prophetic literature includes conspicuous notes of protest. In light of natural evil and human injustice, the prophets repeat the unsettling refrain: Where is God? Modern Jewish atheism and agnosticism are rooted in these biblical themes: opposition to idolatry, a strong tendency toward iconoclasm, the mystery of the hiddenness of God, and the conviction that humans have the right to argue with God. The story of the patriarch Jacob wrestling with God (Genesis 32:23–33) is an enduring emblem of the Jewish intellectual tradition. The Bible's wisdom literature, especially the book of Ecclesiastes with its meditations on the futility of life, acquaint the modern reader with a strain of ancient Hebrew skepticism.

Classical Judaism advanced belief in a singular God but not in a uniform way. The rabbinic lineage, informed by the postbiblical literary treasury of Jewish wisdom called the Talmud (completed around 500 CE), recognized multiple paths to God and reinforced the legitimacy of dissent and debate in Jewish thought. Jewish mysticism, magic, astrology, and alchemy in the Middle Ages, especially in the esoteric Kabbalah tradition, explored nontraditional avenues of theism. Some affirmed the notion of an impersonal divine spark within human consciousness, some the reality of the *shekhinah*, or feminine sacred presence, permeating the natural world. All demonstrated the living quality of Judaism's intellectual culture and its relative freedom from ancient biblical constraints. Periodic heretical movements, often centered around purported Messiah figures, further manifested the decentralized and malleable nature of premodern Jewish spirituality.

A dominant feature of the modern Jewish experience has been the reimagining and reevaluation of theism. Science and enhanced sensitivity to the universal problem of suffering, prime threats to the tenet of divine providence, have contributed significantly to this process. Enlightenment skepticism confronted conventional notions of supernaturalism and monotheism's cardinal premise of a personal, omniscient, omnipotent, and loving God overseeing the world. The Bible's image of God became a problem in itself. Early modern critiques of the Bible almost always led with criticism of its jealous and erratic God and the ancient scripture's moral vision that sanctioned the subordination of women, the enslavement of enemies, the hatred of gender-nonconforming individuals, and the slaughter of pagan adversaries young and old. Thinkers associated with the *Haskalah*, or Jewish Enlightenment, pondered the prospects of a relevant modern Judaism relieved of the psychic and moral burden of traditional theism. Intellectuals from Baruch Spinoza to Karl Marx and Freud sought to discover the origins, nature, and function of theism in human experience. Spinoza came away with pantheist conclusions, seeing God in all things. Marx and Freud's conclusions were atheist, but for different reasons. In their article on atheism in the *Jewish Encyclopedia* (1901–1906), American Jewish leaders Kaufmann Kohler and Emil Hirsch concluded that modern Judaism harbored "Atheism of every kind."

The chronicle of anti-Jewish persecution, from the Babylonian destruction of Jerusalem's original temple (586 BCE) to the rise of modern antisemitism, put increasing pressure on the age-old enterprise of theodicy—the attempt, set forth in the book of Job, to reconcile faith in divine mercy with the facts of undeserved misery. Jews who were convinced atheists, such as Theodor Herzl, author of *The Jewish State* (1896), were the principal leaders of the effort to create a Jewish nation-state. Their Zionism and in some cases their atheism were responses to modern anti-Jewish persecution, unchecked by a divine judge. For many Jews, the twentieth-century Holocaust, or Shoah, the systematic, state-sponsored, and internationally ignored murder of six million Jewish adults and children, constitutes the ultimate trial of traditional Judaism's God. Auschwitz, the name of perhaps the most notorious death camp, has become synonymous with the problem of the suffering of the innocent.

Jewish responses to these challenges have ranged across a broad span of options. The Reform movement, organized in the nineteenth century and still popular in Europe and North America, offers a God shorn of ancient limitations and a community hospitable to individuals of various beliefs. Reconstructionist Judaism, initiated by Mordecai Kaplan, author of *The Meaning of God in Modern Jewish Religion* (1937), rejects traditional theism but retains the word *God* as a symbol for the highest aspirations of Jewish culture and human existence as a whole. Felix Adler's Ethical Culture movement, inaugurated in 1876, and Sherwin Wine's Humanistic Judaism, organized in the 1960s, continue to contribute to the growing varieties of religious, nontheist humanism. In the United States, some Jews express their atheist, agnostic, humanist, and secular identities in Unitarian Universalism's noncreedal environment. Feminists in all Jewish communities have found belief in patriarchy's God untenable. Harold Kushner's popular book *When Bad Things Happen to Good People* (1981) represents the best-known case for belief in a caring but powerless God—a position found in multiple sectors of the worldwide Jewish community, organized and unorganized. Abraham Joshua Heschel, who said Auschwitz and Hiroshima never left his mind, identified the highest Jewish vision of God not with omnipotence but with pathos, divine suffering with humanity.

The experience of the death of God has been recognized and registered in many different religious traditions. It has profoundly affected Jewish life and thought. In *Eclipse of God* (1952), Martin Buber, well known for his classic *I and Thou* (1923), framed the experience in terms of the absence of God rather than the nonexistence of God. For others, the experience has signaled the impossibility, even immorality, of collusion with conventional belief. Reflections on the death of God have taken multiple forms—in philosophy, history, psychology, art, poetry, music, fiction, theater, film, and autobiography, especially since the publication of Elie Wiesel's memoir *Night* (1958). Jewish atheism and agnosticism have complex sources. Much of contemporary Judaism's experimentation in nontheist and post-theist theology—or atheology—springs from the conviction driving Richard Rubenstein's *After Auschwitz* (1966): "God really died at Auschwitz."

See also: Christianity, Atheism and Agnosticism in; Feminism, Atheism and Agnosticism and; Islam, Atheism and Agnosticism in

Further Reading

Buber, Martin. *Eclipse of God*. New York: Harper and Brothers, 1952.

Fackenheim, Emil L. *To Mend the World: Foundations of Post-Holocaust Jewish Thought*. Bloomington: Indiana University Press, 1994.

Feiner, Shmuel. *The Jewish Enlightenment*. Trans. Chaya Naor. Philadelphia: University of Pennsylvania, 2004.

Freud, Sigmund. *Moses and Monotheism*. Trans. Katherine Jones. New York: Vintage Books, 1967.

Guttchen, Robert S. *Felix Adler*. New York: Twayne, 1974.

Kaplan, Mordecai. *Judaism as a Civilization: Toward a Reconstruction of American-Jewish Life*. New York: Macmillan, 1934.

Kaplan, Mordecai. *The Meaning of God in Modern Jewish Religion*. Detroit: Wayne State University Press, 1994.

Kasimow, Harold. *Interfaith Activism: Abraham Joshua Heschel and Religious Diversity*. Eugene, OR: Wipf and Stock, 2015.

Kaufmann, Walter. *The Faith of a Heretic*. Garden City, NY: Doubleday, 1961.

Kohler, Kaufmann, and Emil G. Hirsch. "Atheism." *The Jewish Encyclopedia*. 12 vols. New York: Funk and Wagnalls, 1906. II: 262–265. https://www.jewish encyclopedia.com/articles/2081-atheism.-

Kushner, Harold. *When Bad Things Happen to Good People*. New York: Schocken Books, 2001.

Morgan, Michael J. *Beyond Auschwitz: Post-Holocaust Jewish Thought in America*. Oxford: Oxford University Press, 2001.

Rubenstein, Richard. *After Auschwitz: Radical Theology and Contemporary Judaism*. New York: Macmillan, 1966.

Sagi, Avi. *Prayer after the Death of God: A Phenomenological Study of Hebrew Literature*. Boston: Academic Studies Press, 2016.

Wine, Sherwin T. *Humanistic Judaism*. Buffalo, NY: Prometheus Books, 1978.

Wine, Sherwin T. *Judaism beyond God: A Radical New Way to Be Jewish*. Hoboken, NJ: KTAV, 1996.

K

Kristeva, Julia

Julia Kristeva (b. 1941) is an award-winning literary critic, psychoanalyst, biographer, and novelist. She is best known for her feminist rereadings of Sigmund Freud and her research in the philosophy of language, especially her innovations in the interdisciplinary study of signs and symbols drawing from diverse schools of psychological, anthropological, and linguistic theory. The author of dozens of books and articles, Kristeva has also contributed significantly to new, evolving understandings of humanism, informed by what she has called a "mystic atheism," a nontheist worldview transcending conventional categories of belief and unbelief. At the invitation of Pope Benedict XVI, she became the first openly humanist intellectual to address an official interfaith conference sponsored by the Roman Catholic church.

Kristeva was born in Nazi-dominated Bulgaria and grew up under Soviet domination during the Cold War. She studied linguistics at the University of Sofia and, after immigrating to France, completed her doctoral work at the École Pratique des Hautes Études in Paris, writing her dissertation on "Revolution in Poetic Language." Since the 1970s, Kristeva has served as professor of linguistics at the University of Paris VII-Denis Diderot and has been the recipient of numerous academic honors and prizes. Her many publications, such as *Powers of Horror* (1982), *In the Beginning Was Love: Psychoanalysis and Faith* (1987), *Black Sun: Depression and Melancholia* (1989), *Strangers to Ourselves* (1991), *New Maladies of the Soul* (1995), and *Hatred and Forgiveness* (2010), explore the dynamic intersections of art, literature, politics, cultural studies, and psychology. The aim of all her work has been the illumination of the sources of language and consciousness in the evolution of the human species and the development of the individual human person. Biographies of political philosopher Hannah Arendt, Freudian rival Melanie Klein, and taboo-breaking French writer-actress Colette have established Kristeva as one of the most incisive interpreters of independent and trendsetting twentieth-century women in the contemporary academy. Her fiction, including *Teresa, My Love* (2008), an imagined life of sixteenth-century Spanish mystic Teresa of Avila, demonstrates, sometimes within the format of metaphysical detective stories, her ability to plumb the mysteries of personal experience in the boundary lands shared by reality and fantasy.

In one of her most provocative books, *This Incredible Need to Believe* (2009), Kristeva investigates what she calls a prereligious drive to believe. She traces the roots of this universal impulse to the heart of human existence—to the core of what makes human beings "speaking beings"—and concludes that it represents an intuitive grasp of a truth preceding and laying the foundation for the critical inquiries of empirical science. It is, she argues, a fundamental trust that makes possible an individual's meaningful and meaning-making relationship with the world beyond the boundaries of the ego. Kristeva approaches the topic of believing from a secular perspective, but hers is a secularism with a difference. It is nonreligious without being antireligious. Humanism—Christianity's "rebellious child," as she puts it—has its origins in religion. Likewise, the disciplines of the humanities, the locations for her lifelong scholarly residence, are natural outgrowths of the historic Christian intellectual tradition, representing at its best a curiosity about the "all things" mentioned in the church's Nicene Creed. For Kristeva, modern atheism and agnosticism exist in continuity, not discontinuity, with the Western world's broad intellectual heritage.

This commitment to humanism and nonconfessional empathy toward religion's legacy made Kristeva a natural choice for the roster of speakers selected to participate in the Vatican's fourth global interfaith summit, held in Assisi, Italy. Since the 1980s, the church's Pontifical Council for Interreligious Dialogue has been scheduling periodic assemblies of clergy, activists, and educators from all the religions of the world to address issues of international peace and solidarity. The 2011 gathering, featuring approximately two hundred leaders representing traditions from Buddhism to Zoroastrianism, was the first to include on the program a delegate communicating a nonreligious point of view. Kristeva's lecture, "Principles for the Humanism of the Twenty-First Century," is one of the new millennium's most forceful calls for an engaged humanism advancing beyond its rationalist, skeptical past. Its thesis of an obligatory "wager" on a boldly refounded humanism, shaped by dedication to ethical globalization, steadfast feminism, and care for the earth, represents a summary of Kristeva's far-reaching vision.

See also: Freud, Sigmund; Humanism

Further Reading

Beardsworth, Sara. *Julia Kristeva: Psychoanalysis and Modernity*. Albany: SUNY Press, 2004.

Kristeva, Julia. *Black Sun: Depression and Melancholia*. Trans. Leon S. Roudiez. New York: Columbia University Press, 1989.

Kristeva, Julia. *Hannah Arendt*. Trans. Ross Guberman. New York: Columbia University Press, 2001.

Kristeva, Julia. *Hatred and Forgiveness*. Trans. Jeanine Herman. New York: Columbia University Press, 2012.

Kristeva, Julia. *This Incredible Need to Believe*. Trans. Beverly Bie Brahic. New York: Columbia University Press, 2011.

Moi, Toril, ed. *The Kristeva Reader*. Oxford: Basil Blackwell, 1986.

Kurtz, Paul

Paul Kurtz (1925–2012) was a crucial figure in the history of twentieth-century humanism. He was a philosopher, professor, author, and editor, overseeing multiple magazines and journals, encouraging generations of new writers, and penning dozens of books and hundreds of articles of his own. He was also an intellectual with profound leadership skills and a matchless sense of cultural timing. He started numerous scholarly institutes, centers, and councils, giving contemporary humanism a much-needed skeletal structure. He established Prometheus Books, giving humanism a much-needed voice. Without him, humanism today would look and sound dramatically different.

Kurtz grew up in a nonobservant Jewish home in Newark, New Jersey, and was briefly affiliated with the Unitarian church. He attended public schools and studied economics, political science, and philosophy at New York University before pursuing graduate degrees in philosophy at Columbia. Pausing his undergraduate study during World War II, he served in the U.S. Army, seeing action in the Battle of the Bulge and later serving survivors at Nazi death camps. For all of his adult life, he identified as an atheist and a humanist. For most of his long career, he taught philosophy at the State University of New York at Buffalo.

By the 1970s, as the United States was heading toward a major culture war, Kurtz was emerging as an eminent public intellectual, taking the humanist message to the general reader and the defense of humanism to radio and television. He edited *Humanist* magazine, was instrumental in drafting the second Humanist Manifesto (1973), and promoted humanism as a positive view of life with a compelling, even joyful, moral vision. He became even more institutionally engaged as the New Religious Right began to gain influence, bringing to the public square its sense of Christian exceptionalism mixed with a set of anxieties linked to shifting moral standards, changing sexual mores, increasing secularization at home, and decreasing American power abroad.

In 1976, dubbed the "Year of the Evangelical" due to Southern Baptist Jimmy Carter's successful bid for the White House, Kurtz founded the Committee for the Scientific Investigation of Claims of the Paranormal (now the Committee for Skeptical Inquiry). In 1980, the year after fundamentalist Jerry Falwell launched the Moral Majority, Kurtz created the Council for Democratic and Secular Humanism (later renamed Council for Secular Humanism). The two organizations merged in 1991 to form the Center for Inquiry, the humanist think tank in Amherst, New York, publisher of the journals *Free Inquiry* and *Skeptical Inquirer* and the site for numerous lectures, conferences, symposia, and research projects. Throughout the turbulent years of the Reagan administration, Kurtz was the United States' best-known representative of *secular humanism*, a term he was largely responsible for introducing into the nation's vocabulary.

Kurtz was an indefatigable writer, authoring or editing over fifty books. Some important foundational works include *A Secular Humanist Declaration,* originally released in 1980 and endorsed by over fifty signatories, *In Defense of Secular Humanism* (1983), *Neo-Fundamentalism: The Humanist Response* (1988), *Forbidden Fruit: The Ethics of Secularism* (1988), *The New Skepticism* (1992), and *What is Secular Humanism?* (2007). He published, however, more books than he ever wrote. In midcareer, he started his own publishing company dedicated to a broad, inclusive humanist message and an expanding market interested in material promoting reason, science, and freedom of conscience. Named after the Greek mythological hero who stole fire from the gods, Prometheus Books, founded in 1969, has become one of the leading disseminators of atheist, agnostic, secularist, and humanist literature worldwide. With a back list of some 2,500 titles, it has published notable authors such as Harold Bloom, J. T. Joshi, Judith Little, Anthony B. Pinn, and Victor Stenger.

A rare entrepreneur among intellectuals, Kurtz received many awards, including the 1999 International Humanist Award from the International Humanist and Ethical Union (now Humanists International) and the 2007 Humanist Lifetime Achievement Award from the American Humanist Association. He was also a fellow of the American Association for the Advancement of Science. In one of his final speeches, he praised what he called the Promethean virtues—"our use of the arts and sciences to better the human situation."

See also: Humanism; Humanist Manifestos; Media, Atheism and Agnosticism and the; Organizations, Atheist and Agnostic

Further Reading

Kurtz, Paul. *Forbidden Fruit: The Ethics of Secularism.* Amherst, NY: Prometheus Books, 2008. Originally published in 1988.

Kurtz, Paul. *Humanist Manifesto 2000: A Call for a New Planetary Humanism.* Amherst, NY: Prometheus Books, 2000.

Kurtz, Paul, ed. *Humanist Manifestos I and II.* Buffalo, NY: Prometheus Books, 1973.

Kurtz, Paul. *Multi-Secularism: A New Agenda.* New York: Routledge, 2017.

Kurtz, Paul. *A Secular Humanist Declaration.* Buffalo, NY: Prometheus Books, 1983.

Shook, John R., ed. *Paul Kurtz: Exuberant Skepticism.* Amherst, NY: Prometheus Books, 2010.

L

LGBTQ+ Persons, Atheist and Agnostic

Members of the LGBTQ+ community and members of atheist and agnostic communities often find themselves on the same sides of issues. Fighting for the freedom to love, the freedom to express personal identities, the freedom to articulate points of view without harassment, and the freedom simply to exist unites people from many different social and cultural locations. In *Queer Disbelief* (2017), queer activist and atheist Camille Beredjick calls LGBTQ+ individuals and unbelievers natural allies in contemporary society. In a number of cases, the concerns intersect in the same person. Today, 26 percent of adults in the United States are religiously unaffiliated (4 percent self-describing as atheist, 5 percent as agnostic, and 17 percent as "nothing in particular"). Nearly half of the unaffiliated population (41 percent) identifies as LGBTQ+.

The same pattern of intersection has been evident throughout modern Western history. Early advocates for religious toleration and freedom of speech were also among the first to question restrictive notions of gender, marriage, and sexual behavior. One way to oppose the Abrahamic belief systems, especially Judaism and Christianity, was to resist the sexual mores of their moral codes. Critics proposed alternative approaches to family, love, and personal identity, frequently based on insights from modern science and evolving feminist principles. In the early twentieth century, proponents of atheism and agnosticism were among the most prominent voices advocating for the decriminalization of homosexuality.

Few things have unnerved the traditional Western mind more than doubts about God and deviations from the heterosexual norm. Historians have argued that both atheophobia and homophobia issue from an anxiety at the core of the monotheist worldview—an uneasiness revealed in missionary exclusivism, domination of women, religiously motivated crusades, suspicion of sex, and the persecution of heretics. In societies where church and state have exercised unified or cooperative power, traditional punishments for theological and sexual nonconformity have included public humiliation, incarceration, banishment, and death, both legal and extralegal.

In contemporary American culture, LGBTQ+ individuals of all ages regularly contend with faith-related homophobic threats and hate crimes ranging from the reparative or conversion therapies of antigay ministries to family disavowal, abuse, and murder. Christian televangelists have blamed everything from hurricanes to terrorist attacks on the presence of LGBTQ+ people in society. Westboro Baptist Church, an extremist group based in Kansas, is infamous for its antigay hate speech often exhibited at funerals of military personnel and celebrities. Aggression can take other forms too. In some religious communities, lesbian, gay, bisexual, transgender, queer, intersex, asexual, and pansexual individuals are routinely dismissed or simply unacknowledged, their testimonies contradicted, their pronouns ignored.

Some faith keepers within religious organizations have attempted to eradicate homophobic elements from their traditions and convert hostility to hospitality. Controversies typically revolve around same-sex marriage and the ordination of openly LGBTQ+ individuals as leaders. Reform Judaism, Humanistic Judaism, Unitarian Universalism, and welcoming congregations in some mainline Protestant denominations have sought to make all aspects of community life LGBTQ+-affirming. The Metropolitan Community Church, established in 1968 by Troy Perry, author of *The Lord Is My Shepherd and He Knows I'm Gay* (1972), was the first Protestant denomination specifically organized to serve the needs of LGBTQ+ people and promote LGBTQ+ leadership. New Ways Ministry, founded by religious sister Jeannine Gramick and priest Robert Nugent in 1977, advocates for LGBTQ+ people in the Roman Catholic community. In the 1980s, AIDS activist Jimmy Creech endeavored to convince his fellow United Methodists that heterosexism is just as sinful as racism. Reform movements within the classic dharma traditions of Asian spirituality have pursued similar courses. The Two-Spirit identity and role in some Native American cultures honors nonbinary gender experience as sacred and serves as a model for anyone who imagines all religions as necessarily antagonistic to LGBTQ+ well-being. Annual Pride events sometimes include interfaith services or celebrations.

Religious scholarship has also been shaped by appreciation for LGBTQ+ life and thought. Historians, such as John Bosworth, author of

Christianity, Social Tolerance, and Homosexuality (1980), have worked to recover forgotten patterns of same-sex union and other forms of multigender-acceptance in the Christian past. Groundbreaking religious thinkers have developed queer theologies, interpreting scriptures through the lens of LGBTQ+ experiences and reviewing traditional doctrine and moral teaching in light of current science and LGBTQ+ perspectives.

Still, a significant number of LGBTQ+ people find religious belonging untenable. Many see homophobia, biphobia, and transphobia as irredeemable components of religious experience with too many ties to legacies of injustice. Strategies of supposed tolerance founded on slogans such as "love the sinner, hate the sin" and "don't ask, don't tell" only mask worldviews incapable of embracing LGBTQ+ persons in their fullness and integrity. Increasingly, individuals, nonconforming in belief and gender, choose "none of the above" when it comes to both faith and heteronormative notions of embodied being. Full freedom means total separation from institutions and ideas linked to ancient taboos.

People who self-describe as both LGBTQ+ and atheist or agnostic point out the distinctive features of that intersection in a variety of ways. Many speak of the formidable challenges of coming out twice—once as LGBTQ+, once as an unbeliever or secular person. Some use the term *gaytheist* (also the name of a metal band) to highlight the unique dynamics of navigating these multiple identities. African American LGBTQ+ nonbelievers often see themselves as members of a triple minority.

Organizations of LGBTQ+ people and their allies recognize the seriousness of these challenges and offer diverse types of support and advocacy. GLAAD (www.glaad.org), formerly known as the Gay and Lesbian Alliance against Defamation, and PFLAG (www.pflag.org), originally known as Parents, Families, and Friends of Lesbians and Gays, provide focused resources for LGBTQ+ people who are atheists, agnostics, humanists, freethinkers, or Nones. The American Humanist Association sponsors the LGBTQ Humanist Alliance (www.lgbtqhumanists.org), dedicated to the promotion of LGBTQ+ rights. Every year it honors a notable activist or theorist with its LGBTQ Humanist Award. The first recipient, in 2011, was Candace Gingrich-Jones, queer equality activist, sibling of former U.S. Speaker of the House Newt Gingrich, and author of *The Accidental Activist: A Personal and Political Memoir* (1996). Other awardees include writer and actor Mara Wilson, poet and performing artist Staceyann Chin, and atheist blogger and pansexual, sex-positive feminist Greta Christina, author of *Coming Out Atheist* (2014).

See also: Atheism and Agnosticism, African American; Atheophobia; Christina, Greta; Feminism, Atheism and Agnosticism and; Nones; Organizations, Atheist and Agnostic

Further Reading

Beredjick, Camille. *Queer Disbelief: Why LGBTQ Equality Is an Atheist Issue.* N.p.: Friendly Atheist Press, 2017.

Bosworth, John. *Christianity, Social Tolerance, and Homosexuality: Gay People in Western Europe from the Beginning of the Christian Era to the Fourteenth Century.* Chicago: University of Chicago Press, 1980.

Brewster, Melanie Elyse. "Atheism, Gender, and Sexuality." In *The Oxford Handbook of Atheism.* Ed. Stephen Bullivant and Michael Ruse, pp. 511–524. Oxford: Oxford University Press, 2013.

Christina, Greta. *Coming Out Atheist: How to Do It, How to Help Each Other, and Why.* Durham, NC: Pitchstone, 2014.

Gaylor, Annie, ed. *Women without Superstition: "No Gods—No Masters": The Collected Writings of Women Freethinkers of the Nineteenth and Twentieth Centuries.* Madison, WI: Freedom from Religion Foundation, 1997.

Gingrich-Jones, Candace. *The Accidental Activist: A Personal and Political Memoir.* New York: Scribner, 1996.

Gorham, Candace R. M. *The Ebony Exodus Project: Why Some Black Women Are Walking Out on Religion—and Others Should Too.* Durham, NC: Pitchstone, 2013.

Greenberg, Steven. *Wrestling with God and Men: Homosexuality in the Jewish Tradition.* Madison: University of Wisconsin Press, 2004.

Greenough, Chris. *Queer Theologies: The Basics.* New York: Routledge, 2019.

Gregorio, I. W. *None of the Above.* New York: Balzer and Bray, 2015.

Harris, W. C. *Slouching towards Gaytheism: Christianity and Queer Survival in America.* Albany: State University of New York Press, 2014.

Henderson, Bruce. *Queer Studies: Beyond Binaries.* New York: Harrington Park Press, 2019.

Kugle, Scott Siraj al-Haqq. *Living Out Islam. Voices of Gay, Lesbian, and Transgender Muslims.* New York: New York University Press, 2014.

Leyland, Winston, ed. *Queer Dharma: Voices of Gay Buddhists.* Vol. 1. San Francisco: Gay Sunshine Press, 1998.

Lightsey, Pamela. *Our Lives Matter: A Womanist Queer Theology.* Eugene, OR: Pickwick Publications, 2015.

Ozment, Katherine. *Grace without God: The Search for Meaning, Purpose, and Belonging in a Secular Age.* New York: Harper Collins, 2016.

Tonstad, Linn Marie. *Queer Theology: Beyond Apologetics.* Eugene, OR: Cascade Books, 2018.

Marx, Karl

Karl Marx (1818–1883) was one of the most influential thinkers of all time. His ideas are a major part of the intellectual currency of the contemporary world, and his writings are treated as near oracles by millions of people around the globe. His last name alone inspires extremes of reverence and revulsion but never indifference. Variants of his name, *Marxist* and *Marxian*, refer to a vast family of interpretive methods illuminating aspects of human experience from literature and art to psychology and family life. He is best known as one of the prime architects of modern social, political, and economic theory. His *Communist Manifesto* (1848), one of the most important books in the history of the world, has changed the course of nations and empires. His unforgettable image of religion as the "opium of the people" has, for over a century and a half, sparked great interest in the ways religious beliefs and organizations aid and abet oppression in society.

Marx was born between two major revolutions—in a Europe reacting to the cataclysm of the French Revolution and almost exactly a hundred years before the Russian Revolution that, as American journalist John Reed said, "shook the world." A third major upheaval, fully in progress at the time of his birth, served as the source for many of Marx's ideas: the Industrial Revolution. Marx did not invent the modern notion of revolution, but he gave it a conceptual basis that he and his followers thought scientifically persuasive and politically explosive.

Raised in a German territorial colony of Prussia, Marx grew up in an assimilated Jewish family newly affiliated by baptism with the Lutheran tradition. Both his grandfathers were rabbis. His lawyer father gravitated more toward the *philosophes* of the Enlightenment than the prophets of the Hebrew scriptures. Marx shared his father's intellectual inclinations and followed the latest trends in liberal thought throughout his education. He studied law and philosophy at the Universities of Bonn and Berlin and wrote his doctoral dissertation, submitted to the University of Jena, on a debate between the ancient Greek materialists Democritus and Epicurus. He was particularly drawn to the works of the German thinker Georg Wilhelm Friedrich Hegel, who dominated European philosophy after the death of Immanuel Kant in 1804. Along with other left-leaning Young Hegelians, including Ludwig Feuerbach, whose *Essence of Christianity* (1841) pronounced God a projection of the human imagination, Marx mined Hegel's insights into the dynamics of history for resources to address the social problems of the present and arouse hope for the future.

Critiques of individualism, calls for communitarian living, reevaluations of private property, and schemes for earthly utopias were all part of the Enlightenment's visionary legacy and the Romantic reaction to what poet William Blake called the "dark Satanic Mills" of industrialism. Themes of progress and development were attracting Europe's most original minds years before Charles Darwin enshrined evolution as the nineteenth century's intellectual hallmark. Reformers such as Charles Fourier, Henri de Saint-Simon, Robert Owen, and Pierre-Joseph Proudhon advocated various models of socialism, communism, and anarchism, some hearkening back to early Christianity's practice of the community of goods. These ideas stimulated the imaginations of many troubled by the rise of new authoritarian regimes in Europe after the French Revolution. The negative effects of unchecked free enterprise—and its companion, colonialism—especially stirred resentment among those on the bottom rungs of the social ladder and incensed those who believed the purpose of society to be justice itself. Capitalism's much touted "invisible hand," supposedly guiding fluctuating markets, was not fostering the greater benevolence many expected but ushering the urban poor toward degradation and the earth toward grave danger.

Marx's endorsement of these new progressive currents of thought made him typical of his age. What made him stand out was the unique configuration of ideas he set forth. At the heart of his vision was a fundamental rethinking of Hegel's notion of how history worked. Hegel saw the forward motion of human history as one massive dialectical, or conflict-driven, conversation between competing ideas and the emergence of new and better epochs out of that contest—all guided by his own version of an "invisible hand," what he called the absolute Idea or Spirit that gave coherence to the world. Future textbooks would reduce Hegel's thought to a three-part formula: affirmation/negation/new affirmation. A *thesis* is challenged by an *antithesis*, and out of this confrontation a new *synthesis* arises, beginning the process all over again. Marx changed this approach, bringing Hegel's idealism down to earth. He declared class struggle the foremost rivalry in history, economics the driving engine of history, the working class (or proletariat) the agent of a new revolutionary era, economic crisis the trigger for revolution, and a classless society the ultimate goal of history—with no God or cosmic Spirit overseeing any of it.

What became known as Marx's theory of dialectical materialism spread rapidly after the release of *The Communist Manifesto*, coauthored with Marx's collaborator: historian and business leader Friedrich Engels. Published in a year of violent revolutions sweeping European cities, the slim but powerful document focused on class antagonism as the dominant plot of the human drama. Its opening line sent shock waves through boardrooms and drawing rooms of the rich and powerful: "A specter is haunting Europe—the specter of Communism." The *Manifesto*'s keen insights into capitalism's never-ending quest to create new markets, the alienation of workers from their labor, and the transformation of labor into a commodity itself resonate with similar concerns in twenty-first-century social criticism. In the lead-up to the turbulent period of 1848–1849, Marx renounced his Prussian citizenship, participated in secret meetings of insurgents, and helped to organize the international Community League. He was arrested, tried, and briefly imprisoned but did not fight on the barricades in the streets of Paris, Berlin, Vienna, or Rome. By the 1850s, he was Europe's most radical theorist, well known for his role in founding the International Working Men's Association—later known in socialist parlance as the First International. Since the nineteenth century, many have called the grandson of rabbis one of the world's greatest secular prophets.

Marx's atheism prevented him from achieving his early dream of an academic career. He worked primarily as an independent scholar, journalist, and newspaper editor, living in forced exile, often in poverty, in Cologne, Paris, Brussels, and London. Today, his chair in the reading room of the British Museum is a tourist attraction. He initiated numerous literary projects but brought few to completion. Most of his books—such as *The Holy Family*, *The German Ideology*, and *The Poverty of Philosophy*—read more like denunciation of opponents than proposals for social change. The most mature statement of his economic thought is found in his unfinished *Capital* (the first volume published in 1867 and volumes 2 and 3, edited by Engels, after his death).

World leaders such as Vladimir Lenin, Joseph Stalin, Mao Zedong, Jawaharlal Nehru, Fidel Castro, and Ho Chi Minh have seen themselves as enlargers and refiners of Marx's insights. A vast number of writers, artists, and activists, including figures as diverse as Leon Trotsky, Eugene Debs, Rosa Luxemburg, George Bernard Shaw, Bertrand Russell, W. E. B. Du Bois, Alfred Adler, Simone de Beauvoir, Dmitri Shostakovich, Richard Wright, Che Guevara, and Shulamith Firestone, have applied Marxist principles to a broad range of social and cultural questions. Many of the first Zionists were socialists.

Today, Marx's legacy is as hotly debated as the legacies of the diverse socialist and communist movements worldwide that have claimed the mantle of his authority. Marxisms and Neo-Marxisms abound. Critics point to unresolved tensions in his thought, his unsocialist devotion to a bourgeois-bohemian lifestyle, his use of racist epithets for people of African descent, and his failure to support fully the nineteenth-century women's movement. Generations of biographers have labored to understand the ambivalence he expressed regarding his Jewish ancestry.

Marx's contribution to the development of modern atheism is distinctive. Drawing from Feuerbach's theory of projection, he, too, saw the world of religion as an invention of the human mind. Instead of focusing on its illusory quality, though, Marx highlighted religion's roots in human anguish and alienation. He concentrated on religion's practical function in society rather than the abstract question of the existence of God. He gave impetus not only to the rise of the social sciences but to the specialty field of the sociology of religion, today a thriving academic enterprise.

In his *Critique of Hegel's Philosophy of Right* (1843), Marx described religion as an opiate or drug that dulls the pain caused by exploitation and, impairing the senses, distracts people from their true plight in society. Interpreters have claimed that he borrowed the image—especially striking in the age of Britain's imperial Opium Wars with China—from the atheist theologian Bruno Bauer or the philosopher Moses Hess or the poet Heinrich Heine. Whatever its source, Marx made effective use of the metaphor, speaking eloquently of religion as the sigh of the abused and a devious form of social control exercised by the ruling class. For Marx, religion is both a tool of the oppressor and a survival strategy of the oppressed. The end of earthly injustice, he conjectured, will render the hope of heaven irrelevant. At his funeral, German socialist leader Wilhelm Liebknecht said Marx had unleashed forces that would destroy not only capitalism but also the "idols and lords of the earth, who, as long as they live, will not let God die."

See also: Beauvoir, Simone de; Besant, Annie; Du Bois, W. E. B.; Feminism, Atheism and Agnosticism and; Feuerbach, Ludwig; Goldman, Emma; Russell, Bertrand; Sartre, Jean-Paul

Further Reading

Avineri, Shlomo. *Karl Marx: Philosophy and Revolution*. New Haven, CT: Yale University Press, 2019.

Breckman, Warren. *Marx, the Young Hegelians and the Origins of Radical Social Theory: Dethroning the Self*. Cambridge: Cambridge University Press, 1999.

Carver, Terrell, ed. *The Cambridge Companion to Marx*. Cambridge: Cambridge University Press, 1991.

Chadwick, Owen. *The Secularization of the European Mind in the 19th Century*. Cambridge: Cambridge University Press, 1975.

Eagleton, Terry. *Why Marx Was Right*. New Haven, CT: Yale University Press, 2011.

Marx, Karl. *Capital: A Critique of Political Economy*. 3 vols. New York: Penguin Classics, 1992–1993.

Marx, Karl. *Critique of Hegel's Philosophy of Right*. Trans. Joseph O'Malley. Cambridge: Cambridge University Press, 2009.

Marx, Karl, and Friedrich Engels. *The Communist Manifesto*. Trans. Samuel Moore. London: Penguin, 1967.

Reed, John. *Ten Days That Shook the World*. New York: Penguin Classics, 2007.

Robinson, Cedric J. *Black Marxism: The Making of the Black Radical Tradition*. 2nd ed. Chapel Hill, NC: University of North Carolina Press, 2005.

Singer, Peter. *Marx: A Very Short Introduction*. New York: Oxford University Press, 2018.

Sperber, Jonathan. *Karl Marx: A Nineteenth-Century Life*. New York: Liveright, 2013.

Media, Atheism and Agnosticism and the

Atheism and agnosticism have long been associated with freedom of thought and freedom of expression. Free thought, often questioning the foundational claims of social and religious systems, has been communicated in different ways—in print, in image, and through recorded, broadcast, and livestreamed word and act. The history of modern unbelief corresponds with the history of modern media.

Books have played an immensely important role in the dissemination of atheist and agnostic ideas. After the appearance of the Gutenberg Bible

(1455), the first book produced with movable metal type, many of the first mass-produced books in the West openly attacked or questioned points of political or religious orthodoxy—issues such as the divine right of monarchs, the legitimacy of the papacy, the doctrine of the Trinity, the divinity of Christ, and the union of church and state. Countercultural books challenged ideas about God, the reasonableness of the Bible, the coherence of creeds, and the moral reputations of church, priesthood, and empire. Until the nineteenth century, though, virtually no book challenged the existence of God head-on.

Historians debate the question of the appearance of the first book in Western literature written from an atheist point of view. *Theophrastus redivivus*, an anonymous text from the seventeenth century, is often cited as the first published defense of unambiguous nontheism in modern times. A collection of Latin treatises, whose title borrows the persona of Aristotle's student Theophrastus (*theos + phrázein*, "divine phrase"), the book questions the rationality of belief in any god.

Arguably, the first explicitly atheist book with an identifiable author is a manuscript penned by the eighteenth-century French Catholic priest Jean Meslier: *Memoir of the Thoughts and Feelings of Jean Meslier: Clear and Evident Demonstrations of the Vanity and Falsity of All the Religions of the World*. Discovered after the author's death in 1729, it shocked its first readers by the boldness of its conclusions regarding the ignorance and deceit at the root of all religions, including Meslier's own Christian tradition.

The attempt to generate a full list of early atheist books in Western history also results in scholarly debate. Works typically appearing in such lists include the following: Erasmus's *In Praise of Folly* (1511), Niccolò Machiavelli's *The Prince* (1513), François Rabelais's five-volume *Gargantua and Pantagruel* (1532–1564), Giordano Bruno's *De l'infinito, universo e mondi* (1584), Thomas Hobbes's *Leviathan* (1651), Pierre Bayle's *Pensées diverses sur la comète* (1682) and *Dictionnaire historique et critique* (1697–1702), Anthony Collins's *Discourse on Freethinking* (1713), Denis Diderot's multiauthored *Encyclopédie* (1751–1772), Voltaire's *Dictionnaire philosophique* (1764), Baron d'Holbach's *Système de la nature* (1770), Edward Gibbon's *History of the Decline and Fall of the Roman Empire* (1776–1788), David Hume's *Dialogues Concerning Natural Religion* (1779), Marquis de Sade's *Dialogue between a Priest and a Dying Man* (1782), Joseph Priestley's *A History of the Corruptions of Christianity* (1782), Mary Wollstonecraft's *A Vindication of the Rights of Woman* (1792), and Thomas Paine's three-part *Age of Reason* (1794, 1795, 1807).

These books took a number of different approaches to the topic of religion: detached examination, impassioned polemic, unrestrained curiosity, sparkling satire, and irreverent indifference. Their targets were usually the superstition, irrationality, clericalism, and hypocrisy that their authors found in the Christian churches of Reformation and post-Reformation Europe and its colonies.

Many of the books were condemned by civil and ecclesiastical authorities. Many were placed on the Vatican's new Index of Forbidden Books (established in 1559). Some were burned. Hobbes's books were burned at Oxford, Voltaire's in Paris. Paine's books were burned in mock execution by Britain's public hangman. Joseph Priestley witnessed a mob torch his entire personal library, Bibles included. Giordano Bruno, condemned for insisting the earth revolved around the sun, saw his books go up in flames just before he himself was burned at the stake.

The authors were all branded as heretics or apostates or irresponsible minds flirting with dangerous ideas. Theirs was an age that assumed that good people could be infected with bad ideas and that bad ideas could destroy civilization. Some of the authors' reputations were tarred with a word just entering European languages in their era: *atheist*. At the time, the word was a term of derision, not a label adopted voluntarily by an individual and not even a name designating a particular position on the question of God's existence. It functioned as *witch*, *communist*, and *fundamentalist* have in different times and places—more as an all-purpose insult than a technical term. English writer John Wingfield's *Atheism Closed and Open* (1634) was typical of the period. It employed *atheist* to denounce the wicked and proud, not individuals who held a specific opinion on the subject of a supreme being. The concept of God was so ingrained in the Western worldview that few people could even imagine someone not believing in God at all. *Atheist* had imprecise meaning, but its charge communicated *subversive*.

Because of subsequent shifts in the meaning of *atheist* and the many blasphemy laws that did not allow any writer to speak with complete candor, the task today of determining the exact mental starting point of these important early modern authors is fraught with difficulty. Voltaire, while fending off accusations of atheism himself, criticized other people for spreading atheism. In many respects, these writers appear to have been deists, undogmatic theists, agnostics (before the term was invented), or reforming or dissenting Christian iconoclasts seeking simpler, more reasonable, less supernaturally dependent versions of faith—if not for themselves, at least for believers in their society.

In the twenty-first century, these authors have been frequently identified as protoatheists. Some interpreters call them the modern West's original atheists, intellectual ancestors of present-day unbelievers and nonreligious. If the term "original atheists" applies at all, they were covert or closet atheists or near atheists. In their time, their writings were often mixed, in street peddlers' carts, with other clandestine works of the early modern literary underground. Antireligious tracts mingled with erotica and the first mass-produced pornography. The full reality of their individual outlooks will likely never be known. With fearless scrutiny and withering ridicule, their books helped to make the future publication of forthright atheist and agnostic books possible—especially as Western societies came to agree with Thomas Jefferson, accused of atheism himself, who declared that all attempts to coerce the mind with temporal punishments only "beget habits of hypocrisy and meanness."

Published books with the contemporary sense of atheism began to appear after the American, French, and Haitian Revolutions of the late eighteenth century. The previously unthinkable overthrow of empires had a tremendous effect on a generation whose forebears had assumed God to be a permanent fixture of the moral architecture of the universe. Texts such as Wollstonecraft's *Vindication of the Rights of Woman* made it clear that patriarchy, too, was not as invincible or self-evident as it had once seemed.

Two milestones were *The Necessity of Atheism* (1811) and *A Refutation of Deism* (1814) by Percy Bysshe Shelley, the romantic writer who married Wollstonecraft's daughter Mary, author of *Frankenstein* (1818), and who thought poets the true legislators of the world. Known as the "Eton Atheist" due to his adolescent rejection of conventional faith, Shelley was expelled from Oxford for publicly disavowing God. He was famous for his vegetarianism, pacifism, and especially his association of free love with free thought. He arguably gave atheism greater press than any writer before him. His early Gothic novel *Zastrozzi* (1810) features what may be the first atheist protagonist in Western fiction.

After Shelley, the nineteenth became the Western world's first century of open atheism and religious doubt. Blasphemy, obscenity, and sedition laws remained on the books but were enforced with decreasing severity and consistency. The incorporation of religious toleration and freedom of conscience into legal codes raised for the first time the possibility of juridical protection for unbelief. Censorship, however, was still a reality in many countries. Widespread prejudice continued to link atheism with immorality. The 1869 introduction of *agnostic* into the modern vocabulary by Thomas Henry Huxley, "Darwin's Bulldog," helped to give broader range and nuance to the types of unbelief available to the open mind. Despite still significant obstacles, the century witnessed a record public flowering of atheist and agnostic thought. Arthur Schopenhauer, Ludwig Feuerbach, Karl Marx, Charles Darwin, Robert Ingersoll, Annie Besant, Charles Bradlaugh, John Stuart Mill, Friedrich Nietzsche, Elizabeth Cady Stanton, and many others put what was previously unprintable into print. Their works now represent the core of the modern Western nonreligious canon.

The twentieth century—from H. L. Mencken's *The Philosophy of Friedrich Nietzsche* (1907), the first book on Nietzsche in English, to Dutch philosopher Herman Philipse's *Atheïstisch Manifest* (1995)—represented the greatest harvest of atheist and agnostic publication in literary history. Building on themes established in the nineteenth century, twentieth-century writers reached new audiences with mass market and trade paper editions of works promoting unqualified science education, greater church-state separation, unlimited free-speech protections, reproductive freedom, and deepening ties between nonbelievers and global movements for peace and social justice. By the dawn of the new millennium, atheism and related expressions of unbelief had successfully claimed a greater share of freedom and secured a permanent place in mainstream literary culture.

Today, especially stimulated by the early twenty-first-century New Atheist movement and the rise of the Nones, books on atheism, agnosticism, and all forms of free thought and nonreligion flood the market—in traditional print, e-book, and audio formats. Books, in and out of harmony with the New Atheist agenda, include critiques of religious belief and behavior, defenses of nontheism, autobiographical accounts of conversion and deconversion, histories of nonreligion, experiments in post-theist fiction and poetry, and self-help books addressing relationships, parenting, and life-cycle ceremonies from a variety of god-free perspectives. The most striking feature of the twenty-first-century literature of unbelief is the rising prominence of the voices of women, LGBTQ+ persons, young adults, and people of color. Courtney Lynn's *I'm an Atheist and That's OK* (2014), Gene Weingarten's *Me and Dog* (2014), and Jessica Thorpe's *Atheism for Kids* (2016) represent a new wave of books for children.

Books, however, are not the only purveyors of modern unbelief and doubt. Magazines, newspapers, newsletters, pamphlets, and other forms of ephemeral literature have long played a role in disseminating atheist and agnostic ideas to the broader public. For centuries, skeptics and critics of religion have exhibited mastery in the production of the provocative pamphlet, a document often tied to a specific event or based on a controversial speech or debate. In some circumstances, the anonymous pamphlet has been the only way to communicate a nontheist message in an inhospitable cultural environment. Newsletters have accompanied the rise and fall of atheist and humanist organizations. Magazines, an invention of the Enlightenment period and coterminous with modern atheism, remain a vital part of the nonreligious population's life, connecting unbelievers with like-minded colleagues and allies and building community through common rhetoric, shared concerns, and joint action. *The Truth Seeker*, established in the United States in 1873 and recognized as the oldest continually published free-thought periodical in the world, concentrates principally on celebrating the heritage of humanist and nonreligious life and thought. *The Little Freethinker*, launched in 1892 by ex-Quaker atheist Elmina D. Slenker, may have been America's first nonreligious magazine for children.

Today, print and virtual publications include *American Atheist Magazine*, created by American Atheists founder Madalyn Murray O'Hair, the Center for Inquiry's *Free Inquiry*, the American Humanist Association's *The Humanist*, the Rationalist Association's *New Humanist*, and Atheist Alliance International's *Secular World*. *Secularism and Nonreligion*, overseen by the Nonreligion and Secularity Research Network, is the first open-access, scholarly journal to publish peer-reviewed articles advancing research in the academic study of atheism, agnosticism, and related political and social issues.

Increasingly mainstream organs of news and opinion recognize atheism and agnosticism as serious and complex features of the contemporary cultural landscape. Nonreligious journalism has joined the once-standard church beat. *Time* magazine's 1966 Easter issue, with its "Is God Dead?" cover in red and black, was the beginning of a trend. It was followed quickly by *Playboy*'s publication of radical theologian William Hamilton's essay "God Is Dead." Susan Jacoby's "Spirited Atheist" column for the *Washington Post* (2010–2012), provided an unprecedented platform for a positive and forthright message of nonreligion's value in the public sphere.

Unsung heroes in the history of atheist and agnostic media interactions have been the publishers and printers who risked life and livelihood for the cause of freedom of thought and speech. Even before radical printer Richard Carlile accompanied Rev. Robert Taylor, the "Devil's Chaplain," on his 1829 "Infidel Home Mission Tour" of Great Britain's universities, including young Darwin's Cambridge, individuals who literally constructed countercultural books and magazines worked closely with the writers who conceived the countercultural messages. Sites for book printing and selling frequently functioned as spaces for nonconformists to gather and share ideas. Anarchist William Godwin and feminist Mary Wollstonecraft launched their romance at radical printer-entrepreneur Joseph Johnson's bookshop/workshop in London. The spaces, however, were never completely safe. The history of atheophobia includes the history of hostility to literary and business accomplices sympathetic to visionary and controversial thinkers. The burning of books and destruction of printing presses are two parts of one story. Voltaire's books were burned; his publisher-dealer was subjected to the public punishment of the pillory.

Over the years, many atheist and agnostic writers have found it extremely difficult to find printers willing to take the economic and political risks entailed in the pursuit of unpopular ventures. The examples of Marx and Nietzsche self-publishing their works and selling only a handful of copies are not atypical. As modern publishing houses developed in the nineteenth and early twentieth centuries, few editors justified financial commitments to otherwise intellectually engaging projects that could negatively impact the corporate enterprise. Since the middle of the twentieth century, special-interest publishing firms have emerged, devoted to works articulating atheist, agnostic, and secular insights. Free Press, Freedom from Religion Foundation, American Atheist Press, Oak Hill Free Books, Pitchstone, Dirty Heathen Publishing, and Infidel Books currently publish some of the most popular titles in nonreligious thought. Prometheus Books, founded in 1969 by American philosopher Paul Kurtz, editor of *The Humanist* for over ten years, is the preeminent company in the field.

Proponents of atheist and agnostic viewpoints have also made impressive use of the full complement of electronic and social media technologies. In the twenty-first century, secular and nonreligious websites compete in cyberspace with religious sites for ingenuity, efficiency, relevance, and audacity. Atheism United Wiki (www.atheismunited.com) provides a wide array of resources, as does the Secular Web, sporting the URL www .infidels.org. The ever-growing Celebrity Atheist List can be found at www.celebatheists.com. Videos showcase scores of lectures, interviews, testimonials, and debates on unbelief old and new. Philosopher Alain de

Botton's landmark 2011 TED talk "Atheism 2.0" continues to attract a steady stream of viewers. Former high school teacher Hemant Mehta's *Friendly Atheist* blog and weekly podcasts bring commentary on politics and popular culture from an upbeat, faith-free point of view. Self-declared "science nerd" Rebecca Watson's *Skepchick* blog and website thrive at the intersection of skepticism and feminism. Other popular secular-pitched blogs and podcasts include *The Thinking Atheist, The Scathing Atheist, The Non-Prophets, Atheists on Air, Atheist Nexus, Poetic Atheism, Godless Bitches, Cellar Door Skeptics, Queereka,* and *I, Medusa* (hosted by atheist witch Anna Mist). YouTube videos by "Atheist Codger" David Goza, accompanied by the playful cat Endocene, dominate an unbelief-meets-serious-musicology lane in social media.

Talk radio and the twenty-first-century transformation of web-based television have brought atheist and agnostic outlooks into the listening and viewing spaces of millions of people around the world. A new breed of teleatheists rival and mimic televangelists; some, former Christian clergy, apply the skills honed in their previous profession to their new secular vocation. Media personality Ron Reagan's signature "not afraid of burning in hell" commercial spots for the Freedom from Religion Foundation (www.ffrf.org) have arguably raised greater awareness for nontheism in sixty seconds than any number of freethinking publications with hundreds of pages and footnotes.

While the concept of the atheist or agnostic film is a matter of ongoing debate, so-called unbeliever-friendly movies include the 1960 classic *Inherit the Wind,* based on the Jerome Lawrence and Robert E. Lee play about the 1925 antievolution Scopes trial, and a cluster of films released in the early 2000s: *The Da Vinci Code* (2006); *Jesus Camp* (2006); *The Golden Compass* (2007), based on Philip Pullman's *His Dark Materials* trilogy; *The Great Debaters* (2007), based on the career of African American humanist and Wiley College professor Melvin B. Tolson; *Religulous* (2008); *The Stoning of Saroya M.* (2008); *Agora* (2009); *The Invention of Lying* (2009); and *Creation* (2009), telling the story of the death of Charles Darwin's young daughter and his uneasy relationship with his religiously devout wife. The documentary *Hug an Atheist* (2013) by British filmmaker Sylvia Broeckx offers an empathetic portrait of the lives of god-free people in the twenty-first century.

See also: Agnosticism; Atheism, New; Atheism 2.0; Atheophobia; Darwin, Charles; Deism; Feminism, Atheism and Agnosticism and;

Feuerbach, Ludwig; Friendly Atheist, The; Huxleys, The; Jacoby, Susan; Kurtz, Paul; LGBTQ+ Persons, Atheist and Agnostic; Marx, Karl; Nietzsche, Friedrich

Further Reading

Armstrong, Karen. *A History of God: The 4000-Year Quest of Judaism, Christianity and Islam*. New York: Alfred A. Knopf, 1993.

Christie-Murray, David. *A History of Heresy*. Oxford: Oxford University Press, 1991.

Febvre, Lucien. *The Problem of Unbelief in the Sixteenth Century: The Religion of Rabelais*. Trans. Beatrice Gottlieb. Cambridge, MA: Harvard University Press, 1982.

Gauna, Max. *Upwellings: First Expressions of Unbelief in the Printed Literature of the French Renaissance*. Rutherford, NJ: Fairleigh Dickinson University Press, 1992.

Hecht, Jennifer Michael. *Doubt: A History*. San Francisco: HarperSanFrancisco, 2003.

Hunter, Michael, and David Wootton, eds. *Atheism from the Reformation to the Enlightenment*. Oxford: Clarendon Press, 1992.

Joshi, S. T., ed. *The Original Atheists: First Thoughts on Nonbelief*. Amherst, NY: Prometheus Books, 2014.

Mansfield, Harvey C., Jr., ed. *Thomas Jefferson: Selected Writings*. Arlington Heights, IL: Harlan Davidson, 1979.

Mehta, Hemant. *The Friendly Atheist: Thoughts on the Role of Religion in Politics and Media*. Englewood, CO: Patheos Press, 2013.

Reiman, Donald H., and Sharon B. Powers, eds. *Shelley's Poetry and Prose*. New York: W. W. Norton, 1977.

Warburton, Nigel. *Free Speech: A Very Short Introduction*. Oxford: Oxford University Press, 2009.

N

Nietzsche, Friedrich

Friedrich Nietzsche (1844–1900) is one of the most quoted and least understood writers in modern history. The issues he addressed—self-discovery, the adventure of independent thinking, the fearless transgression of taboos—all contribute to his high profile in the academy and in popular culture. His penchant for first-person writing, where nonfiction and near fiction overlap, especially in concise provocative aphorisms, nurtures what has become a seemingly unshakable legacy of misunderstanding. His fateful and unwitting tendency to attract disciples on the Far Right—from Hitler's philosophers to today's alt-right pundits—only feeds the frequency with which interpreters assign him to the category of enigma. His lapse into mental illness during his last decade grants his already eccentric life an unfinished and undefinable quality. One thing is beyond dispute: Nietzsche crossed a line in the Western mind. God is dead, he declared. For over a century, this electric proclamation, difficult to comprehend fully, has spoken to untold numbers of individuals who confront the West's largely Christian heritage with suspicion, dissatisfaction, and outrage.

Nietzsche was phenomenally productive during his brief career. He was forty-four years old when he collapsed and was committed to an asylum. He was fifty-six when he died, paralyzed and speechless. He was a professor for only ten years. During the period of his most intense creativity, dogged by insomnia, deteriorating eyesight, digestive trauma, and multiday migraines, he wrote over ten books in a highly personalized style, revolutionizing philosophy in both form and substance. He philosophized with a hammer, he said, but also with a skillfully wielded stiletto. He was master of the miniature, packing much into small spaces. His signature phrases—the transvaluation of all values, the will to power, the

Übermensch (rendered variously as "overman" and "superman"), "Live dangerously!"—now have a life of their own, rousing and repelling readers in all cultures.

Nietzsche's background did not augur a future as prophet of the death of God. Born in Saxony, the heart of Martin Luther country, he was raised by parents with deep roots in German Protestant tradition: his father a pastor, and his mother the daughter of a pastor. After his father's struggle with mental illness and premature death, the young Nietzsche attended single-sex boarding schools, where his record was notable but unexceptional. In Gymnasium, or secondary school, he began to demonstrate greater intellectual promise and achieved impressive proficiency in classical languages and music, both piano performance and composition. At the University of Bonn, Nietzsche pursued interests in theology and what would become his area of expertise: philology, the study of the origin, structure, and function of (mainly ancient) languages. Following a beloved mentor to the University of Leipzig, he left behind theology—and Christian faith—and prepared for a teaching career in his chosen field.

Nietzsche gained the respectable position of professor of philology at the University of Basel in Switzerland but never quite fit into academic culture. Even his early writings did not conform to the narrow standards of research then dominating the profession. From the beginning, his interests ranged far beyond his discipline, and he ignored unspoken expectations regarding scholarly style. His tenure was interrupted by aggravating illness, service as a medical orderly during the Franco-Prussian War, and a distracting infatuation with the musical genius Richard Wagner, at the time revolutionizing the world of opera. An amateur philosopher and confirmed atheist, Wagner was reading post-Christian thinkers such as Ludwig Feuerbach and Arthur Schopenhauer when he made Nietzsche an intimate in his inner circle. Nietzsche wrote four books about the composer, increasingly antagonistic, and eventually abandoned their complex relationship because of Wagner's mounting Germanic chauvinism and antisemitism.

After retiring from Basel for health reasons at age thirty-four, Nietzsche ventured upon an independent and iconoclastic writing career, never enjoying a permanent home, technically stateless, and always seeking new medical treatments, at times self-medicating with opium. He had intense and unsteady relationships with a handful of friends, most notably the closet-atheist theologian Franz Overbeck and the future psychoanalyst Lou Andreas-Salomé, author of *Friedrich Nietzsche in His Works* (1894), *The Erotic* (1910), and *Struggling for God* (1885), a fictional account of her ill-fated love triangle with Nietzsche and Jewish atheist philosopher Paul Rée. Queer theorists and gay-affirmative biographers have connected Nietzsche's experiences and his emerging concept of the death of God with the deep history of modern gay liberation. By all accounts, he met only disappointment in his romantic ambitions. Historical speculation identifies the cause of his decline and death as either sexually transmitted disease or brain cancer.

In his books, published at the rate of about one a year, Nietzsche blurred the boundaries between poetry and prose, philosophy and art, analysis and autobiography. His style became increasingly oracular. He declaimed and never explained, leaving the hard work of figuring out what he was saying to his readers. He adopted a prophet, the ancient Persian seer Zarathustra (Zoroaster), as his chosen mouthpiece.

Nietzsche's most important works include *The Gay Science* (1882), *Thus Spoke Zarathustra* (1883–1885), *Beyond Good and Evil* (1886), *On the Genealogy of Morals* (1887), *Twilight of the Idols* (1888), *The Antichrist* (1888), and *Ecce Homo: How One Becomes What One Is* (1888)—all of which have had a transformative influence on a host of writers, scholars, artists, actors, and therapists worldwide. Page after page he advanced his argument against what he thought were the life-denying aspects of Christianity and its "spider" deity: the negation of human instinct, the denigration of all things earthly, and especially the shame and resentment he detected in middle-class Christian morality.

Lingering charges of racism and fascism, exacerbated by Nazi fawners and his sister Elisabeth's opportunistic misreading of his work, have been disproved in recent decades. Nietzsche was an uncompromising opponent of nationalism and antisemitism. Feminist scholars have long condemned the negative view of women on display in his texts. As philosopher Mary Daly put it, his priceless prophetic work was "short-circuited" by unexamined misogyny. Some specialists in gender studies suggest that Nietzsche, in the dense code of his individualized language, was actually dismantling the gender dualism he inherited from Christianity. As a professor, he offered a course on Sappho, the ancient Greek poet whose name is virtually synonymous with lesbianism. No student registered for it.

Nietzsche's atheism encompasses a vast range of insights and emotions. He came to his atheism, or it came to him, through the trials of experience and intuition rather than inference or inquiry. The message of the death of God in *Gay Science* and *Zarathustra*—announced in one by a madman, in the other by a mocked prophet—is a revelation of humanity unmoored and adrift, unsponsored but also liberated. For Nietzsche, atheism is not the conclusion of a rational syllogism. It is the stunning realization of human responsibility, awesome opportunity, and the prospect for unprecedented joy. Some see Nietzsche's atheism as a mysticism without God. In his 1900 memorial address in Berlin, Rudolf Steiner, freethinking mystic and founder of eurhythmy and Waldorf education, called Nietzsche the "poet of the new world conception."

See also: Christianity, Atheism and Agnosticism in; Feuerbach, Ludwig; Proofs for God, Atheist and Agnostic Critiques of

Further Reading

Daly, Mary. *Beyond God the Father: Toward a Philosophy of Women's Liberation.* Boston: Beacon Press, 1985.

De Lubac, Henri. *The Drama of Atheist Humanism.* Trans. Edith M. Riley, Anne Englund Nash, and Mark Sebanc. San Francisco: Ignatius Press, 1995.

Diethe, Carol. *Nietzsche's Women: Beyond the Whip.* Boston: Walter de Gruyter, 1996.

Kaufmann, Walter. *Nietzsche: Philosopher, Psychologist, Antichrist.* 4th ed. Princeton, NJ: Princeton University Press, 1974.

Kaufmann, Walter, ed. and trans. *The Portable Nietzsche.* New York: Penguin, 1982.

Köhler, Joachim. *Zarathustra's Secret: The Interior Life of Friedrich Nietzsche.* Trans. Ronald Taylor. New Haven, CT: Yale University Press, 2002.

Nietzsche, Friedrich. *Beyond Good and Evil.* Trans. R. J. Hollingdale. London: Penguin, 1990.

Nietzsche, Friedrich. *The Gay Science.* Trans. Walter Kaufmann. New York: Vintage Books, 1974.

Nietzsche, Friedrich. *On the Genealogy of Morals and Ecce Homo.* Trans. Walter Kaufmann and R. J. Hollingdale. New York: Vintage Books, 1969.

Nietzsche, Friedrich. *Twilight of the Idols and The Anti-Christ.* Trans. R. J. Hollingdale. New York: Penguin, 1979.

Oppel, Frances Nesbitt. *Nietzsche on Gender: Beyond Man and Woman.* Charlottesville: University of Virginia Press, 2005.

Prideaux, Sue. *I Am Dynamite! A Life of Nietzsche.* New York: Tim Duggan Books, 2018.

Sherratt, Yvonne. *Hitler's Philosophers.* New Haven, CT: Yale University Press, 2013.

Steiner, Rudolf. *Friedrich Nietzsche: Fighter for Freedom.* Trans. Margaret Ingram deRis. Blauvelt, NY: Garber, 1985.

Tanner, Michael. *Nietzsche: A Very Short Introduction*. New York: Oxford University Press, 2001.

Vickers, Julia. *Lou von Salomé: A Biography of the Woman Who Inspired Freud, Nietzsche and Rilke*. Jefferson, NC: McFarland, 2008.

Nones

Nones (rhymes with *nuns*) represent one of the newest forms of nonreligion or unconventional spirituality in U.S. culture. Nones may be atheists or agnostics by another name. They may also be theists of one sort or another. What unites them, at least in theory, is not a belief system but resistance to or dissatisfaction with a cluster of factors that fall under the category of organized religion. Rapidly growing, though constituting a group only in abstract statistical terms, Nones offer great insight into the future of both religion and nonreligion.

American religious and intellectual history has always been characterized by plurality, fluidity, and creativity. U.S. culture has long been a fertile seedbed for new religious movements and new philosophies of life. Prophets, seers, reformers, and critics, often with entrepreneurial spirit, have energized every period of the nation's history. Some have paid dearly for their innovation, despite popular allegiance to individualism and constitutional guarantees of freedom of religion and speech. Many have sought refinements of, rediscoveries of, or new variations on existing traditions. Even skeptics and freethinkers have expressed their criticisms in terms borrowed from the traditions they have found so problematic. Nones signal something new. Appearing just as the United States was ceasing to be a majority Protestant nation, Nones have ignored or bypassed the culture's religions more than they have sought to assail or correct them.

None entered the U.S. vocabulary during the first decade of the twenty-first century. *American Nones: The Profile of the No Religion Population* (2009), produced by Barry A. Kosmin and researchers at the Institute for the Study of Secularism in Society and Culture at Trinity College in Hartford, Connecticut, introduced the term to the general public. The Pew Research Center's report *"Nones" on the Rise* (2012) consolidated its place in the American lexicon. *None* is social-scientific shorthand for a person unaffiliated with a religious tradition or institution, alluding to the "none of the above" option that often completes a list of choices in a sociological survey. In the early years of the new millennium, researchers detected acute growth in levels of nonaffiliation, especially among young adults. As the century has progressed, the number of Nones in all age brackets has increased significantly.

The first signs of change came in 2008, with the release of the U.S. Religious Landscape Survey produced by the Pew Forum on Religion and Public Life. It documented core features of the American religious experience: Americans tend to be believers, they are relatively undogmatic when it comes to doctrine, and many exhibit a propensity to switch religions at least once over a lifetime. The survey also confirmed the shrinking of mainline Protestantism, once considered the backbone of U.S. religious life. The most striking feature of the document concerned the status of the religiously unaffiliated: 16.1 percent of the adult population. Including atheists (1.6 percent), agnostics (2.4 percent), and people who identified with "nothing in particular" (12.1 percent), the group outnumbered the nation's Buddhist, Hindu, Jewish, Mormon, Muslim, and Unitarian Universalist populations combined.

By 2019, the religiously unaffiliated portion of the population—now dubbed Nones—had jumped to 26 percent of all U.S. adults, with atheists at 4 percent and agnostics at 5 percent. The greatest rate of growth was identified in individuals eighteen to twenty-nine years of age, almost half of whom professed no affiliation. Today, many observers call "no faith" the nation's fastest-growing faith. The content of that uncommon faith, however, remains ill defined.

Nones avoid organized religions for a variety of reasons, frequently because of the religions' age-old connections with racism, sexism, anti-LGBTQ+ hatred, authoritarianism, and limitations on intellectual freedom. They also express impatience with the concept of religious membership itself, often seeing it as a relic of colonial or capitalist distortions of genuine faith. Some Nones, like other Americans, participate in unofficial multiple religious belonging or experiment with hyphenated religious identities, such as Jewish-Buddhist. Some take a cafeteria approach to religion, borrowing elements from a wide array of religious and philosophical sources. Some self-describe as "spiritual but not religious" (SBNR in sociological jargon). Some say the terms of religion—revelation, ritual, spiritual experience—are meaningless for them, as are perennial debates between belief and unbelief.

Such complex identities defy the data categories of social science research. The phenomenon of the Nones challenges the once unquestioned binary opposition of religion and nonreligion.

See also: Atheism, New; LGBTQ+ Persons, Atheist and Agnostic

Further Reading

Baggett, Jerome P. *The Varieties of Nonreligious Experience: Atheism in American Culture.* New York: New York University Press, 2019.

Brewster, Melanie E., ed. *Atheists in America.* New York: Columbia University Press, 2014.

Drescher, Elizabeth. *Choosing Our Religion: The Spiritual Lives of America's Nones.* New York: Oxford University Press, 2016.

Epstein, Greg. *Good without God: What a Billion Nonreligious People Do Believe.* New York: HarperCollins, 2009.

Gray, John. *Seven Types of Atheism.* New York: Farrar, Straus and Giroux, 2018.

Kosmin, Barry A., Ariela Keysar, Ryan T. Cragun, and Juhem Navarro-Rivera. *American Nones: The Profile of the No Religion Population.* Hartford, CT: Institute for the Study of Secularism in Society and Culture, 2009.

Moore, R. Lawrence, and Isaac Kramnick. *Godless Citizens in a Godly Republic: Atheists in American Public Life.* New York: W. W. Norton, 2018.

Niose, David. *Nonbeliever Nation: The Rise of Secular Americans.* New York: Palgrave Macmillan, 2012.

Ozment, Katherine. *Grace without God: The Search for Meaning, Purpose, and Belonging in a Secular Age.* New York: Harper Collins, 2016.

Pew Forum. *U.S. Religious Landscape Survey.* Washington, DC: Pew Forum on Religion and Public Life, 2008.

Zuckerman, Phil. *Living the Secular Life: New Answers to Old Questions.* New York: Penguin, 2014.

Zuckerman, Phil. *What It Means to Be Moral: Why Religion Is Not Necessary for Living an Ethical Life.* Berkeley, CA: Counterpoint, 2019.

Zuckerman, Phil, Luke W. Galen, and Frank L. Pasquale. *The Nonreligious: Understanding Secular People and Societies.* New York: Oxford University Press, 2016

Zuckerman, Phil, and John R. Shook, eds. *The Oxford Handbook of Secularism.* New York: Oxford University Press, 2017.

O

O'Hair, Madalyn Murray

Madalyn Murray O'Hair (1919–1995) was one of the best-known and most dynamic advocates for unbelievers in the history of the United States. An unrelenting proponent of strict church-state separation and an unrepentant propagandist for nonbelief, she engaged in litigation for First Amendment rights, promoted awareness of atheist perspectives, and founded American Atheists, one of the nation's first organizations dedicated to the networking and support of nonreligious and antireligious individuals. Because of her high public profile, her confrontational style, and the controversies she sparked, *Life* magazine anointed her "the most hated woman in America" (echoing earlier censures of anarchist Emma Goldman). O'Hair's improbable rise to prominence and her horrific death—outdone by few true-crime stories—make hers one of the most remarkable lives in the American experience.

At one point in her career, O'Hair was even called the most famous atheist in the world. Her early years, however, if noteworthy, were far from extraordinary. A native of Pittsburgh, she was raised in a middle-class Protestant family of Irish and German ancestry. She earned her undergraduate degree from Ashland University and a law degree from South Texas College of Law, serving during World War II as a commissioned officer in the Women's Army Auxiliary Corps in Europe. What began to set her apart from her neighbors after the war was her involvement in libertarian causes and her unconventional lifestyle. She opposed the anticommunist crusade of Sen. Joseph McCarthy as well as the United States' military involvement in Korea, and she snubbed popular norms regarding marriage, family, and gender roles.

In the early 1960s, O'Hair became a household name virtually overnight. The decade prior had witnessed what many in government and business were touting as a postwar return to religion. The National Advertising Council launched its "Back to God" campaign. Mainline denominations boasted record-breaking levels of affiliation and attendance. The U.S. Congress added "under God" to the Pledge of Allegiance, and President Eisenhower made "In God We Trust" the country's official motto. Catholic bishop Fulton J. Sheen topped the TV ratings charts, and evangelical Cold War crusader Billy Graham preached his way toward the unprecedented title of "America's pastor." Huge numbers of Americans routinely referred to the United States as a Christian nation. Mandatory prayer and reading of the Bible were standard practices in tax-supported schools.

O'Hair, at the time an obscure homemaker, contributed as much to the breaking of the mood of the allegedly placid '50s as any beatnik or communist sympathizer. Her unlikely saga began with concern for religiously motivated discrimination against her son in school. In 1960, she filed a lawsuit that eventually led to U.S. Supreme Court decisions determining prayer and Bible reading in public schools to be unconstitutional. Over the course of the next two decades, O'Hair initiated similar legal challenges to a host of other uncritically accepted and protected practices and institutions: the banning of atheists on the airwaves, religious services in the White House, prayers before legislative sessions, the broadcasted reading of scripture by U.S. astronauts orbiting the moon, holiday religious displays on government property, and tax-supported chaplains at public hospitals. At the peak of her career, she was perhaps best known for her unsuccessful 1978 case against "In God We Trust" on U.S. currency.

By the '70s, O'Hair's unmistakable cause and unforgettably brash style were familiar features on the university lecture circuit and on television news and talk shows. It was a time when popular assumptions still associated atheism with immorality. Her founding of American Atheists in 1963 put unbelief on a firm structural basis in the United States. She used the organization as a platform for a radio program, a cable TV show, a newsletter and magazine, and the publication of books and pamphlets. Her writings, such as *Freedom under Siege* (1974) and *Why I Am an Atheist* (1991), concentrated on intellectual freedom, the rights of nonbelievers, and explanations of atheist perspectives for a popular audience.

O'Hair's adult life was never free from controversy or crisis, including the events surrounding her tragic and grisly death. In the 1980s, she was in the public eye because her first son, William Murray, converted to Christianity and became a vocal critic of her life work, publishing his tell-all autobiography *My Life without God* (1982). In 1995, she was in the headlines again, this time due to her mysterious disappearance and that of her second son, Jon Garth Murray and of William's estranged daughter, Robin Murray O'Hair—along with thousands of dollars from the accounts of American Atheists. Painstaking criminal investigation led to a robbery-kidnapping-murder plot hatched by a former employee of American Atheists. Six years after the disappearance, law enforcement authorities discovered the decomposed and dismembered bodies of O'Hair and her two relatives, buried in a remote field in Texas.

Once dreaded and derided, O'Hair is now recognized as a seminal figure in the history of American unbelief and the nation's evolving understanding of constitutional rights and liberties. Her contribution to public recognition and acceptance of nonreligion is of immense significance. She set the stage for an organized, activist atheism, unapologetic and unafraid. Today, American Atheists (www.atheists.org), with nearly 400,000 members and over 170 local affiliates across the country, continues her legacy of tenacious education and engagement.

See also: Goldman, Emma; "In God We Trust"; Media, Atheism and Agnosticism and the; Organizations, Atheist and Agnostic; "Under God"

Further Reading

Dracos, Ted. *UnGodly: The Passions, Torments, and Murder of Atheist Madalyn Murray O'Hair*. New York: Free Press, 2010.

LeBeau, Bryan F. *The Atheist: Madalyn Murray O'Hair*. New York: New York University Press, 2003.

Murray, William J. *My Life without God*. Washington, DC: WND Books, 2012.

O'Hair, Madalyn Murray. *Freedom under Siege: The Impact of Organized Religion on Your Liberty and Your Pocketbook*. Los Angeles: J. P. Tarcher, 1974.

O'Hair, Madalyn Murray. *Why I Am an Atheist*. 2nd rev. ed. Austin, TX: American Atheist Press, 1991.

Seaman, Ann Rowe. *America's Most Hated Woman: The Life and Gruesome Death of Madalyn Murray O'Hair*. New York: Continuum Books, 2003.

Organizations, Atheist and Agnostic

The experience of being atheist or agnostic can be highly individual. It can even be secretive. The prevalence of atheophobia, fear or hatred of unbelievers, has contributed significantly to the solitary nature of the nonreligious life. Typically, it has been the lone individual, intellectually and emotionally distant from the assumptions of the age, who has questioned received wisdom and cultivated unpopular ideas—often at great risk. While religions have been almost constitutionally social, atheism and agnosticism have historically represented views of the world explored in relative isolation or shared with considerable discretion.

Atheism and agnosticism, however, are not by definition private affairs. From the coffeehouses and salons of the Enlightenment *philosophes* to the meetups and internet encounters of the twenty-first century, modern doubt and disbelief have consistently bred networks and communities for independent thinkers outside the religious mainstream. Scores of nontheist and nonreligious groups dot the current cultural landscape. Some mimic religious bodies with creed-like statements and charismatic leaders. Some function as alternative academies. Some agitate for social change. Others have less intensive agendas, attempting to offer like-minded individuals opportunities to socialize and express themselves in safe, supportive environments.

Some versions of atheist and agnostic organized life are informal, fostering face-to-face relationships. Others are comparatively impersonal, intricately structured and highly regulated. Some are local, some national, some international. Some are nongovernmental organizations (NGOs) associated with the United Nations.

Most of the earliest freethinking organizations have been lost to history—such as the Friends of Mental Liberty and the Society for Moral Philanthropists from America's colonial and early national periods. Two of the first modern organizations explicitly associated with atheism and agnosticism were products of Britain's age of Victorian dissent. The National Secular Society was founded in 1866 by Charles Bradlaugh, Britain's first openly atheist member of Parliament. Its journal, *National Reformer*, was coedited by Bradlaugh and radical writer Annie Besant, both of whom faced obscenity charges for publishing banned birth control material. The Rationalist Association, established as the Rationalist Press Association in 1885, remains, along with its *New Humanist* magazine, an important contributor to secular and skeptical discourse in the United Kingdom.

An example of an atheist organization aligned with a particular nation-state is the League of Militant Atheists, active in the Soviet Union from 1925 to 1947. Commissioned by the USSR's Communist Party secretary-general Joseph Stalin to "storm the heavens," it functioned as a propaganda instrument, publishing critiques of traditional religious doctrines and practices—including the ringing of church bells—and attempting to demonstrate the superiority of farms and factories run by self-declared godless workers and administrators in contrast to those maintained by laborers and overseers associated with Russian Orthodox Christianity. At its height, the League's membership numbered in the hundreds of millions.

The premier global organization for nonreligious people today is Humanists International (https://humanists.international), formerly called the International Humanist and Ethical Union, an NGO based in London. Since 1952, it has served as a consortium of atheist, agnostic, humanist, and free-thought groups from all over the world. Its purpose is multi-pronged, committing resources to work in the areas of support, education, research, and social action. It concentrates on campaigns to protect the rights of the nonreligious and abolish blasphemy and apostasy laws. The organization hosts an annual World Humanist Congress, promotes the celebration of June 21 as World Humanist Day, and publishes the annual Freedom of Thought Report, documenting human rights abuses around the globe. Its Amsterdam Declaration, released in 1952 and revised in 2002, is one of the core documents of humanism's evolving canon, summarizing the basic principles of the humanist vision.

Another global organization is Atheist Alliance International (www.atheistalliance.org), with offices in California and Washington. Launched in 1991 as a U.S. nonprofit called Atheist Alliance, it has added affiliates in other countries, changing its name in 2001 to reflect its enlarged scope as a multinational coalition of atheist groups. Known for its "right to be secular" initiative, Atheist Alliance International supports educational projects and legal aid for individuals endangered by blasphemy laws, atheophobic travel restrictions, and other repressive regulations. It publishes *Secular World*, maintains a robust social media presence, and holds regular international conferences.

The United States is home to a vast array of organizations serving the country's diverse nontheist and nonreligious community. American Atheists (www.atheists.org) was inaugurated in 1963 by Madalyn Murray O'Hair, one of the most controversial unbelievers in U.S. history. With nearly 400,000 members and over 230 local affiliates, American Atheists has continued and expanded O'Hair's legacy of tenacious education, activism, and political pressure. Through its *American Atheist* magazine, its social media communications, and its provocative "Skip Church" and "You Know It's a Myth" holiday billboard campaigns, the organization tracks violations of church-state separation, provides coverage of anti-atheist prejudice, offers commentary on issues from anti-LGBTQ+ discrimination to pseudoscience trends in popular culture, and keeps the atheist message in the popular imagination. It sponsors a yearly national convention featuring celebrity speakers and entertainers and is headquartered in the American Atheists Center in Cranford, New Jersey.

The American Humanist Association (https://americanhumanist.org), with its motto "Good without a God," is the foremost body of humanists in the United States. Based in Washington, DC, it exists to raise awareness about humanism as a way of life, advocate for humanism in the public sphere, and support the needs and rights of individuals who identify as humanist with a broad set of services and resources. The roots of the American Humanist Association go back to the Humanist Fellowship of the 1920s and '30s, a circle of Unitarian and like-minded professors and students at the University of Chicago who laid the groundwork for the first Humanist Manifesto (1933). Renamed the Humanist Press Association in 1935, the organization became the American Humanist Association in 1941. Today, members and their allies represent a range of outlooks stretching from religious humanism to secular humanism. With 180 chapters and 32,000 members nationwide, the association organizes annual conferences and publishes *Humanist* magazine and (with the Institute for Humanist Studies) *Essays in the Philosophy of Humanism*. It also offers a certificate and graduate degree in humanist studies through its Center for Education, trains and authorizes humanist celebrants for weddings and funerals, and selects a leading humanist thinker, artist, or activist to receive its Humanist of the Year award.

A growing number of U.S. organizations address issues of inclusion and equity and strive to serve marginalized populations within the larger atheist and agnostic community. Driving most is mounting concern over explicit and implicit racism, sexism, and homophobia within nonreligious groups and movements. The American Humanist Association sponsors four working groups: the Black Humanist Alliance, the Feminist Humanist Alliance, the Latinx Humanist Alliance, and the LGBTQ Humanist Alliance. Organizations formed in the early twenty-first century, building on the historic African American humanist tradition, include Black Atheists of America, Black Freethinkers, People of Color Beyond Faith, and African Americans for Humanism (www.AAHumanism.net). Two of the most active organizations are groups founded by women: Black Nonbelievers Inc. (www.blacknonbelievers.com), started by Mandisa

Thomas, named 2019 Person of the Year by the Unitarian Universalist Humanist Association, and Black Skeptics of Los Angeles, founded by Sikivu Hutchinson, author of *Humanists in the Hood* (2020).

Secular Woman Inc. (https://secularwoman.org), registered as a nonprofit in 2012, represents one of the organizations formed by and for nonreligious women. Ayaan Hirsi Ali's nonprofit AHA Foundation (www .theahafoundation.org), founded in 2007, works to promote the rights of women, believing and unbelieving, within Islamic cultures. Atheism Plus, or Atheism+, initiated in 2012 by Jennifer McCreight, a blogger associated with the Secular Student Alliance, has been an important response to sexism and sexual harassment in contemporary atheist culture. It seeks to advance the cause of atheism in solidarity with feminism and social justice activism and in opposition to racism, homophobia, and transphobia.

Related groups in the United States, some not specifically limited to nontheist or nonreligious individuals, include Americans United for the Separation of Church and State, founded in 1948; Secular Coalition for America, founded in 2002; Foundation Beyond Belief, a humanist charitable organization, established in 2010; and Freedom from Religion Foundation (https://ffrf.org), started in 1978. Organized by Anne Nicol Gaylor and housed in Freethought Hall in downtown Madison, Wisconsin, Freedom from Religion Foundation is a communications and publishing enterprise, famous for its television commercials featuring President Ronald Reagan's radio host son with his one-of-a-kind sign-off: "Ron Reagan, lifelong atheist, not afraid of burning in hell."

Organizations supporting the atheist and agnostic community with research and scholarship include the Atheist Research Collaborative, the Humanist Institute (now in partnership with the American Humanist Association), and the Institute for Humanist Studies (http://humaniststudies .org), based in Washington, DC, and directed by Anthony B. Pinn, author and editor of groundbreaking studies, including *By These Hands: A Documentary History of African American Humanism* (2001). The Center for Inquiry (https://centerforinquiry.org), headquartered in Amherst, New York, is a bastion of humanist intellectual life, publishing the journals *Free Inquiry* and *Skeptical Inquirer* and the podcast *Point of Inquiry*. The Center is the result of the 1991 merger of two organizations created by philosopher and secular humanist entrepreneur Paul Kurtz: the Committee for the Scientific Investigation of Claims of the Paranormal (now the Committee for Skeptical Inquiry) and the Council for Democratic and Secular Humanism (renamed Council for Secular Humanism). A division of the

Center for Inquiry is the Richard Dawkins Foundation for Reason and Science (www.richarddawkins.net), created in 2006. The Foundation promotes science education, secularism, and multifaceted support for individuals, including professional religious leaders, exploring and adopting non-supernatural worldviews.

The first academic professional society devoted to the study of atheism, agnosticism, and related phenomena is the international Nonreligion and Secularity Research Network (https://nonreligionandsecularity .wordpress.com), founded by University of Kent scholar Lois Lee in 2008. It convenes annual scholarly conferences and publishes *Secularism and Nonreligion*, an interdisciplinary, open-access platform featuring peer-reviewed articles, essays, and book reviews. The Secular Student Alliance (https://secularstudents.org), organized in 2001, also plays an important role in the academy. The first nationwide group for atheists, agnostics, humanists, and Nones in higher education, it seeks to empower nonreligious university students as they express their identities and pursue their educational goals and activist agendas.

Two examples of atheist and agnostic groups designed to contribute to specific religious communities are the Society for Humanistic Judaism (https://shj.org), conceived by Rabbi Sherwin T. Wine in 1969, and the Unitarian Universalist Humanist Association (http://www.huumanists .org), established in 1962 as the Fellowship of Religious Humanists. Special-purpose groups, exhibiting the rich diversity within the U.S. atheist and agnostic community, include the Military Association of Atheists and Freethinkers (https://militaryatheists.org), addressing the needs of nonreligious individuals in the U.S. armed forces, and Secular Pro-Life (https://secularprolife.org), an educational and activist organization for nonbelievers opposed to abortion.

See also: Amsterdam Declarations; Atheism and Agnosticism, African American; Atheophobia; Besant, Annie; Bradlaugh, Charles; Dawkins, Richard; Feminism, Atheism and Agnosticism and; Humanism; Humanist Manifestos; Humanist of the Year; Hutchinson, Sikivu; Kurtz, Paul; Media, Atheism and Agnosticism and the; O'Hair, Madalyn Murray; Pinn, Anthony B.

Further Reading

Gibbons, Kendyl L. R., and William R. Murry, eds. *Humanist Voices in Unitarian Universalism*. Boston: Skinner House Books, 2017.

Husband, William. *Godless Communists: Atheism and Society in Soviet Russia, 1917–1932*. DeKalb: Northern Illinois University Press, 2000.

Hutchinson, Sikivu. *Humanists in the Hood: Unapologetically Black, Feminist, and Heretical*. Durham, NC: Pitchstone, 2020.

Peris, Daniel. *Storming the Heavens: The Soviet League of the Militant Godless*. Ithaca, NY: Cornell University Press, 1998.

Pinn, Anthony B., ed. *By These Hands: A Documentary History of African American Humanism*. New York: New York University, 2001.

P

Pinn, Anthony B.

Anthony B. Pinn (b. 1964) is a prolific historian of the African American religious experience and the premier interpreter of African American humanism. The first African American individual to hold an endowed chair at Rice University in Houston, Texas, he has earned a reputation as an academic innovator and a committed mentor of aspiring young scholars. The author, coauthor, or editor of nearly thirty books, Pinn is one of the leading nontheist humanist thinkers in the United States.

Pinn narrates his intellectual development in his autobiography *Writing God's Obituary: How a Good Methodist Became a Better Atheist* (2014). He grew up in the evangelical Protestant tradition in upstate New York, became a child-prodigy preacher before his teenage years, and was formally ordained to the ministry by the end of his high school experience. Undergraduate and graduate study in the Ivy League, however, dramatically challenged his spiritual worldview and his sense of life calling. Influenced by a variety of writers and thinkers such as James Cone, Alice Walker, Cornel West, and Harvard's naturalist theologian Gordon Kaufman, Pinn abandoned traditional theism and cut ties with organized Christianity but not with his intellectual curiosity in Christianity's ideals of cultural engagement and social justice. He is currently affiliated with the Unitarian Universalist (UU) tradition.

Pinn's books include original explorations of post-theist theology, scholarly and popular applications of humanist principles, critical studies of contemporary culture, including rap and hip-hop, and one novel, a crime suspense story called *The New Disciples* (2015). Pinn's investigations into the intersections of the humanist tradition and race have been especially influential. Criticism of Black theology's fundamental contention that God sides with the oppressed is a cornerstone of his work. His documentary history of African American humanism *By These Hands* (2001)—including essays from James Baldwin, W. E. B. Du Bois, Zora Neale Hurston, Richard Wright, Walker, and over a dozen other major figures—has effectively showcased a rich dimension of Black intellectual life only minimally recognized by experts on the Black church and historians of the humanist establishment, largely white, male, and elitist.

Pinn is a prominent presence on the international lecture circuit, both in person and virtually, and is active in his adopted UU tradition, especially the UU Humanist Association. The recipient of the Council for Secular Humanism's 1999 African American Humanist Award and Harvard Humanist Chaplaincy's 2006 Humanist of the Year Award, Pinn is also director of research for the Institute of Humanist Studies in Washington, DC.

See also: Du Bois, W. E. B.; Humanism; Hurston, Zora Neale; Hutchison, Sikivu; Organizations, Atheist and Agnostic

Further Reading

McGowan, Dale, and Anthony B. Pinn, eds. *Everyday Humanism*. Sheffield, UK: Equinox, 2014.

Pinn, Anthony B. *African American Humanist Principles: Living and Thinking Like the Children of Nimrod*. New York: Palgrave MacMillan, 2004.

Pinn, Anthony B., ed. *By These Hands: A Documentary History of African American Humanism*. New York: New York University, 2001.

Pinn, Anthony B. *The End of God-Talk: An African American Humanist Theology*. Oxford: Oxford University Press, 2012.

Pinn, Anthony B. *Humanism: Essays on Race, Religion and Popular Culture*. New York: Bloomsbury Academic, 2015.

Pinn, Anthony B. *What Is Humanism and Why Does It Matter?* London: Routledge, 2014.

Pinn, Anthony B. *When Colorblindness Isn't the Answer: Humanism and the Challenge of Race*. Durham, NC: Pitchstone, 2017.

Pinn, Anthony B. *Writing God's Obituary: How a Good Methodist Became a Better Atheist*. Amherst, NY: Prometheus Books, 2014.

Proofs for God, Atheist and Agnostic Critiques of

The history of Western thought is a long reflection on and long debate about God. Over the centuries, prominent thinkers have produced a series of arguments for God's existence. Often called proofs for the existence of God, they are not proofs in the ordinary sense. Rather, they are attempts to demonstrate, according to their authors and advocates, the different ways in which belief in God can be determined to be reasonable or even demanded by reason. Made possible by the unique synthesis of Greek philosophy and Christian faith that undergirds the Western worldview, the arguments have been developed and advanced by various thinkers throughout Western intellectual history, especially in the period from the eleventh century to the nineteenth century. Today, the arguments represent standard problems to be addressed in academic philosophy, especially in the training of professional philosophers. In different times and different places, atheists and agnostics, along with dissenting religious thinkers of many sorts, have offered numerous criticisms of the traditional proofs.

The theist proofs do not seek to establish the rationality of belief in multiple gods or any conceivable kind of deity. They refer to a specific God or type of God (in English almost always referred to with a capital *G*): the God of Western theism. The God that the traditional proofs have in mind can be defined as the infinite, uncreated intelligence that is the singular source of all that exists. Individuals who endorse one or more of the arguments, especially writers whose frame of reference is the Christian tradition, claim that this God possesses or might possess other defining features but that these additional qualities can be established only on the basis of supernatural revelation, not rational analysis. The God of the proofs is a *what*, not a *who*—the "God of the philosophers," as Blaise Pascal put it, not the personal God of biblical narrative or religious faith.

Three types of arguments have predominated in this field since the Middle Ages, all now with traditional names and long lineages of critical literature: the ontological argument, the cosmological argument, and the teleological argument. Most proofs for God discussed in the academy and in the public marketplace of ideas can be described as variants of these three much-analyzed lines of argumentation.

The ontological argument is best associated with the thought of the eleventh-century Benedictine monk and bishop Anselm, who sought to make a case for the existence of God on the basis of reason alone, independent of scripture and church teaching. Anselm's proof, called ontological because it turns on the concept of being (*ontos* in Greek), claims that sorting through the proper understanding of God itself provides sufficient grounds for affirmation of the existence of God. Just as *triangle* necessarily indicates a three-sided figure, the word *God*, Anselm argued, means a being (and the universe's only being) whose essence includes existence. Anselm called God the being "than which nothing greater can be conceived." The greatest possible being, he said, exists by definition—otherwise, it would not be the greatest.

Since first appearing in his book *Proslogion*, the ontological argument has attracted many thinkers, and Anselm has stimulated a long line of imitators, most notably René Descartes and Gottfried Wilhelm Leibniz. Even skeptics have admired the proof's ingenuity and beauty. In his autobiography, Bertrand Russell describes a moment when, as a university student going out to buy a tin of tobacco, he was suddenly struck by the argument's evident soundness.

For over two centuries, the argument has been subjected to great scrutiny. Since Immanuel Kant's negative appraisal in *Critique of Pure Reason* (1781), the ontological proof has been viewed by many, believers and unbelievers alike, as captivating but unconvincing. The principal criticism leveled against it is the charge that it misunderstands existence itself. Generations of critics have balked at the idea of a being's necessary existence—existence that is engineered into that entity's very definition. The question of a thing's definition, they insist, is separate from the question of its existence. Typically, philosophers bring up unicorns. God is no different, they say; define *God*, and then determine whether God exists.

The cosmological argument reverses the direction established by Anselm's proof. It starts not with a definition of God but with observation of the world. It was an effort to read the book of nature in order to understand its author. Reflecting the influence of Aristotle and Europe's first serious encounter with Islamic thought, the argument was put into its classic form in the thirteenth century. In his nearly two-million-word-long *Summa Theologiae*, intended to be a summary of Christian knowledge for his age, the Dominican friar and University of Paris professor Thomas Aquinas proposed his "five ways" of demonstrating the existence of God, four of which were versions of the cosmological proof.

Beginning with the cosmos, the world available to the human senses, the cosmological argument recognizes that all things, animate and inanimate, are limited—dependent upon something else, caused by something else, set in motion by something else. It further states that all such beings exist in a series or network of similarly limited beings, none of which caused its own existence or motion, and none of which possessed or possesses the ability to alter or control its finitude. Ruling out the possibility of infinite regress (a chain of cause and effect extending backward unendingly into the past), Aquinas, following Aristotle, concluded his argumentation with the conviction that the human mind, observing this state of affairs in the cosmos, naturally turns to the thought of an uncaused cause or unmoved mover at the beginning of the series—"and this," he said, "we call God."

Since the thirteenth century, Aquinas has been an enduring touchstone in the debate over God's existence. Critics have accused him of not fully embodying the true philosophical spirit, not exhibiting a willingness to follow the evidence wherever it might lead. Others, even those who reject his conclusions, have revered him as one of the greatest minds of all time. Many critics of his theist proofs have concentrated on questions such as why an eternal universe should be judged to be so unimaginable and why an uncaused cause should be construed necessarily as God and not as a set of gods or other types of forces. All readers today, theist and otherwise, acknowledge that his proofs presume the standards of premodern science— ideas that predate modern physics. In *Dialogues Concerning Natural Religion* (1779), David Hume, sometimes thought to be a covert atheist, identified the notion of causation itself as a problem. For him, and for subsequent critics of Aquinas, causation is not a description of a definite relationship between agents found in nature but rather a mental construct employed by humans to help make sense of the complexity of their natural environment.

The teleological argument for the existence of God continues in the vein of the cosmological proof, basing its thoughts on claims about the intelligibility of the universe. Instead of concentrating on dependence and causation, it focuses on the presumed order found throughout the universe. Often called the argument from design, it seeks to argue from the observation of natural order to the existence of a supernatural designer of order. All beings, the proof's advocates contend, appear to act toward an end or goal (*telos* in Greek), and this sense of purpose, they say, provides evidence of a creative mind behind the body of the universe.

The argument from design enjoyed immense popularity in the era of early modern science and among the religious rationalists and deists of the Enlightenment period. Its notion of an architect God informs Enlightenment ideas of natural law, social movements such as freemasonry, references to "Nature's God" and "divine Providence" in the American Declaration of Independence, and the neoclassical monuments of the U.S. capital's federal cityscape. Today, the argument plays a vital role in religiously motivated antievolution schools of thought such as creationism and intelligent design. Its most widely accepted presentation was made by Anglican priest and philosopher William Paley in his *Natural Theology* (1802), with long chapters on plants, bones, muscles, and insects. Paley's modern parable of a person chancing upon a watch on the seashore and inferring from its intricacy and manifest purpose the existence of a watchmaker is still the best-known shorthand version of the teleological proof.

Other historic proofs for God include the moral argument and arguments from religious experience. The moral argument, advanced by Kant, maintains that a sense of value in human consciousness, a perception that there is moral order to the world and a feeling of ethical obligation in the human heart, suggests the existence of a universal source of goodness, which could be described as Goodness itself. Arguments from experience, ranging from reports of alleged miracles and visions to inklings of self-transcendence and life-transforming insight, come in many forms and are often dependent upon an individual's unique background and relationship to nature and society. Pascal's famous claim that a bet on atheism is far riskier than a wager on theism is much quoted but rarely cited by anyone as the cause of a profound change of mind.

Theists in the twentieth and twenty-first centuries have set forth numerous modifications and modernizations of the classic arguments. Many have sought to update the proofs in light of ongoing scientific developments after Charles Darwin and Albert Einstein. Others have attempted to answer objections from particular schools of philosophical thought such as logical positivism and existentialism. Christian philosophers of religion William Lane Craig and Quentin Smith, often in debate and dialogue with atheist thinkers, have attempted to demonstrate the relevance of the medieval Islamic *kalām* argument, a variant of the cosmological proof, contending that what is normally referred to as the Big Bang constitutes an event requiring a cause—as many have suggested, a Big Banger.

Some religious figures have rejected the entire project of proving God's existence. They find the impulse to rationalize faith unfitting or futile. Mystics have indicted the proofs for exaggerating the capabilities of reason and ignoring the poetic dimension of religion, the mystery of what they call the "God within." Fideists, grounding belief solely on faith in scripture or church authority, insist that rational approaches to the divine lead only to false gods.

Atheists, agnostics, humanists, and other skeptics have offered many responses to the traditional proofs for God. They have identified flaws in definitions, fallacies in reasoning, unacknowledged prejudices, outworn conceptual models, and failures to take contrary evidence into account.

Many focus on what they find to be the incoherence of God-talk itself, especially the concept of a transcendent immaterial God creating or interacting with a world of time and space. Logical positivism, communicated in A. J. Ayer's classic *Language, Truth and Logic* (1936), maintained that the question of God was unprovable because it was incomprehensible. In *A Path from Rome* (1986), philosopher Anthony Kenny, former Catholic priest and expert in Aquinas's "five ways," spoke for many when he said that responsible faith could not be possible without rational justification of belief in God—something, he concluded, the proofs did not deliver.

The course of modern science has multiplied such intellectual verdicts. The theory of evolution's commanding role in natural science has exerted a profoundly negative impact on the effectiveness of the traditional proofs, for people of faith and no faith. The image of the teeming "tangled bank," with which Darwin concluded *The Origin of Species* (1859), though published just a half century after *Natural Theology*, seems worlds away from the portrait of Paley's watchmaker deity. Likewise, principles of uncertainty and indeterminacy in modern physics have significantly threatened the foundations of the worldview presupposed by the proofs.

Modern social sciences have also challenged the relevance of any kind of argument for God. At the beginning of the twentieth century, economist and sociologist Max Weber recognized how some individuals were simply "religiously unmusical." Some people, he said, seemed to have a naturally or socially infused taste for religion, some not. No empirical evidence suggests that reason or conscience leads universally to belief in God or gods. William James's *The Varieties of Religious Experience* (1902) formally inaugurated the field of the psychology of religion, investigating human religiosity independent of the question of the truth or falsity of the historic proofs. Between James's milestone and the publication of Sigmund Freud's *The Future of an Illusion* (1927), Weber's *The Protestant Ethic and the Spirit of Capitalism* (1904–1905), and Emile Durkheim's *The Elementary Forms of the Religious Life* (1912) advanced the scientific study of religion without recourse to notions of first causes or unmoved movers. By the 1930s, many intellectuals in the West had abandoned interest in the reasonableness of beliefs and had turned instead to the quest for the sources of gods in the dynamics of society and the depths of the unconscious.

Just as theist proofs include arguments from experience, atheist and agnostic arguments against theism include scores of experience-based testimonies witnessing to the nonexistence or absence of God. The problems of evil and suffering have loomed large in this genre of modern literature. Voltaire's poem on the 1755 Lisbon earthquake, which left a death toll in the tens of thousands, provided a somber counterweight to the optimism entailed within the cosmological and teleological proofs and their thoughts about "Nature's Lord." A century later, Friedrich Nietzsche's vision of the death of God signaled the dawn of an unforeseen age in which rational arguments for—and against—God would appear to be souvenirs from a far-off land, written in a foreign tongue.

See also: Christianity, Atheism and Agnosticism in; Darwin, Charles; Deism; Flew, Antony; Islam, Atheism and Agnosticism in; Judaism, Atheism and Agnosticism in; Nietzsche, Friedrich; Russell, Bertrand

Further Reading

Ayer, A. J. *Language, Truth and Logic.* 2nd ed. New York: Dover, 1952.

Charlesworth, M. J., ed. *St. Anselm's Proslogion.* Notre Dame, IN: University of Notre Dame, 1979.

Craig, William Lane. *The Kalām Cosmological Argument.* New York: Harper and Row, 1979.

Craig, William Lane, and Quentin Smith, eds. *Theism, Atheism and Big Bang Cosmology.* Oxford: Oxford University Press, 1993.

Hick, John H., ed. *The Existence of God.* New York: Macmillan, 1964.

Hick, John H. *Philosophy of Religion.* 4th ed. Englewood Cliffs, NJ: Prentice Hall, 1990.

Kenny, Anthony. *A Brief History of Western Philosophy.* Oxford: Blackwell, 1998.

Kenny, Anthony. *The Five Ways: St. Thomas Aquinas' Proofs for God's Existence.* Notre Dame, IN: University of Notre Dame Press, 1980.

Kenny, Anthony. *A Path from Rome: An Autobiography.* Oxford: Oxford University Press, 1986.

Küng, Hans. *Does God Exist? An Answer for Today.* Trans. Edward Quinn. New York: Doubleday, 1980.

Redman, Ben Ray, ed. *The Portable Voltaire.* New York: Penguin, 1977.

Russell, Bertrand. *Autobiography.* London: Routledge, 1998.

R

Rand, Ayn

Ayn Rand (1905–1982), the author of blockbuster fiction and founder of a singular school of philosophy, was a prominent champion of free enterprise and a forerunner of contemporary libertarianism. Her advocacy of individualism, so characteristic of her American experience, sprang from her childhood rejection of conventional faith and her negative reaction to the upheavals caused by World War I and the Russian Revolution. Opposed to both religious altruism and secular collectivism, Rand has been variously idolized and dismissed by leaders in the arts, the academy, and government. In her heyday, she moved seamlessly from Hollywood and late-night television to Ivy League schools and the Oval Office. Today, her books remain immensely popular. She and her ideas continue to fuel a wide range of emotions—from fierce antagonism to unquestioning loyalty.

Born Alissa Rosenbaum, Rand was raised in a Jewish home in St. Petersburg during the twilight of the Russian empire. Her father was a pharmacist and her mother a sometime tutor and book translator. With her entire family, she experienced racial prejudice and the traumas of the violent era, spending years of her youth dodging Bolshevik rebels, renegade soldiers, and antisemitic Russian Orthodox mobs. A desire to be a writer was instilled in her during her early education, and her future signature ideas first found expression in childhood experiments with self-reliance and self-determination. The origins of her chosen name remain obscure— Ayn, perhaps a variant of a Hebrew nickname, and Rand, still mystifying her followers. She changed her name after immigrating to the United States in 1926.

Before leaving Russia, Rand studied at Petrograd State University, reading history, literature, and philosophy, all the while writing drafts of novels and storylines for silent movies. She was attracted to the pragmatic realism of Aristotle but repelled by the idealism of Immanuel Kant and G. W. F. Hegel, and she developed an appreciation for Friedrich Nietzsche, especially his concept of the Übermensch—at the time, often rendered into English as "superman." A Soviet purge of faculty and students interrupted her education, but she was able to reenroll and finish her degree in 1924. Dreaming of a future in the burgeoning film industry, she completed her formal education at a state-run performing arts school, pursuing interests in cinematography and screenwriting.

In the United States, Rand developed her system of ideas and established herself as a figure in the national literary and entertainment scene. As a novelist, playwright, and screenwriter, she was notable for her unfashionable emphasis on ideas rather than action, sentiment, or uplift. As an independent political and economic thinker, in an era when most U.S. intellectuals leaned toward progressive values, she was notorious for her adamant endorsement of conservative policies.

Rand called her philosophy objectivism and disseminated its theories in *For the New Intellectual* (1961), *The Virtue of Selfishness* (1963), *Capitalism: The Unknown Ideal* (1966), *The Romantic Manifesto* (1969), *Introduction to Objectivist Epistemology* (1979), and *Philosophy: Who Needs It* (1982), the book-length version of her 1974 speech at West Point. Individual rights, the primacy of reason, and the alleged evils of the welfare state are themes that run through all her works. She served as a friendly witness for the U.S. House Committee on Un-American Activities, supported Senator Joseph McCarthy's anticommunist crusade, criticized President Kennedy's New Frontier as "fascist," and campaigned for conservative Barry Goldwater. Ever the contrarian, she opposed the Vietnam War, defended a woman's right to abortion, and ridiculed scientific creationism and the New Religious Right, but she expressed no sympathy for the nascent gay rights movement. The essence of her vision was captured in the dollar-sign pin that, along with her designer cape and cigarette holder, became part of her costume and, by extension, her public persona. Notable disciples of Rand's thought include Nathaniel Branden, originator of the self-esteem movement in psychology, and economist Alan Greenspan, former chair of the Federal Reserve. A number of individuals in American government, including Paul Ryan, former Speaker of the U.S. House of Representatives and vice presidential candidate, speak of Rand's influence on their life and thought.

Rand's ideas are best seen in her fictional narratives: *We the Living* (1936), *Anthem* (1938), and especially her epic best sellers *The*

Fountainhead (1943) and *Atlas Shrugged* (1957). Her works are dense novels of ideas featuring long philosophical monologues, high stakes, often sexually charged plotlines, and memorable characters exhibiting firmly etched moral profiles. Each book revolves in its own way around the author's conviction that the sovereign individual who courageously defies conformity is not only the true hope of society but also the ultimate portrait of the genuine human being. *The Fountainhead*'s Howard Roark, modeled in part on modernist architect and designer Frank Lloyd Wright (and played by Gary Cooper in the 1949 film version), is the brilliant visionary who refuses to compromise his standards, no matter what the cost. John Galt, the mysterious hero of *Atlas Shrugged*, is the genius-inventor who inspires the most talented of his generation to secede from mainstream society and thrive in their free-market utopia far from the mediocrity of humanity's rank and file. Over a half century after their release, both of Rand's chief works continue to lead polls celebrating the greatest novels of the twentieth century, and both continue to attract an enthusiastic—critics would say, cultlike—readership.

Though atheism was never the most prominent part of Rand's thought, it served as the necessary precondition for her worldview of egoism and rational self-interest. She judged the classic arguments for God to be irrational if not irrelevant and the moral record of religions in history beneath contempt and beyond redemption. The nonexistence of God not only did not rule out human freedom and happiness, she said, but actually made those things possible. The exceptional individual, exercising reason with audacity and resolute integrity, is the sole source of meaning in the world and the closest thing to a deity one will ever encounter. Rand's philosophy of life, founded on no-nonsense nontheism, made humanity—or some members of it—truly the center of all and the measure of all.

See also: Nietzsche, Friedrich

Further Reading

Burns, Jennifer. *Goddess of the Market: Ayn Rand and the American Right.* Oxford: Oxford University Press, 2011.

Heller, Anne C. *Ayn Rand and the World She Made.* New York: Anchor Books, 2009.

Hull, Gary, ed. *The Ayn Rand Reader.* New York: Penguin, 1999.

Rand, Ayn. *Anthem.* New York: Dutton, 1995.

Rand, Ayn. *Atlas Shrugged.* New York: Signet, 2005.

Rand, Ayn. *The Fountainhead.* New York: New American Library, 1993.

Rand, Ayn. *Introduction to Objectivist Epistemology*. Expanded 2nd ed. New York: Meridian, 1990.

Rand, Ayn. *The Virtue of Selfishness*. New York: Signet, 1964.

Rand, Ayn. *We the Living*. New York: New American Library, 2011.

Reason Rally

Reason Rally is the name of two twenty-first-century mass outdoor gatherings of atheists, agnostics, and allies on the National Mall in Washington, DC. The first was held on March 24, 2012, the second on June 4, 2016. The events were organized by the Reason Rally Coalition, a nationwide network of humanist, freethinking, and secularist organizations promoting intellectual freedom, the rights of unbelievers, separation of church and state, and unhindered science education. Contributing organizations included American Atheists, the American Humanist Association, the Center for Inquiry, the Freedom from Religion Foundation, the Richard Dawkins Foundation for Reason and Science, and the Secular Coalition for America.

Both public assemblies featured prominent scholars, entertainers, activists, and politicians seeking to raise awareness about the growth and diversity of nonreligion in the United States, to dispel stereotypes regarding unbelief, and to combat atheophobic trends and policies in U.S. government, business, and education. Each event was organized around a particular theme: "Atheists and Secularists Gather" in 2012 and "Speak Up for Reason" in 2016. The speaker roster for the first Reason Rally included Representative Pete Stark, comedian Bill Maher, evolutionary biologist and New Atheist celebrity Richard Dawkins, *Friendly Atheist* blogger Hemant Mehta, author and activist Greta Christina, and Adam Savage, cohost of the Discovery Channel's *Mythbusters* show. The second Reason Rally's program showcased Representative Tulsi Gabbard, public television science personality Bill Nye, Rice University's humanist scholar Anthony Pinn, and the Gay Men's Chorus of Washington, DC.

Kelly Damerow, representing the Secular Coalition for America, and David Silverman, president of American Atheists, served as the principal organizers of both capital city rallies. According to the Reason Rally Coalition website (www.reasonrally.org), one of the organization's main purposes is the demonstration of the U.S. secular population's potential political strength.

Participants in the Reason Rallies came from a variety of locations across the country and represented a broad array of interests and concerns. Attendance figures for the two gatherings differ greatly. Unofficial estimates for the first event range from eight thousand to thirty thousand. All sources agree that participation for the second rally came in under the fifteen thousand to twenty thousand expected turnout.

See also: Atheism, New; Christina, Greta; Dawkins, Richard; Friendly Atheist, The; Media, Atheism and Agnosticism and the; Organizations, Atheist and Agnostic; Pinn, Anthony B.; Skepticon

Rushdie, Salman

Salman Rushdie (b. 1947) is a leading voice in contemporary world literature, best known for *The Satanic Verses* (1988), one of the most controversial books of all time. He is the author of fourteen novels, two documentary films, and several volumes of short stories and nonfiction. He is also a distinguished educator and commentator, the recipient of numerous awards and honorary doctorates. Rushdie's reputation as a champion of free speech and critic of censorship and religious fundamentalism is unsurpassed. In 2019, he was named Humanist of the Year by the American Humanist Association.

Rushdie grew up in a devout, liberal, and tolerant Muslim home in Mumbai (Bombay), in the Indian state of Maharashtra. He attended elite private schools in India and England and earned an MA in history from King's College, Cambridge. After a brief stint in television work, he committed himself to the vocation of writing. The success of his second novel, *Midnight's Children* (1981), won him a Booker Prize and a privileged place in the upper tier of international literary fame. His lectureships and visiting professorships have included writer-in-residence posts at Emory University and New York University.

The course of Rushdie's life overlaps with the historical career of the Islamic Revival, the resurgence of Muslim self-determination sparked in part by the post–World War II dismantling of Western colonial empires and the 1948 founding of the state of Israel. The Revival added a new set of Muslim nations to the global map and aligned, for millions of Muslim believers, antimodern zeal to the heart of Islamic identity. The first signs of Rushdie's celebrity coincided with Ayatollah Ruhollah Khomeini's successful 1979–1980 Islamic Revolution in Iran and the genesis of a new age of Islamic rage and superpower revenge. Khomeini's infamous 1989 fatwa, or legal judgment, against the alleged blasphemies of *The Satanic Verses* spawned assassination threats from all quarters of the Muslim world and plunged Rushdie into more than a decade of fugitive hiding. A publisher and a translator of the book were brutally attacked. Its Japanese translator was murdered by a knife-wielding terrorist. Rushdie's memoir *Joseph Anton* (2012), named after his alias of those years, gives a full personal account of the tragic chapter in literary history now known universally as the "Rushdie affair."

Mixing fantasy and realism, *The Satanic Verses* narrates a story revolving around the phenomenon of modern terrorism and the many contradictory forces competing for dominance within the late-capitalist mind. Its title derives from the early Muslim legend about lines, inspired by the devil, that the prophet Muhammad mistakenly incorporated into his recitation of the revelations that eventually became the Qur'an. Banned for years in India, Pakistan, South Africa, and every Arab country, the novel is today recognized as a world classic and a masterpiece of Rushdie's inimitable craft and imagination.

Rushdie's career has also coincided with the rise of New Atheism, the early twenty-first-century movement attacking the purported absurdities and evils of religion and defending the rights and rationality of unbelief. Writer, world traveler, and atheist provocateur Christopher Hitchens, one of the so-called four horsemen of the movement, was a member of Rushdie's inner circle. He devoted an entire chapter in his memoir *Hitch 22* (2011) to his friendship with the novelist. Rushdie himself has made no secret of his quarrel with religious intolerance and its negative impact on culture and the arts. In the *Humanist* magazine, he spoke of religion as "a kind of childhood of the human race." A self-described "hardline atheist," he sees secular society as the most hospitable environment for the free mind and the creative imagination.

See also: Atheism, New; Hitchens, Christopher; Humanist of the Year; Islam, Atheism and Agnosticism in

Further Reading

Bradley, Arthur, and Andrew Tate. *The New Atheist Novel: Philosophy, Fiction and Polemic after 9/11*. New York: Continuum, 2010.

Hitchens, Christopher. *Hitch 22: A Memoir*. New York: Twelve, 2011.
Rushdie, Salman. *Joseph Anton*. New York: Random House, 2012.
Rushdie, Salman. *Midnight's Children*. New York: Random House, 2006.
Rushdie, Salman. *The Satanic Verses*. New York: Random House, 2008.

Russell, Bertrand

Bertrand Russell (1872–1970) was one of the most provocative public intellectuals of the twentieth century. His achievements in mathematics and logic won him international acclaim. His advocacy of unpopular social causes such as pacifism and free love landed him in near-permanent controversy. In the first sentence of his autobiography, he defined his life as an enduring quest for three things: love, knowledge, and the relief of human suffering. In the last sentence of his *History of Western Philosophy* (1945), he defined philosophy as a way of life—not an ivory tower subject—that can advance human understanding and minimize evil. For many the preeminent face of twentieth-century atheism, Russell put his passionate skepticism into the service of a career dedicated to intellectual freedom and social reform.

Born into the British aristocracy, Russell was raised by his grandparents and educated by private tutors. His home environment was infused with a mixture of Victorian morality, Enlightenment freethinking, and the influences of Anglican and Unitarian Christianity. His interests ranged from history and literature to classical languages and mathematics. As an adolescent, especially after reading John Stuart Mill's *Autobiography* (1873), in which the utilitarian thinker revealed his lifelong natural bent toward nonbelief, Russell gradually lost all semblance of religious faith. He recorded his escalating doubts on the existence of God and immortality in a secret notebook written in Greek characters. By the time he entered Trinity College, Cambridge, aside from a brief phase of then-fashionable Hegelian idealism, he was a convinced and confident atheist.

At Cambridge, Russell excelled in mathematics and philosophy. He was inducted into the elite discussion group called the Apostles, befriending members of the avant-garde Bloomsbury literary circle, including Virginia Woolf, Lytton Strachey, and Ottoline Morrell. Early recognized for his brilliance, he became a lecturer at Trinity and was one of the founders of the analytic school of philosophy, the dominant approach to philosophical issues in English-speaking countries during the twentieth century.

Like its subfield, Vienna-based logical positivism, analytic philosophy rejected all forms of metaphysics and concentrated the philosophical task on questions of method, logic, and the operation of language in ordinary experience. In the context of this intellectual ferment, Russell served as the chief mentor for the philosophical iconoclast Ludwig Wittgenstein, author of *Tractatus Logico-Philosophicus* (1922).

Russell launched his impressive publishing career with *The Principles of Mathematics* (1903), seeking the philosophical underpinnings for mathematics, and secured his place in the discipline of philosophy with the massive and magisterial *Principia Mathematica* (1910–1913), coauthored with his former teacher, mathematician and process philosopher Alfred North Whitehead. For the next sixty years, Russell published scores of books, articles, reviews, pamphlets, and public letters, including treatises on erudite points in the philosophy of science along with popular works such as *Marriage and Morals* (1929), *The Conquest of Happiness* (1930), *Unpopular Essays* (1950), and *Satan in the Suburbs* (1953), a collection of short stories. In 1950, he received the Nobel Prize in Literature in recognition of his persistent campaigns for human rights and freedom of thought.

Social activism was always a part of Russell's sense of personal vocation. His parents, who died when he was a child, had energetically worked in Britain and the United States for women's rights and reproductive freedom. Russell was initially thrust into notoriety during World War I, when his antiwar and anti-imperial sentiments earned him both a six-month prison sentence and dismissal from the Trinity faculty. From then until his nineties, with his pipe and flowing white hair often at the head of a mass march, rally, or sit-in, Russell became a symbol of the thinking individual contending with the forces of state-sponsored militarism. He promoted internationalism, education reform, civil disobedience, the liberalization of divorce laws, and acceptance of homosexuality. He became an early critic of nuclear armament, publishing with Albert Einstein an antiwar manifesto and sending telegrams to John F. Kennedy and Nikita Khrushchev to defuse the 1962 Cuban missile crisis. In 1966, after forming the Bertrand Russell Peace Foundation, he organized, along with French philosopher-writer Jean-Paul Sartre, an international tribunal on American war crimes in Vietnam. His daughter, Katharine Tait, called him a passionate moralist who in another age would have been considered a saint. Though consistently aligned with progressive efforts for a lifetime, he harbored little hope of solving the problem of the "core of loneliness" that he detected at the heart of each person's life.

Russell's atheism played a major role in both his public and private life and was never far from the minds of his critics and admirers. An early period piece, "A Free Man's Worship" (1903), portrays humanity, illuminated by a flickering divine spark, struggling to lead a life of meaning in a bleak and senseless cosmos. Subsequent essays—in *What I Believe* (1925), *Religion and Science* (1935), *Why I Am Not a Christian* (1957), and *Essays in Skepticism* (1963)—reveal a less morose and more sardonic Russell turning wit and reason on the dishonesty, hypocrisy, superstition, and irrationality that he thought endemic to religion, especially Christianity. He discerned much to appreciate in the classical proofs for the existence of God but judged them ultimately unconvincing and insincere—the conclusions being rigged in advance. Likewise, he perceived nobility in Jesus (along with character flaws) but wondered why so few Christians followed their Lord's teachings regarding peacemaking and freedom from material possessions. His 1948 BBC radio debate with Jesuit priest-philosopher Frederick Copleston, author of the eleven-volume *History of Philosophy* (1946–1975), is celebrated as one of the greatest atheist-theist encounters of all time.

Russell saw the legacy of religion crowded with cruelty, intolerance, absurdity, and fear, and he found no evidence suggesting religious people to be happier, smarter, or more virtuous than their unbelieving neighbors. When, in the 1940s, City College of New York pronounced him morally unfit to teach, he knew religious organizations enjoyed no monopoly on bigotry. He summed up the good life in these terms: "inspired by love and guided by knowledge."

See also: Proofs for God, Atheist and Agnostic Critiques of; Sartre, Jean-Paul

Further Reading

Egner, Robert E., and Lester E. Denonn, ed. *The Basic Writings of Bertrand Russell*. London: Routledge, 1992.

Grayling, A. C. *Russell: A Very Short Introduction*. Oxford: Oxford University Press, 2002.

Griffin, Nicholas, ed. *The Cambridge Companion to Bertrand Russell*. Cambridge: Cambridge University Press, 2003.

Monk, Ray. *Bertrand Russell: The Ghost of Madness 1921–1970*. New York: Free Press, 2016.

Monk, Ray. *Bertrand Russell: The Spirit of Solitude 1872–1921*. New York: Free Press, 1996.

Moorehead, Caroline. *Bertrand Russell: A Life*. New York: Viking, 1992.

Russell, Bertrand. *Autobiography*. 2nd ed. New York: Routledge, 2000.

Russell, Bertrand. *Essays in Skepticism*. New York: Philosophical Library, 1962.

Russell, Bertrand. *The History of Western Philosophy*. New York: Simon and Schuster, 1972.

Russell, Bertrand. *On God and Religion*. Ed. Al Seckel. Amherst, NY: Prometheus Books, 1986.

Russell, Bertrand. *Religion and Science*. New York: Oxford University Press, 1961.

Russell, Bertrand. *Why I Am Not a Christian and Other Essays on Religion and Related Subjects*. Ed. Paul Edwards. New York: Simon and Schuster, 1957.

Tait, Katharine. *My Father Bertrand Russell*. New York: Harcourt Brace Jovanovich, 1975.

Wood, Alan. *Bertrand Russell: The Passionate Skeptic*. New York: Simon and Schuster, 1958.

S

Sartre, Jean-Paul

Jean-Paul Sartre (1905–1980), one of the premier voices of twentieth-century thought, defined an era in modern experience. Revolutionary novelist, philosopher, playwright, biographer, and social activist, he set the tone for much of intellectual life from World War II through the first decades of the Cold War. Few literary figures have had such an impact on both culture and politics, East and West. His vision of engaged literature dramatically reconceived the role of the writer in society. The existentialist movement in philosophy, intimately related to his life and outlook, challenged academic and popular notions about what philosophers do and who qualifies as a philosopher. Committed to what he called the "long-range affair of atheism," Sartre saw frank acceptance of the absence of God as the core value shaping an evolving humanist vision of hope for people in the modern world.

In his autobiography *The Words* (1964), published the same year he refused the Nobel Prize in Literature, Sartre said he began his life as he imagined he would end it—among books. Without a doubt, he was one of the great literary personalities of modern Western culture. Despite the consistency, his career was filled with conspicuous paradoxes. He sparked one of the most significant court insurrections in the academy but was never really a professional scholar; many questioned his philosophical credentials. He shook the foundations of modern fiction and drama, but critics found his artistry wanting. Dedicated to anticapitalist and anticolonial social change around the globe, he logged thousands of hours at his urban apartment desk, writing voluminous and still largely unread works of literary history—and all by hand. Anglo-Irish philosopher-novelist Iris Murdoch captured some of these paradoxes in her label for Sartre: "romantic rationalist."

Raised in French bourgeois culture, Sartre spent most of his life in and around Paris, never owning a home and never learning to drive a car. He was educated in his grandparents' home and at two elite lycées, or secondary schools. Early in his development, he felt a call to the literary life—what he described as a substitute for the Catholicism he was temperamentally and intellectually unable to embrace. His reputation as a promising author was uncontested during his postsecondary studies at the École Normale Supérieure, where he befriended the equally gifted future writer and feminist thinker Simone de Beauvoir. Sartre's lifelong and romantically open relationship with Beauvoir, scandalous in their day, formed one of the greatest literary partnerships of all time. Together they served as the archetype of the literary couple and the guiding figures in the early existentialist movement.

Like many in his generation, Sartre divided his life into two parts: before and after World War II. Following a brief stint in teaching and a year devoted to research in continental philosophy, he served in the French army, spent nine months in a German prison camp, and participated in the anti-Nazi and anticollaborationist resistance, writing for the underground newspapers *Les Lettres Françaises* and Albert Camus's *Combat*. By the end of the war, Sartre was recognized as a major force in a new age of French literature. His first novel *Nausea* (1938) set the standard for existentialist fiction and unveiled the movement's new antihero figure, the citizen of the secular city who knows the tragedy and absurdity of life and suffers from psychological and metaphysical homelessness. Sartre's first major nonfiction publication, *Being and Nothingness* (1943), rocked the scholarly establishment and attracted the attention of a war-weary generation seeking a new philosophical language with which to articulate a mood of anxiety, restlessness, and hope.

The demanding vocabulary of that new tongue—with catchphrases such as "being *en-soi*" (in itself) and "being *pour-soi*" (for itself), the precedence of existence, "bad faith," and the condemnation to freedom—was both exhilarating and mystifying. Enthusiasts took it to be revelation. The postwar press, picking up on black turtlenecks, dungarees, and dirndl skirts as canonized vestments, spoke of Sartre and Beauvoir in ecclesiastical terms—the pope of existentialism and its high priestess. The last thing Sartre intended, however, was a new creed. Both his 1945 lecture on "Existentialism as a Humanism" and his speech on "The Responsibility of the Writer" at the 1946 opening session of the United Nations Educational

Scientific and Cultural Organization (UNESCO) stressed the open-ended and never-ending quality of the project of being human.

Sartre's novels and plays, most famously *The Flies* (1943), *No Exit* (1944), and *The Age of Reason* (1945), presented situations and problems, not schemes or solutions. His politics also never ceased to be experimental, even improvisational. Always radical but unorthodox in his Marxism, Sartre treated social ethics as art rather than science. Anguish and the agony of decision, he declared, defied systematization. Despite the myths he inspired and generated, he was the independent intellectual, keeping leaders of developing countries guessing as much as guardians of Western capitalist empires. He never fully appropriated the feminist insights of Beauvoir, nor did he ever clear his thought from the charge of fad or fashion.

Sartre identified his work as the attempt to draw conclusions for life from a consistently atheist point of view. In *The Words*, he spoke of how the idea of God evaporated from his adolescent mind. In his last interview with Beauvoir, he reflected on the "long-drawn-out work" of following the path of an evolving and deepening sense of God's absence. His unbelief was neither reluctant nor self-congratulatory. Other philosophers debated, defended, and celebrated atheism. Sartre wondered what a philosophy based on atheism might say to humans burdened with the task of making their own meaning.

See also: Beauvoir, Simone de; Marx, Karl

Further Reading

Beauvoir, Simone de. *Adieux: A Farewell to Sartre*. Trans. Patrick O'Brian. New York: Pantheon Books, 1984.

Cohen-Solal, Annie. *Sartre: A Life*. Trans. Anna Cancogni. New York: Pantheon Books, 1987.

Flynn, Thomas R. *Sartre: A Philosophical Biography*. Cambridge: Cambridge University Press, 2014.

Fullbrook, Edward, and Kate Fullbrook. *Sex and Philosophy: Rethinking De Beauvoir and Sartre*. London: Continuum, 2008.

Howells, Christina, ed. *The Cambridge Companion to Sartre*. Cambridge: Cambridge University Press, 1992.

Murdoch, Iris. *Sartre: Romantic Rationalist*. London: Penguin, 1987.

Sartre, Jean-Paul. *Being and Nothingness*. Trans. Hazel E. Barnes. New York: Washington Square Press, 1992.

Sartre, Jean-Paul. *Existentialism Is a Humanism*. Trans. Carol Macomber. New Haven, CT: Yale University Press, 2007.

Sartre, Jean-Paul. *Nausea*. Trans. Lloyd Alexander. New York: New Directions, 1964.

Sartre, Jean-Paul. *The Words*. Trans. Bernard Frechtman. New York: George Braziller, 1964.

Singer, Peter

Peter Singer (b. 1946) is one of the most controversial professional philosophers working today. Journalists have called him the "world's most influential living philosopher." Opponents call him the "most dangerous man in the world." An altruist who advocates for animal rights and a humanist who denies the sanctity of human life, he is both admired and reviled in the academy and the public sphere. Legendary for the clarity of his communication and the audacity of his conclusions, Singer is recognized as a guiding figure in the animal rights movement and a revolutionary force in contemporary bioethics. In its 2020 list of "50 Top Atheists in the World Today," TheBestSchools.org ranked Singer number one.

A native of Australia, Singer was raised in a nonreligious Jewish household by refugees from Nazi-ravaged Europe. In *Pushing Time Away: My Grandfather and the Tragedy of Jewish Vienna* (2003), he told the story of David Oppenheim, a member of Sigmund Freud's inner circle, one of three of Singer's grandparents killed in the Holocaust. An atheist from childhood, Singer refused to participate in a bar mitzvah ceremony as an adolescent.

Singer studied at the University of Melbourne, his hometown, and at Oxford, where he wrote his thesis on civil disobedience. The distinctive course of his career has led to professorships in philosophy at numerous universities around the world and to his current endowed chairs at Princeton and the Centre for Applied Philosophy and Public Ethics at his Australian alma mater. He is the author, coauthor, or editor of over fifty books, many of them translated into a dozen or so languages.

Singer launched his career with *Animal Liberation* (1975) and *The Expanding Circle* (1981). In these two works, his entire philosophical program can be seen in embryonic form. Singer's area of specialization is practical or applied ethics. Since his student days, he has been primarily concerned with the moral ramifications of how humans eat, how humans make their livings, how humans treat each other (especially in extreme cases such as infancy, old age, and illness), and how humans interact with other beings and with the earth itself.

Singer maintains that the proper foundation for ethics is an understanding of humanity's place in the biological process of evolution. He is a staunch proponent of utilitarianism, judging actions to be moral if their consequences promote the greatest degree of well-being for the greatest number of individuals. He is also a fervent critic of speciesism, the belief that human beings occupy the superior or a privileged rank of living things in the natural order. Much of his philosophical reflection concentrates on a being's capacity to express preference and to experience suffering. Singer argues that nonhuman animals deserve moral treatment on par with humans and that in some circumstances the moral claims of nonhumans outweigh those of humans.

Singer defends the full gamut of reproductive freedoms and the moral justifiability of some forms of euthanasia. He has been most provocative when questioning the personhood of discrete classes of human beings, such as the unborn, the elderly, and the severely ill. Antiabortion groups and organizations advocating for the rights of people with disabilities frequently protest his public appearances. Critics in the academy and the media point to what they believe to be serious fallacies and contradictions in his thought. Defenders see him as a near-prophetic figure, radically rethinking the role of philosophy in contemporary society. Very open about his personal habits, such as his vegan diet, his charitable giving, and his refusal to wear clothing made from animal products, Singer is often the target of ad hominem attacks.

Through his foundation, called The Life You Can Save (www.thelifeyoucansave.org), a registered nonprofit organization cofounded by former business executive Charlie Bresler, Singer currently addresses issues of global wealth inequality, extending the vision of "smart giving" he presented in his book *The Life You Can Save* (2009) and his 2013 TED talk "The Why and How of Effective Altruism." In 2004, the Council of Australian Humanist Societies named Singer Australian Humanist of the Year.

Further Reading

Jamieson, Dale, ed. *Singer and His Critics.* Oxford, UK: Wiley-Blackwell, 1999.

Regan, Tom, and Peter Singer, eds. *Animal Rights and Human Obligations.* Englewood Cliffs, NJ: Prentice-Hall, 1976.

Schaler, Jeffrey A., ed. *Peter Singer under Fire: The Moral Iconoclast Faces His Critics*. Chicago: Open Court, 2009.

Singer, Peter. *Animal Liberation*. New York: Harper Perennial, 2009.

Singer, Peter. *A Darwinian Left: Politics, Evolution, and Cooperation*. New Haven, CT: Yale University Press, 2000.

Singer, Peter. *Democracy and Disobedience*. New York: Oxford University Press, 1974.

Singer, Peter. *The Expanding Circle: Ethics, Evolution, and Moral Progress*. Princeton, NJ: Princeton University Press, 2011.

Singer, Peter. *Hegel: A Very Short Introduction*. Oxford: Oxford University Press, 2001.

Singer, Peter. *How Are We to Live? Ethics in an Age of Self-Interest*. Oxford: Oxford University Press, 1997.

Singer, Peter. *The Life You Can Save: Acting Now to End World Poverty*. New York: Random House, 2009.

Singer, Peter. *Marx: A Very Short Introduction*. Oxford: Oxford University Press, 2000.

Singer, Peter. *The Most Good You Can Do: How Effective Altruism Is Changing Ideas about Living Ethically*. New Haven, CT: Yale University Press, 2015.

Singer, Peter. *One World Now: The Ethics of Globalization*. New Haven, CT: Yale University Press, 2016.

Singer, Peter. *Rethinking Life and Death: The Collapse of Our Traditional Ethics*. Oxford: Oxford University Press, 1995.

Singer, Peter, with Jim Mason. *The Ethics of What We Eat: Why Our Food Choices Matter*. Emmaus, PA: Rodale, 2006.

Skepticon

Skepticon (https://skepticon.org) is the largest free conference for atheists, agnostics, humanists, and freethinkers in the United States. Held annually in Missouri, it combines serious intellectual engagement with lighthearted in-group solidarity, billing itself as a "celebration of truth, justice, and dinosaurs." The event is part conference, part festival, part strategy session, sponsored by American Atheists, the American Humanist Association, and individual benefactors. It features invited speakers and entertainers and attracts a cross-section of the contemporary American secular community.

Skepticon originated in meetings of secular and nonreligious students at Missouri State University (formerly Southwest Missouri State University) in 2008. It has evolved into a professionally run, multiday convention showcasing atheist and freethinking celebrity bloggers, speakers, authors, and activists. Prominent speakers, some repeat guests, have included Skepchick.org founder Rebecca Watson, author and scholar Sikivu Hutchinson, Black Nonbelievers Inc. founder Mandisa Thomas, church-state separation activist Jessica Ahlquist, biologist and science blogger PZ Myers, *Friendly Atheist* blogger Hemant Mehta, and feminist activist and sex writer Greta Christina. Programs include plenary speeches, workshops, book and merchandise sales, and professional and personal networking. In 2020, the eleventh Skepticon, originally scheduled to be held in St. Louis, was held virtually due to the coronavirus pandemic.

See also: Christina, Greta; Friendly Atheist, The; Hutchinson, Sikivu; Media, Atheism and Agnosticism in; Organizations, Atheist and Agnostic; Reason Rally

U

"Under God"

The phrase "under God" is the most controversial part of the Pledge of Allegiance to the flag of the United States. It was added to the pledge, already an authorized ceremony of the federal government, by legislative decision and presidential approval in 1954. Two years later, "In God We Trust" became the official motto of the nation, displacing the earlier, unofficial *e pluribus unum* ("out of many, one"). Both decisions, both including government-sanctioned use of the word *God*, have sparked decades of debate in American society.

The Pledge of Allegiance dates back to a brief flag-recognition rite published in 1892 by a private citizen: Boston-based former Baptist minister, journalist, and Christian socialist educator Francis Bellamy, famous for his provocative "Jesus was a socialist" speeches. Bellamy designed his flag pledge as a contribution to the many celebrations taking place across the country during 1892 and 1893 in observation of the four hundredth anniversary of Christopher Columbus's first transatlantic voyage. Bellamy's aim was to foster patriotism among young people and generate support for official approval of a federal Columbus Day holiday. His original twenty-two-word profession of loyalty, published in the *Youth's Companion* magazine, invited participants to pledge allegiance to "my Flag and the Republic for which it stands." It did not mention God.

By the early twentieth century, Bellamy's pledge ceremony, along with the fully extended arm salute (later abandoned due to its likeness to the Nazi "Heil, Hitler" gesture), was gaining popularity with U.S. educators and civic leaders. It became a near-universal American morning ritual in public schools. Organizations such as the American Legion and Daughters of the American Revolution promoted widespread use of the pledge and gradually changed the language of the pledge to say "the flag

211

of the United States of America." In 1942, the U.S. Congress voted to include the augmented pledge in the nation's official Flag Code.

The phrase "under God" was added to the pledge during the same Cold War religious revival that stimulated increasing support for "In God We Trust" as the country's motto. The religious revival of the late 1940s and '50s was the high-water mark of Protestant influence in American culture. Prayer and Bible reading were conspicuous parts of public life and the shared culture of public education. Churchgoing was fashionable and encouraged by the White House. The National Advertising Council inundated the press with "Back to God" and "Back to Church" slogans. The annual National Prayer Breakfast became part of routine of life in Washington, DC. Evangelical, anticommunist crusader Billy Graham captured the support of media mogul William Randolph Hearst. Supreme Court justice William O. Douglas declared American institutions dependent upon a supreme being. The Senate Judiciary Committee considered, but eventually rejected, the latest in a long line of proposed Christian amendments to the Constitution seeking political recognition of "the authority and law of Jesus Christ, Saviour and Ruler of nations."

The period also witnessed the mainstreaming of Roman Catholicism in the United States. Long perceived to be a foreign religion at odds with basic democratic values, especially religious liberty and free speech, Catholicism was gaining ground as America's second way of being Christian. The shift in attitude was due largely to the patriotic performance of Catholic Americans side by side with Americans of other creeds in the battle zones of World War II and the classrooms of American academia under the GI Bill. Bishop Fulton J. Sheen's best-selling book *Peace of Soul* (1949) and his Emmy-winning television show *Life Is Worth Living* (1952–1957) brought new respectability to the tradition many Protestant Americans once associated with the Dark Ages and immigrant ghettoes. Hollywood films such as *Knute Rockne, All American* (1940), starring Ronald Reagan, and *The Bells of St. Mary's* (1945), featuring Bing Crosby and Ingrid Bergman, did much to enhance the public profile and acceptability of Catholicism in American life.

The more favorable status of the Catholic church set the stage for the incorporation of "under God" into the Pledge of Allegiance. Seeking to showcase American exceptionalism in light of the Soviet Union's much-discussed atheism, the Knights of Columbus, an all-male Catholic lay organization founded in 1882, launched a nationwide campaign to expand the text of the official pledge and underscore what it perceived to be the

United States' special covenant with God. Louis Rabaut, Democratic congressman from Detroit and devout Catholic father of a Jesuit priest and three nuns, introduced a resolution to expand the pledge's text. In tune with rising public opinion, Congress was receptive and in 1954 passed legislation containing the words "under God." President Dwight D. Eisenhower signed the bill into law on June 14 of that year, the day established thirty-eight years earlier by President Woodrow Wilson as the nation's annual Flag Day. Festivities included a congressional "Back to God" ceremony on the U.S. Capitol steps, broadcast live on television with laudatory commentary from CBS news anchor Walter Cronkite.

Legal opposition to the amended text of the pledge—and the pledge itself—has come from different quarters of the American public. Religious opposition has concentrated on the pledge as a state-mandated imitation-religious ceremony, an impediment to the free exercise of religion guaranteed by the First Amendment of the U.S. Constitution. Jehovah's Witnesses, whose numbers ironically once included the young Eisenhower, consistently refuse to participate in pledge rites and see the action as a violation of their freedom of conscience and an unwelcome temptation to engage in idolatry. Secular and humanist opposition has focused on the pledge and its invocation of God language as violations of the establishment clause of the First Amendment prohibiting a state-sponsored religion. Higher and lower courts have recognized the rights of dissent and voluntary nonparticipation. Critics maintain that "under God" creates an environment hostile to unbelievers and their worldview, in effect undergirding a form of spiritual apartheid and relegating the nonreligious to second-class-citizen status. The U.S. justice system has consistently defended, but rarely explained, the ceremonial use of God language in American public life. Saluting (since the '40s, with hands on hearts) what writer Sylvia Plath called the "aerial altarcloth over the teacher's desk"—with ritual repetition of the word *God*—remains a contested part of life in the United States.

See also: Atheophobia; "In God We Trust"

Further Reading

Ellwood, Robert S. *1950: Crossroads of American Religious Life*. Louisville, KY: Westminster John Knox Press, 2000.

Ellwood, Robert S. *The Fifties Spiritual Marketplace: American Religion in a Decade of Conflict*. New Brunswick, NJ: Rutgers University Press, 1997.

Kruse, Kevin M. *One Nation under God: How Corporate America Invented Christian America*. New York: Basic Books, 2015.

Moore, R. Lawrence, and Isaac Kramnick. *Godless Citizens in a Godly Republic: Atheists in American Public Life*. New York: W. W. Norton, 2018.

Plath. Sylvia. *Johnny Panic and the Bible of Dreams: Short Stories, Prose, and Diary Excerpts*. New York: HarperCollins, 2000.

Warburton, Nigel. *Free Speech: A Very Short Introduction*. Oxford: Oxford University Press, 2009.

Z

Zuckerman, Phil

Phil Zuckerman (b. 1969) is an internationally acclaimed academic, writer, speaker, blogger, and organizer. He is best known as an expert in and advocate for secularity and the secular life. A trained social scientist, he is primarily interested in documenting the ascent of nonreligion in the twenty-first century and offering firsthand accounts of the advantages of post-theist approaches to family, society, work, leisure, and self-expression. He is widely recognized as the founder of the first academic department of secular studies in U.S. higher education.

Zuckerman was raised in the United States, in a nonreligious Jewish home in California. He studied at the University of Oregon, receiving his PhD in sociology in 1998. His dissertation on fractures in modern Judaism was published as *Strife in the Sanctuary: Religious Schism in a Jewish Community* (1999). Since his graduate work, he has devoted most of his career to the study of life outside the physical and psychological boundaries of religious sanctuaries. He is a professor of sociology at Pitzer College in California, where he teaches courses on secularism, sociology and film, and Scandinavian culture. He has also taught at Claremont Graduate University and Aarhus University, in Denmark.

Zuckerman is the author, coauthor, editor, or coeditor of several books on atheism, humanism, and secularity, including a collection of W. E. B. Du Bois's essays on religion. He is a popular conference speaker and an active contributor to scholarly journalism, offering social commentary for various media as well as blogging regularly on "The Secular Life" for *Psychology Today*. His special concerns revolve around the long-familiar claims that happiness, moral responsibility, and social well-being depend upon belief in God. In numerous articles and interviews, he supplies data to confirm that the least religious parts of the United States and the world enjoy the lowest rates of crime and the highest rates of education, employment, political involvement, and health.

As an academic leader, Zuckerman has been particularly effective in creating and supporting institutional structures for the study of secularity. He has played a key role in the founding and cultivation of the international Nonreligion and Secularity Research Network and its journal *Secularism and Nonreligion*, respectively the first academic professional society and the first interdisciplinary, open-access platform devoted to the study of atheism, agnosticism, and related issues. The Institute for the Study of Secularism in Society and Culture at Trinity College in Connecticut, founded by Barry Kosmin in 2005, was the first program in American academia to promote research and curriculum development in secular studies. Zuckerman's secular studies venture at Pitzer, inaugurated in 2011, is the nation's first interdisciplinary program in the field leading to degree opportunities for undergraduate students. Largely because of Zuckerman's efforts at Pitzer, the American Humanist Association selected the college for its 2016 University Award.

Much of Zuckerman's distinction depends on rising interest in the phenomena of the Nones and New Atheism. He has consistently distanced himself from debates over the existence of God and from all forms of antireligious and proatheist militancy. In what is arguably his most popular book, *Living the Secular Life* (2014), he speaks in first person about the positive, nonargumentative quality of secular existence—a way of life to be understood on its own terms, not as a rejection or negation of something else. He confesses his discomfort with shopworn terms such as *atheist*, *agnostic*, and *secular humanist*, recognizing their historic importance and relative utility but admitting their eventual inability to communicate a distinctive way of engaging life in its fullness.

In the book's final chapter, he offers the alternative *aweist*—that is, someone, according to Zuckerman's definition, whose life is driven by an expansive sense of awe not unlike the feeling of transcendence that accompanies moments of great insight, heroism, social uprising, and love. Manifestos abound in the history of atheism and agnosticism, a history marked by both brilliance and brutality. Zuckerman's abstract for aweism is a draft declaration for the next generation of seekers unsatisfied with the choice between God-obsessed belief and God-haunted unbelief. "A lack of belief in God does not render this world any less wondrous, lush, mystifying, or amazing," he says. "Quite the contrary. One need not have God to feel and experience awe. One just needs life."

See also: Atheism, New; Du Bois, W. E. B.; Nones; Organizations, Atheist and Agnostic

Further Reading

Zuckerman, Phil, ed. *Atheism and Secularity*. 2 vols. Westport, CT: Praeger, 2010.

Zuckerman, Phil, ed. *Du Bois on Religion*. Walnut Creek, CA: AltaMira Press, 2000.

Zuckerman, Phil. *Faith No More: Why People Reject Religion*. New York: Oxford University Press, 2011.

Zuckerman, Phil. *Invitation to the Sociology of Religion*. New York: Routledge, 2003.

Zuckerman, Phil. *Living the Secular Life: New Answers to Old Questions*. New York: Penguin, 2014.

Zuckerman, Phil, ed. *The Social Theory of W. E. B. Du Bois*. Thousand Oaks, CA: Pine Forge, 2004.

Zuckerman, Phil. *Society without God: What the Least Religious Nations Can Tell Us about Contentment*. New York: New York University Press, 2008.

Zuckerman, Phil. *What It Means to Be Moral: Why Religion Is Not Necessary for Living an Ethical Life*. Berkeley, CA: Counterpoint, 2019.

Zuckerman, Phil, Luke W. Galen, and Frank L. Pasquale. *The Nonreligious: Understanding Secular People and Societies*. New York: Oxford University Press, 2016.

Zuckerman, Phil, and Christel Manning, eds. *Sex and Religion*. Belmont, CA: Wadsworth, 2005.

Zuckerman, Phil, and John R. Shook, eds. *The Oxford Handbook of Secularism*. New York: Oxford University Press, 2017.

Annotated Bibliography

Allen, Norm R., Jr., ed. *African American Humanism: An Anthology*. New York: Prometheus Books, 1991. The first extensive collection of texts from African American humanist writers, assembled by the founder of African Americans for Humanism.

Allen, Norm R., Jr., ed. *The Black Humanist Experience: An Alternative to Religion*. New York: Prometheus Books, 2003. Essays on the distinctive features of African American secular and nonreligious thought.

Altizer, Thomas J. J. *The Gospel of Christian Atheism*. Philadelphia: Westminster Press, 1966. An arresting vision of Christianity by the most original death of God theologian.

Altizer, Thomas J. J. *The New Gospel of Christian Atheism*. Aurora, CA: Davies Group, 2002. An updated version of Altizer's radical theological vision, reasserting the death of God as the essence of Christian faith.

Armstrong, Karen. *A History of God: The 4,000-Year Quest of Judaism, Christianity and Islam*. New York: Alfred A. Knopf, 1993. A magisterial treatment of the evolution of the idea of God in the Abrahamic traditions, including chapters on the death of God and the future of God.

Baggett, Jerome P. *The Varieties of Nonreligious Experience: Atheism in American Culture*. New York: New York University Press, 2019. A groundbreaking study of the postbelief experience of being atheist in the twenty-first century.

Baggini, Julian. *Atheism: A Very Short Introduction*. Oxford: Oxford University Press, 2003. An intentionally concise treatment of atheism as a positive worldview, written for a general audience.

Batchelor, Stephen. *Confessions of a Buddhist Atheist*. New York: Random House, 2010. An autobiographical account of a former Buddhist monk's journey into secular, nontheist Buddhism.

Beredjick, Camille. *Queer Disbelief: Why LGBTQ Equality Is an Atheist Issue*. N.p.: Friendly Atheist Press, 2017. A queer activist and atheist's incisive review of the intersection of LGBTQ+ identity and nonreligion in the contemporary United States.

Berman, David. *A History of Atheism in Britain: From Hobbes to Russell*. New York: Routledge, 2013. The first comprehensive history of British atheism, originally published in 1988, concentrating on major scholarly and popular writers.

Billington, Ray. *Religion without God*. New York: Routledge, 2002. An intriguing exploration of nontheist faith and spirituality by a British philosopher and scholar of Asian thought.

Bloch, Ernst. *Atheism in Christianity: The Religion of the Exodus and the Kingdom*. Trans. J. T. McSwann. London: Verso, 2009. First published in 1968, an unparalleled analysis of the biblical roots of atheism and a critique of the theist/atheist impasse by the celebrated utopian Marxist philosopher.

Bradley, Arthur, and Andrew Tate. *The New Atheist Novel: Philosophy, Fiction and Polemic after 9/11*. New York: Continuum, 2010. A masterful assessment of the literary reception of New Atheism in the works of Ian McEwan, Martin Amis, Philip Pullman, and Salman Rushdie.

Brewster, Melanie E., ed. *Atheists in America*. New York: Columbia University Press, 2014. An effectively designed collection of over twenty-four first-person narratives, revealing the diversity of atheist identities in contemporary U.S. culture.

Bruce, Steve. *God Is Dead: Secularization in the West*. Oxford: Blackwell, 2002. A well-argued overview of the much-contested secularization thesis by one of its most articulate proponents.

Buckley, Michael J. *At the Origins of Modern Atheism*. New Haven, CT: Yale University Press, 1987. A prodigious account of the beginnings of modern Western atheism by a philosophical theologian.

Buckley, Michael J. *Denying and Disclosing God: The Ambiguous Progress of Modern Atheism*. New Haven, CT: Yale University Press, 2004. A refinement and expansion of Buckley's 1987 thesis regarding the roots of modern Western atheism in early modern Christian theology.

Bullivant, Stephen. *Faith and Unbelief*. New York: Paulist Press, 2013. An empathetic study of contemporary nonreligion by a Catholic theologian engaged in Christian-atheist dialogue.

Bullivant, Stephen, and Lois Lee. *Oxford Dictionary of Atheism*. Oxford: Oxford University Press, 2016. A useful subscription-only online resource at https://www.oxfordreference.com, offering brief and up-to-date definitions of terms from *agnostic* to *worldview*.

Bullivant, Stephen, and Michael Ruse, eds. *The Oxford Handbook of Atheism*. Oxford: Oxford University Press, 2013. The best and most thorough one-volume reference work on global atheism.

Cameron, Christopher. *Black Freethinkers: A History of African American Secularism*. Evanston, IL: Northwestern University Press, 2019. A penetrating account of an important strain in Black intellectual life by one of the premier historians of African American humanism.

Carroll, Anthony, and Richard Norman, eds. *Religion and Atheism: Beyond the Divide*. Oxford: Routledge, 2017. A unique set of essays on issues such as rationality, morality, and death, seeking to advance a mutually enriching relationship between religiously oriented and nonreligious thinkers.

Chadwick, Owen. *The Secularization of the European Mind in the 19th Century*. Cambridge: Cambridge University Press, 1975. An impressive but dated contribution to the secularization debate by a master historian.

Christie-Murray, David. *A History of Heresy*. Oxford: Oxford University Press, 1991. A brisk and informative historical survey of alternative and nonorthodox variants in the international Christian tradition.

Christina, Greta. *Coming Out Atheist: How to Do It, How to Help Each Other, and Why*. Durham, NC: Pitchstone, 2014. A candid approach to being and becoming atheist by a creative U.S. culture critic and fiction writer.

Christina, Greta. *The Way of the Heathen: Practicing Atheism in Everyday Life*. Durham, NC: Pitchstone, 2016. An insightful and entertaining investigation of the impact of unbelief on all aspects of life.

Comte-Sponville, André. *The Little Book of Atheist Spirituality*. Trans. Nancy Huston. New York: Penguin, 2007. A generous and personal exploration of nondogmatic atheism by one of France's leading philosophers.

Copson, Andrew. *Secularism: A Very Short Introduction*. New York: Oxford University Press, 2019. An inviting and economical overview of multifaceted secularism by the president of Humanists International.

Copson, Andrew, and A. C. Grayling, eds. *The Wiley Blackwell Handbook of Humanism*. Oxford: John Wiley and Sons, 2015. A collection of nearly two dozen essays addressing humanism and topics such as science, counseling, feminism, architecture, and optimism.

Curran, Andrew S. *Diderot and the Art of Thinking Freely*. New York: Other Press, 2019. A critically acclaimed account of the life and thought of the editor of the eighteenth-century *Encyclopédie*, by an authority on the French Enlightenment.

Dawkins, Richard. *The God Delusion*. Boston: Houghton Mifflin, 2008. One of the best-selling books that sparked the New Atheist movement.

Dawkins, Richard. *Outgrowing God: A Beginner's Guide*. New York: Random House, 2019. A popular introduction to the God idea from one of the world's best-known evolutionary biologists.

De Botton, Alain. *Religion for Atheists: A Non-believer's Guide to the Uses of Religion*. New York: Vintage Books, 2012. A smart and stylish argument for the cultural value of religion by the advocate of Atheism 2.0.

Dennett, Daniel C. *Breaking the Spell: Religion as a Natural Phenomenon*. New York: Viking, 2006. A naturalist interpretation of the origins and career of religion by one of the primary spokespersons for New Atheism.

Dennett, Daniel C., and Linda LaScola. *Caught in the Pulpit: Leaving Belief Behind*. Durham, NC: Pitchstone, 2015. A qualitative study of professional religious clergy who have converted to atheism or agnosticism.

Drescher, Elizabeth. *Choosing Our Religion: The Spiritual Lives of America's Nones*. New York: Oxford University Press, 2016. One of the first serious studies of America's newest religiously unaffiliated generation and the spiritual-but-not-religious (SBNR) movement.

Eagleton, Terry. *Culture and the Death of God*. New Haven, CT: Yale University Press, 2015. A stimulating history, by one of the English-speaking world's great literary theorists, on the erosion of religious faith in Western culture from the Enlightenment to late modernity.

Epstein, Greg. *Good without God: What a Billion Nonreligious People Do Believe*. New York: HarperCollins, 2009. The best-selling case for morality independent of religious belief by Harvard University and MIT's celebrated humanist chaplain.

Erdozain, Dominic. *The Soul of Doubt: The Religious Roots of Unbelief from Luther to Marx*. Oxford: Oxford University Press, 2016. An innovative study discovering the roots of modern doubt and unbelief in the conflicted conscience of Reformation Protestantism.

Febvre, Lucien. *The Problem of Unbelief in the Sixteenth Century: The Religion of Rabelais*. Trans. Beatrice Gottlieb. Cambridge, MA: Harvard University Press, 1982. Originally published in 1942, the classic study of French satirist François Rabelais and the milieu of Renaissance skepticism.

Feuerbach, Ludwig. *The Essence of Christianity*. Trans. George Eliot. New York: Harper and Row, 1957. The landmark publication by one of the nineteenth century's most prominent Christian atheists, portraying God as a projection of human aspiration; translated by the nineteenth-century British novelist Mary Ann Evans.

Flew, Antony. *Atheistic Humanism*. Buffalo, NY: Prometheus Books, 1993. The 1991 Prometheus Lectures and other essays from one of the most influential analytic philosophers of the twentieth century.

Flew, Antony. *The Presumption of Atheism*. New York: Harper and Row, 1976. Flew's most influential philosophical argument, assigning the burden of proof to theism, not atheism.

Flynn, Tom, ed. *The New Encyclopedia of Unbelief*. Amherst, NY: Prometheus Books, 2007. A comprehensive successor to Gordon Stein's 1985 multiauthor encyclopedia of unbelief, with a foreword by New Atheist spokesperson Richard Dawkins.

Gauna, Max. *Upwellings: First Expressions of Unbelief in the Printed Literature of the French Renaissance*. Rutherford, NJ: Fairleigh Dickinson University Press, 1992. A meticulous study of dissent and skepticism in early modern French literature.

Gaylor, Annie Laurie, ed. *Women without Superstition: "No Gods—No Masters"; The Collected Writings of Women Freethinkers of the Nineteenth and Twentieth Centuries.* Madison, WI: Freedom from Religion Foundation, 1997. A treasury of works by atheist and agnostic women, edited by the cofounder and copresident of the Freedom from Religion Foundation.

Gaylor, Anne Nicol, ed. *The World Famous Atheist Cookbook.* Madison, WI: Freedom from Religion Foundation, 1998. Recipes, such as Blasphemous Bran Waffles and Chicken Salad with No Religious Nuts, compiled by the cofounder of the Freedom from Religion Foundation.

Gordon, David J. *Literary Atheism.* New York: Peter Lang, 2002. An interdisciplinary study of changing and conflicting postreligious perspectives in modern Western literature.

Gorham, Candace R. M. *The Ebony Exodus Project: Why Some Black Women are Walking Out on Religion—and Others Should Too.* Durham, NC: Pitchstone, 2013. A landmark publication, by a mental health service provider, based on interviews with women of color who rejected religion and embraced varieties of unbelief.

Gray, John. *Seven Types of Atheism.* New York: Farrar, Straus and Giroux, 2018. A rich exploration of atheism's diverse forms in the contemporary world.

Grayling, A. C. *The God Argument: The Case against Religion and for Humanism.* New York: Bloomsbury USA, 2014. A careful and humane treatment of the perennial arguments by one of Britain's most distinguished philosophers.

Grayling, A. C. *The Good Book: A Humanist Bible.* New York: Walker, 2011. Wisdom from some of the world's greatest humanist writers, arranged in scripture-like chapter-and-verse style.

Grayling, A. C. *Meditations for the Humanist: Ethics for a Secular Age.* Oxford: Oxford University Press, 2002. Brief essays on a wide range of issues, including health, leisure, love, loyalty, and racism.

Harris, Sam. *The End of Faith: Religion, Terror, and the Future of Religion.* New York: W. W. Norton, 2004. An animated critique of religion, inspired by the 9/11 terrorist attacks, often seen as a precursor to the New Atheist movement.

Harris, Sam. *Letter to a Christian Nation.* New York: Vintage, 2008. A fiery epistle to traditional U.S. Christian believers by one of New Atheism's main spokespersons.

Harris, W. C. *Slouching towards Gaytheism: Christianity and Queer Survival in America.* Albany: State University of New York Press, 2014. An uncompromising critique of homophobia and heteronormativity in American Christianity and a plea for queer-affirmative forms of humanism and nonreligion.

Hazleton, Lesley. *Agnostic: A Spirited Manifesto.* New York: Riverhead Books, 2016. An elegant refutation of the caricature of agnosticism as intellectual indecision or cowardice.

Hecht, Jennifer Michael. *Doubt: A History*. San Francisco: HarperSanFrancisco, 2003. A stunning survey of the evolution of doubt from Socrates and Jesus to Thomas Jefferson and Emily Dickinson by a leading atheist historian, blogger, and poet.

Hick, John, ed. *The Existence of God*. New York: Macmillan, 1964. The classic anthology of diverse and opposing readings on arguments for God, edited by one of the twentieth century's outstanding philosophers of religion.

Hirsi Ali, Ayaan. *Infidel*. New York: Atria, 2013. A riveting autobiographical account of abuse and survival by a woman fleeing Islam for the values of modern Western culture.

Hitchens, Christopher. *god is not Great: How Religion Poisons Everything*. New York: Twelve, 2007. The dynamic and damning indictment of religion's record in society by the most literary of the New Atheist "four horsemen."

Hitchens, Christopher, ed. *The Portable Atheist: Essential Readings for the Nonbeliever*. Philadelphia: Da Capo Press, 2007. A helpful anthology of well-known and lesser-known writings from forty-seven atheist, agnostic, and secular writers, thinkers, and activists.

Hitchens, Christopher, Richard Dawkins, Daniel C. Dennett, and Sam Harris. *The Four Horsemen: The Conversation that Sparked an Atheist Revolution*. New York: Random House, 2019. An account of the 2007 dialogue that launched the New Atheism movement.

Hunsberger, Bruce E., and Bob Altemeyer. *Atheists: A Groundbreaking Study of America's Nonbelievers*. Amherst, NY: Prometheus Books, 2006. Fresh insights into the worldviews of self-professed atheists, based on survey data from participants in U.S. atheist organizations.

Hutchinson, Sikivu. *Godless Americana: Race and Religious Rebels*. Los Angeles: Infidel Books, 2013. A forceful defense of science, feminism, racial justice, intellectual freedom, and LGBTQ+ rights by the founder of Black Skeptics of Los Angeles.

Hutchinson, Sikivu. *Humanists in the Hood: Unapologetically Black, Feminist, and Heretical*. Durham, NC: Pitchstone, 2020. Essays envisioning an antiracist, postsexist, and god-free existence for America's new Gen Secular.

Hutchinson, Sikivu. *Moral Combat: Black Atheists, Gender Politics, and the Values Wars*. Los Angeles: Infidel Books, 2011. A wide-reaching critique of conservative Christianity and an impassioned recommendation of the values of the African American humanist tradition.

Huxley, Julian. *Religion without Revelation*. Westport, CT: Greenwood Press, 1979. A proposal for a new vision of religion by a brilliant biologist and one of the signers of Humanist Manifesto II.

Hyman, Gavin. *A Short History of Atheism*. London: I. B. Tauris, 2010. The best single-volume history of atheism, identifying the origins of modern atheism in the complex internal dynamics of late medieval and early modern Christian intellectual culture.

Jacoby, Susan. *The Age of American Unreason in a Culture of Lies*. New York: Vintage Books, 2018. A spirited critique of U.S. anti-intellectualism, originally published in 2008 and updated in the age of Donald Trump, by a prominent journalist and atheist thinker.

Jacoby, Susan. *Freethinkers: A History of American Secularism*. New York: Metropolitan Books, 2004. The story of doubt and dissent in U.S. culture, with a fascinating chapter on the belief and unbelief of Abraham Lincoln.

Jacoby, Susan. *The Great Agnostic: Robert Ingersoll and American Freethought*. New Haven, CT: Yale University Press, 2013. A critical biography of the best-known skeptic in nineteenth-century America.

Joshi, S. T., ed. *Atheism: A Reader*. Amherst, NY: Prometheus Books, 2000. A well-documented collection of thirty-one texts and excerpts from the canon of Western atheist literature, compiled by the former editor of *American Rationalist* magazine.

Joshi, S. T., ed. *The Original Atheists: First Thoughts on Nonbelief*. Amherst, NY: Prometheus Books, 2014. A valuable collection of texts from early modern atheists and skeptics in the French, German, British, and American Enlightenment traditions.

Kaufmann, Walter. *The Faith of a Heretic*. Princeton, NJ: Princeton University Press, 2015. Lucid personal essays from the distinguished Princeton philosopher and Jewish atheist biographer and translator of Friedrich Nietzsche.

Kenny, Anthony. *The Unknown God: Agnostic Essays*. London: Continuum, 2004. Graceful essays on proofs for God, agnostic poetry, John Henry Newman, Ludwig Wittgenstein, and the intellectual humility of agnosticism by a model historian of philosophy.

Kosmin, Barry A., Ariela Keysar, Ryan T. Cragun, and Juhem Navarro-Rivera. *American Nones: The Profile of the No Religion Population*. Hartford, CT: Institute for the Study of Secularism in Society and Culture, 2009. The study that first reported a dramatic increase in the numbers of religiously unaffiliated Americans, based on the American Religious Identification Survey of 2008.

Kramnick, Isaac, and R. Laurence Moore. *The Godless Constitution: The Case against Religious Correctness*. New York: W. W. Norton, 1996. A powerful defense of separation of church and state by two of the United States' most prestigious historians.

Küng, Hans. *Does God Exist? An Answer for Today*. Trans. Edward Quinn. New York: Doubleday, 1980. Still the definitive survey of arguments for and against the existence of God by the twentieth century's most eminent dissenting Catholic theologian.

Kurtz, Paul. *Humanist Manifesto 2000: A Call for a New Planetary Humanism*. Amherst, NY: Prometheus Books, 2000. A personal defense of humanism for the twenty-first century by one of the United States' best-known humanist thinkers and organizers.

Law, Stephen. *Humanism: A Very Short Introduction*. Oxford: Oxford University Press, 2011. An attractive survey of humanism, including humanist ceremonies, by the author of *The Philosophy Gym* (2003) and *Believing Bullshit* (2011).

LeDrew, Stephen. *The Evolution of Atheism: The Politics of a Modern Movement*. New York: Oxford University Press, 2016. A provocative study of New Atheism and the Atheist Right by a Canadian sociologist.

Lee, Lois. *Recognizing the Non-religious: Reimagining the Secular*. Oxford: Oxford University Press, 2015. The presentation of a new framework for the study of nonreligious people by the founder of the Nonreligion and Secularity Research Network and founding editor of *Secularism and Nonreligion*.

Le Poidevin, Robin. *Agnosticism: A Very Short Introduction*. Oxford: Oxford University Press, 2010. A conversational overview of agnostic life and thought by a leading British professor of metaphysics.

Martin, Michael, ed. *The Cambridge Companion to Atheism*. Cambridge: Cambridge University Press, 2007. A collection of eighteen essays by leading scholars on philosophical, historical, sociological, and psychological issues related to atheism.

Marty, Martin E. *Varieties of Unbelief*. New York: Anchor Books, 1966. A classic, still highly relevant, analysis of the types of atheism by one of America's most respected historians.

May, Henry F. *The Enlightenment in America*. New York: Oxford University Press, 1976. Still the standard study of the variants of the international Enlightenment movement in colonial and early national America.

McGowan, Dale. *Atheism for Dummies*. Ontario: John Wiley and Sons, 2013. A lively and accessible introduction to the history and varieties of atheism.

McGowan, Dale, ed. *Parenting beyond Belief: On Raising Ethical, Caring Kids without Religion*. McGraw-Hill Education, 2007. Creative and humane essays on ordinary life without God.

McGowan, Dale, ed. *Voices of Unbelief: Documents from Atheists and Agnostics*. Santa Barbara, CA: Praeger, 2012. Selections from atheist and agnostic literature from the ancient world to the present.

Moore, R. Lawrence, and Isaac Kramnick. *Godless Citizens in a Godly Republic: Atheists in American Public Life*. New York: W. W. Norton, 2018. A captivating narrative account of secular principles and secular people in the United States by the author of *Selling God* (1995) and editor of *The Portable Enlightenment Reader* (1995).

Mullen, Shirley A. *Organized Freethought: The Religion of Unbelief in Victorian England*. New York: Garland, 2018. An important study of the place of doubt across social classes in nineteenth-century Britain.

Niose, David. *Nonbeliever Nation: The Rise of Secular Americans*. New York: Palgrave Macmillan, 2012. A popular critique of religion and defense of secularity by the former president of the American Humanist Association and the Secular Coalition for America.

Norman, Robert. *On Humanism*. London: Routledge, 2004. A well-crafted review of humanist principles and viewpoints, including a useful postscript on organized humanism, by a celebrated British philosopher.

Onfray, Michel. *Atheist Manifesto: The Case against Christianity, Judaism, and Islam*. Trans. Jeremy Leggatt. New York: Arcade, 2011. A translation of the French philosopher's best-selling *Traité d'Athéologie*, an original and stimulating examination of the relationship between atheism and the world's classic monotheisms.

Oppy, Graham. *Arguing about Gods*. Cambridge: Cambridge University Press, 2006. A critical survey of arguments for and against God and/or gods by one of Australia's leading philosophers of religion.

Oppy, Graham. *Atheism and Agnosticism*. Cambridge: Cambridge University Press, 2018. A short and finely tuned explanation of atheism and agnosticism as philosophical positions.

Oppy, Graham. *Atheism: The Basics*. London: Routledge, 2019. A concise and clear introduction to atheism as a worldview assuming the nonexistence of gods.

Oppy, Graham, ed. *A Companion to Atheism and Philosophy*. Oxford: Wiley Blackwell, 2019. A collection of essays by an international team of scholars on individual thinkers, philosophical movements, ethics, politics, and critiques and defenses of atheism.

Ozment, Katherine. *Grace without God: The Search for Meaning, Purpose, and Belonging in a Secular Age*. New York: Harper Collins, 2016. A journalist's firsthand account of the phenomenon of the Nones in contemporary American culture.

Pearce, Jonathan M. S., ed. *Filling the Void: A Selection of Humanist and Atheist Poetry*. Fareham, Hampshire, UK: Onus Books, 2016. An anthology of diverse atheist and humanist voices collected by a popular British philosopher.

Philipse, Herman. *Atheïstisch Manifest en De Onredelijkheid van Religie*. Amsterdam: Uitgeverij Prometheus, 2004. An expanded version of the influential 1995 essay collection by the prominent Dutch philosopher, now a world-famous defense of atheism.

Pinn, Anthony B. *African American Humanist Principles: Living and Thinking like the Children of Nimrod*. New York: Palgrave MacMillan, 2004. The foundational work in the field of African American humanist studies by one of America's most original thinkers.

Pinn, Anthony B., ed. *By These Hands: A Documentary History of African American Humanism*. New York: New York University, 2001. Essays from James Baldwin, Frederick Douglass, W. E. B. Du Bois, Zora Neale Hurston,

Alice Walker, and many other representatives of the multifaceted African American humanist tradition.

Pinn, Anthony B. *The End of God-Talk: An African American Humanist Theology*. Oxford: Oxford University Press, 2012. A superb example of nontheist theology, informed by the African American intellectual tradition.

Pinn, Anthony B. *Humanism: Essays on Race, Religion and Popular Culture*. New York: Bloomsbury Academic, 2015. A set of Pinn's best essays, covering the intersection of humanist perspectives and multiple dimensions of contemporary life.

Pinn, Anthony B. *Writing God's Obituary: How a Good Methodist Became a Better Atheist*. Amherst, NY: Prometheus Books, 2014. A fascinating first-person deconversion/conversion narrative, charting the development of one of the leading scholars of humanism in the United States.

Pospielovsky, Dimistry. *A History of Marxist-Leninist Atheism and Soviet Antireligious Policies*. New York: St. Martin's Press, 1987. A comprehensive study by an expert in Russian Orthodox history and Soviet social and intellectual life.

Russell, Bertrand. *Marriage and Morals*. New York: Liveright, 1970. Twenty-one essays, in Russell's near-perfect mid-twentieth-century prose, addressing subjects such as love, feminism, marriage, prostitution, and divorce.

Russell, Bertrand. *On God and Religion*. Ed. Al Seckel. Amherst, NY: Prometheus Books, 1986. Twenty-one essays, spanning the breadth of Russell's productive career, including the inimitable "The Theologian's Nightmare."

Russell, Bertrand. *Religion and Science*. New York: Oxford University Press, 1997. A collection of Russell's best short works on the conflict between science and traditional religion.

Russell, Bertrand. *Why I Am Not a Christian and Other Essays on Religion and Related Subjects*. Ed. Paul Edwards. New York: Simon and Schuster, 1957. Fifteen essays from Russell's sprawling canon, including his early statement on "A Free Man's Worship."

Ryrie, Alec. *Unbelievers: An Emotional History of Doubt*. Cambridge, MA: Harvard University Press, 2019. A study, by a British historian of Christianity, arguing for the origins of modern unbelief in sixteenth- and seventeenth-century Protestant thought.

Schmidt, Leigh Eric. *Village Atheists: How America's Unbelievers Made Their Way in a Godly Nation*. Princeton, NJ: Princeton University Press, 2016. Four instructive portraits of nineteenth-century American unbelief.

Schweitzer, Bernard. *Hating God: The Untold Story of Misotheism*. Oxford: Oxford University Press, 2010. A fascinating tour of the forms of God-hatred in the works of Algernon Swinburne, Zora Neale Hurston, Rebecca West, Elie Wiesel, Peter Shaffer, and Philip Pullman.

Shea, William M., and Peter A. Huff, eds. *Knowledge and Belief in America: Enlightenment Traditions and Modern Religious Thought*. New York:

Cambridge University Press, 1995. A collection of essays by twelve leading historians, literary critics, philosophers, and religion scholars on the Enlightenment's legacy in U.S. intellectual life.

Sheiman, Bruce. *An Atheist Defends Religion: Why Humanity Is Better Off with Religion Than without It*. New York: Alpha, 2009. A credible case for the cultural significance of religion by a nonparticipant.

Singer, Peter. *The Expanding Circle: Ethics, Evolution, and Moral Progress*. Princeton, NJ: Princeton University Press, 2011. The core text in Singer's work, arguing for a revolution in ethics based on evolutionary science.

Sneddon, Andrew. *A Is for Atheist: An A to Z of the Godfree Life*. Durham, NC: Pitchstone, 2016. A cultural historian's wide-ranging tour of nonreligious life, from "A Very Ordinary Day" to "Xmas," "You," and "Zounds."

Stedman, Chris. *Faitheist: How an Atheist Found Common Ground with the Religious*. Boston: Beacon Press, 2012. A compelling plea for dialogue among believers and unbelievers by a former evangelical Christian and leader in the American humanist community.

Stein, Gordon, ed. *The Encyclopedia of Unbelief*. 2 vols. Amherst, NY: Prometheus Books, 1985. A dated but still valuable multi-author reference work by the editor of *The Encyclopedia of the Paranormal* (1996) and *The Encyclopedia of Hoaxes* (1993).

Stenger, Victor J. *God: The Failed Hypothesis: How Science Shows that God Does Not Exist*. Amherst, NY: Prometheus Books, 2007. A best-selling argument against theism by a physicist associated with New Atheism.

Strousma, Sarah. *Freethinkers of Medieval Islam: Ibn Al-Rāwandī, Abū Bakr Al-Rāzī, and their Impact on Islamic Thought*. Leiden, Netherlands: E. J. Brill, 2016. A critical achievement highlighting the place of skepticism in Islamic intellectual culture by a professor at the Hebrew University of Jerusalem.

Taylor, Charles. *A Secular Age*. Cambridge, MA: Belknap Press of Harvard University Press, 2007. A highly acclaimed work by one of Canada's most prestigious philosophers, arguably the most important inquiry into the meaning of secularity since Max Weber.

Thrower, James. *Western Atheism: A Short History*. New York: Prometheus Books, 2000. An engaging popular account by a scholar of the history of religions.

Turner, James. *Without God, Without Creed: The Origins of Unbelief in America*. Baltimore, MD: Johns Hopkins University Press, 1985. The unsurpassed historical account of the rise of public and widespread atheism and agnosticism in U.S. intellectual life.

Walters, Kerry. *Atheism: A Guide for the Perplexed*. New York: Continuum, 2010. One of the best and most readable introductions to atheism, including chapters on godless morality and atheist spirituality.

Watson, Peter. *The Age of Atheists: How We Have Sought to Live since the Death of God*. New York: Simon and Schuster, 2014. A sweeping narrative of intellectual history charting the variety of reactions to the loss of religious belief in Western culture.

Yolton, John W., Roy Porter, Pat Rogers, and Barbara Maria Stafford, eds. *The Blackwell Companion to the Enlightenment*. Oxford: Blackwell, 1995. An excellent reference guide including scores of signed and unsigned entries on topics from "Absolutism" to "John Zoffany."

Zuckerman, Phil, ed. *Du Bois on Religion*. Walnut Creek, CA: AltaMira Press, 2000. The best collection of essays on religion from W. E. B. Du Bois, the trendsetting sociologist of religion and key figure in the development of African American humanism.

Zuckerman, Phil. *Faith No More: Why People Reject Religion*. New York: Oxford University Press, 2011. A well-argued account of the factors motivating nonreligion by an innovative sociologist and founder of the first department of secular studies in U.S. higher education.

Zuckerman, Phil. *Living the Secular Life: New Answers to Old Questions*. New York: Penguin, 2014. A positive and moving defense of nonreligious identity.

Zuckerman, Phil. *Society without God: What the Least Religious Nations Can Tell Us about Contentment*. New York: New York University Press, 2010. Investigations into the dynamics of nonreligious life, based on research in Scandinavian countries.

Zuckerman, Phil. *What It Means to Be Moral: Why Religion Is Not Necessary for Living an Ethical Life*. Berkeley, CA: Counterpoint, 2019. Discerning reflections on the foundations and meaning of morality in human experience.

Zuckerman, Phil, Luke W. Galen, and Frank L. Pasquale. *The Nonreligious: Understanding Secular People and Societies*. New York: Oxford University Press, 2016. The standard social science textbook for the study of nonreligious people, covering history, geography, behavior, politics, and values.

Zuckerman, Phil, and John R. Shook, eds. *The Oxford Handbook of Secularism*. New York: Oxford University Press, 2017. A distinctive collection of essays by specialists in the interdisciplinary study of secularism.

Index

Page numbers in **bold** indicate the location of main entries in the encyclopedia.

About the Author

PETER A. HUFF is an academic administrator and professor of religious studies at Benedictine University in the Chicago area. He has held endowed chairs at Xavier University and Centenary College of Louisiana. Active in interfaith and intercultural dialogue, he is the author of four books and coeditor of *Knowledge and Belief in America* and *Tradition and Pluralism*.